Before I Forget

Also by Geoffrey Blainey

The Peaks of Lyell
The University of Melbourne: A Centenary Portrait
Johns and Waygood, 1856–1956
A Centenary History of the University of Melbourne
Gold and Paper: A History of The National Bank of Australia
Mines in the Spinifex: The Story of Mount Isa Mines
The Rush That Never Ended: A History of Australian Mining
A History of Camberwell
The Tyranny of Distance: How Distance Shaped Australia's History
Wesley College: The First Hundred Years
The Rise of Broken Hill
Across a Red World
The Steel Master: A Life of Essington Lewis
The Causes of War
Triumph of the Nomads: A History of Ancient Australia
A Land Half Won
The Blainey View
Gold and Paper 1858–1982: A History of the National Bank of Australasia
Our Side of the Country: The Story of Victoria
All for Australia
Making History (with CMH Clark and RM Crawford)
The Great Seesaw: A New View of the Western World, 1750–2000
A Game of Our Own: The Origins of Australian Football
Odd Fellows: A History of IOOF Australia
Blainey, Eye on Australia: Speeches and Essays of Geoffrey Blainey
Sites of the Imagination: Contemporary Photographers View Melbourne and Its People (with Isobel Crombie)
Jumping Over the Wheel
The Golden Mile
A Shorter History of Australia
White Gold: The Story of Alcoa of Australia
In Our Time
A History of the AMP 1848–1998
A Short History of the World
This Land is All Horizons: Australia's Fears and Visions (Boyer Lectures)
A Very Short History of the World
Black Kettle & Full Moon: Daily Life in a Vanished Australia
A Short History of the Twentieth Century
A History of Victoria
Sea of Dangers: Captain Cook and His Rivals
A Short History of Christianity
The Story of Australia's People: The Rise and Fall of Ancient Australia
The Story of Australia's People: The Rise and Rise of a New Australia

Before I Forget

AN EARLY MEMOIR

GEOFFREY
BLAINEY

HAMISH HAMILTON
an imprint of
PENGUIN BOOKS

HAMISH HAMILTON

UK | USA | Canada | Ireland | Australia
India | New Zealand | South Africa | China

Hamish Hamilton is part of the Penguin Random House group of companies
whose addresses can be found at global.penguinrandomhouse.com.

First published by Hamish Hamilton, an imprint of
Penguin Random House Australia Pty Ltd, 2019

Front-cover image: *The Age*
Author image on back jacket flap: Stuart McEvoy/Newspix
Back-cover image: Blainey collection
Cover design by Alex Ross © Penguin Random House Australia Pty Ltd
Text design by Midland Typesetters, Australia
Typeset in Adobe Caslon Pro by Midland Typesetters, Australia
Colour separation by Splitting Image Colour Studio, Clayton, Victoria
Printed and bound in Australia by Griffin Press, part of Ovato, an accredited
ISO AS/NZS 14001 Environmental Management Systems printer.

A catalogue record for this book is available from the National Library of Australia

ISBN 978 1 76089 033 9

penguin.com.au

To all who taught me

CONTENTS

PREFACE

Half of this book is about growing up. Our family consisted of four boys – I came second – and one girl. Our father was a clergyman when the churches were still a most powerful force in the country. Living in what is now called 'rural and regional Australia', we moved every fourth year to a new district. Even in the smaller towns our life – I am surprised to rediscover – was intersected by events and people now of national significance.

In the other half of this book I learn to be a historian: I am still learning. I started young, and by the time I was thirty I had written, as a freelance writer, more books on Australian history than probably had any professor of the time. I am talking about quantity, not quality. This book comes to a halt when I reach about the age of forty. I do not end this memoir of my life for any valid reason; I simply thought that I had written enough.

Actually I wrote much of the book at the start of this century. I had the idea that my memory might become weaker, and that therefore it was sensible to write something sooner rather than later. In fact my memory remains fairly tight, or so I believe. Lately I went back to the pages compiled about fifteen years ago and read them again. Occasionally they were erroneous, and so I verified many episodes with the aid of the pocket diary I kept each year and the letters I had carefully saved. Probably errors will remain in this book though I have tried hard to avoid them. Memory, it is said, is not a skilled worker.

I must express my gratitude especially to the team at Penguin Random House – my publisher Nikki Christer, editors Rachel Scully and Katie Purvis, and designer Alex Ross. I am also indebted to John Day, the notable Wangaratta gardener, with whom I discuss my books at nearly every stage of the writing, and to my wife Ann and my daughter Anna.

Geoffrey Blainey
March 2019

PART ONE

1

REMEMBERED IN BLACK AND WHITE

My mother was born in a bark house in East Gippsland in 1903. Her birthplace was called Buchan South, and its hills were so steep and the road so uneven that horses were harnessed to a sledge in order to haul in the supplies. The nearest post office was about 8 kilometres away and the nearest doctor was at least 30 kilometres away; and when our mother was about to be born the doctor was called by telegram. He arrived on horseback to find the baby alive and well. As our grandfather received the small salary of an up-country teacher he could not easily afford the money to pay the doctor for his travelling time.

Hilda May Lanyon, our mother, was the eldest of six children. Most of her very young years were spent in the schoolhouse at Sugar Loaf Creek, a hamlet near Seymour, a station on the Sydney–Melbourne railway line. At the age of six she first attended school at Corryong in north-eastern Victoria, not far from the source of the Murray River, and later at Gisborne which was on the railway line between Melbourne and Bendigo. Her last years of schooling were as a scholarship girl at the new Melbourne High School which taught boys too. At this time she lived with an aunt who kept a boarding house in St Kilda, near the bay.

Becoming a trainee teacher, she taught in small schools on the dry northern plains and also was a prize winner at the teachers' college. Meanwhile she met my father at a 'social' in the suburban church that her family attended.

My earliest memories are of Mum's affection for us, though – I hope it is not unfair to add – she could be slightly mischievous towards adults who, in her eyes, had lost the right to her affection. Ambitious for her children, she made endless sacrifices to help us. At the same time she encouraged us, to an unusual degree, to become adventurous from an early age. When I was only five she did not worry if I walked far from the small country town where we lived. Though snakes sometimes wriggled across the road on hot days, she ensured as best she could that we were wary of them.

She once held secret literary ambitions, but after her marriage she rarely had the opportunity to pursue them. She enjoyed fluent writing, and loved to read a book for half an hour, though her sense of duty reminded her that she should be washing the clothes or scrubbing the kitchen table. Letters to friends she wrote by the dozen, when she could find the time. Words interested her more than music, especially the classical and religious music that captivated my father. For fine china, fine table linen and the other adornments of domestic life she had a longing but in our house the casualty rate of the china saucers, cups and plates was high, for they were in constant use, serving the numerous people who dropped in to our house for a cup of tea during the course of each week. We have almost forgotten how much a church congregation, particularly Methodists in a country town, formed a fellowship or a kind of tribe, companionable and tightly knit.

Much of my mother's life was spent in the continuous tasks of feeding and clothing and rearing a large family. How hard she worked! She made jam in large quantities, and onion pickles and tomato sauces, along with jars of preserved apricots and plums, so that at the end of the summer her pantry held a few hundred jars and bottles of all shapes and sizes, each carrying a handwritten label signifying that it was chutney or jam and that it was bottled on a certain day. Trays of biscuits were drawn from the oven, and wholesome cakes too. Anything that could be made at home was made there. To save money she bought dozens of eggs when they were cheap and rubbed their shells with a mixture called Keepegg so that they would be relatively edible when winter arrived and fresh eggs rose in price.

Mum did not regard housekeeping as the core of her existence even though it filled most of her waking hours. Many of our clothes and some of her own she made, using a little Singer sewing machine. Numerous pairs of socks she mended each week, for a typical woollen sock during the era before synthetics was inclined to develop holes, especially at the heel. In one room of our house sat a large coloured-cloth bag the size of a huge cushion, and it was full of jumpers and socks waiting to be darned and shirts whose buttons had to be replaced. Washing day on Monday morning was a mammoth event. Later the shirts had to be ironed, because the drip-dry shirt was not yet invented. The irony was that amid all these difficulties people made more effort in those days to be clean and neat, at weekends and especially on Sundays. On Saturday afternoon the spectators at the football, mainly males, were far better dressed than they are today.

Mum was an avid listener to tales about the pioneers of the rural districts in which she lived. When telling us about sad happenings – perhaps a local resident crushed by a falling tree – she might lose her composure for an instant, though her voice cracked only for a word or two: she was a romantic. She admired scenery, especially green paddocks and the wattle in full blossom along a country river. To travel the countryside in a car – she never learnt to drive – was her special pleasure. Of birds, flowers and native and imported trees, her knowledge was far wider than mine ever became. A collector of plants, she enjoyed the memory of where she had scavenged a cutting as much as she enjoyed its sight and scent after it blossomed in new soil. As she moved house often, she was endlessly engaged in the making or reshaping of gardens. Whereas she loved a rambling garden my father preferred the hand-mown lawn and the weeded flowerbed and the patch of tomatoes, each plant being fastened to a wooden stake. In their personalities and their sense of order they were different.

Our father came from California Gully, an evangelical fortress inside the goldfield of Eaglehawk, adjacent to the city of Bendigo. His own father, Samuel Blainey, drove the enormous stationary steam engine that hauled the miners or the skips of rock up the shafts of Bendigo's goldmines which, by world's standards, were very deep. Samuel and his wife were Bible Christians, she by birth and he by marriage. A minor Methodist sect founded in the west of England, and flourishing in many Australian mining towns, it eventually merged with the other Methodists. In contrast my mother's background was mainstream Wesleyan. Ethnically she was Cornish with English and Irish strands.

Christened as Samuel Clifford Blainey, and known always as Cliff, Dad began to conduct religious services when he was only fourteen, preaching his first sermon in the Sparrowhawk Mission Hall near Eaglehawk. Belonging to that special Methodist category called a 'local preacher', he began to preach in tiny country halls and matchbox churches. After a few years at Bendigo High School he won high marks in the exam held to determine who could enter the public service, and thereupon he moved to Melbourne where he became a junior clerk in the police department and then in the audit office. By now his mother was dying of tuberculosis, for which Bendigo and its deep mines were infamous; and soon after her death he went to live in Queen's College within the University of Melbourne in order to study for the Methodist ministry. Unable to afford the fees needed to complete his university degree he was posted at the end of his second year as a student-pastor to the small Mallee town of Hopetoun. There he boarded at the Coffee Palace, and travelled in a horse-drawn jinker to the little churches in the surrounding wheatfields. When he was posted to Orbost in East Gippsland, he bought a bike so that he could ride to preaching places up to 35 kilometres away. Once he was invited to a house to marry a couple, and saw them clamber out of bed to take part in the ceremony. In those days such conduct caused a stir.

After studying more theology and serving in various small towns, he was formally ordained in March 1924 as a minister of what was called the Methodist Church of Australasia. The ceremony took place in the handsome Wesley Church in Melbourne, in the presence of a packed congregation, and I have inherited the leather-bound King James Bible presented to him. It is one of those editions in which a host of printed texts – from 'the most ancient authorities' – cluster in the narrow margins on both sides of each page. The five clerical signatures in the front of his presentation Bible include those of Professor A. E. Albiston, a learned and kindly clergyman, and Reverend Tom Woodfull, the father of the famous Australian cricket captain who, eight years later, was a target, along with Don Bradman, for the aggressive 'bodyline' bowling of Harold Larwood. That episode caused a crisis in English-Australian relations.

My father's first senior posting was at the wheat-belt town of Jeparit, not far from the South Australian border. My mother went there as a new bride. My brother John was born there in January 1928, the first of five children, each of whom was born in a different town. I was second in the family, and two years younger.

In April 1929 our father became the Methodist minister in Terang, which stood on the main railway line between Melbourne and the port of Warrnambool. It was in the heart of the sheep country, with patches of dairying here and there. The Presbyterians owned the grandest and richest church – many of the early sheep-owners had been Scots – while the Methodists must have been the smallest of the four congregations in Terang. On the other hand many Methodists gathered in tiny churches and halls in the volcanic countryside nearby. My father cared for all these Sunday congregations, preaching morning, afternoon and evening. On some Sunday evenings he would give his sermon in Terang and, before the last hymn was sung, slip away and drive quickly into the country where the farmers and their wives, the day's second milking now completed, would be assembling in the local hall for a late-hour service.

In Terang my mother was expecting another baby, and for some medical reason was advised by the sister at the baby health centre not to give birth in the local hospital but to visit Melbourne. As Mum's parents were then living in the suburb of Box Hill, she went there with baby John, still a toddler. I was born on 11 March 1930. When she returned to her mother's home in Harrow Street after the normal fortnight spent in hospital she became perturbed that I was losing weight. I also began to vomit: slightly ominous, it was ejected some distance. I know this because my mother in old age used to send me a letter of reminiscence as a gentle reminder, on my birthday, that I was fortunate to be alive.

Alarmed by the 'projectile vomiting' she carried me to the baby health centre where the presiding sister advised her to see the doctor quickly. My mother then carried me along Whitehorse Road – 'shedding tears as I went', she recalled – to the consulting room of Dr Harry Judkins, a family friend, who looked at me and decided that I could be suffering from pyloric stenosis, a condition that prevented the mother's milk from continuing its journey. It was quickly arranged that Mum should take me to nearby Camberwell where a child specialist and surgeon named Kingsley Norris might be able to help. He prescribed a medicinal mixture, to be fed to me just before breastfeeding began. Apparently it had little effect. Now five weeks old, I was still losing weight, and Norris decided to operate. My mum, knowing that this operation was relatively new, was nervous, but it proved to be a success. I still have the large scar which, when I am examined by doctors of a new generation, causes puzzlement.

My parents were worried, as the weeks went on, about the expense of the medical care. They possessed almost no savings; and in those days the government did not help with medical bills. Fortunately it was the custom for doctors to view clergymen and their families with sympathy, and both Judkins and Norris declined to charge for their skills.

*

I have no memories of my three years in Terang, except those borrowed from an occasional photograph. There I am, gripping the handles of a toy wheelbarrow in which sits a large cuddly toy. I wear rompers, a short bulging kind of trouser that was commonly placed on little children. I look like a young bruiser, strong and outgoing, and behind me stands my older brother John, who looks every bit the intellectual of the family. My hair is short – it must have been the fashion – and I am probably not yet three years old. My younger sister Joan is not visible and two more brothers are not yet born.

In several of these black-and-white photos the stark weatherboard walls of the house can be seen, while nearby grow a few hydrangeas which, at the town pharmacy where the film was developed, were tinted with the colour of baby-blue.

My mental pictures of childhood are in black and white – unless I consciously set out to restore to them the colour that must have been present. My dreams are not in colour. My memory, even of today's events, is more often a detailed map of places, objects and people than a coloured scene. Though I am intensely aware of colour and scenery when I am out of doors, the colour – I feel pretty sure – is not usually stored in my memory. Perhaps for that reason I am more inclined than many historians to devote a few words to recreating and describing the coloured landscape in which important events took place.

2

THAT GIPPSLAND TOWN

My earliest memories are of Leongatha, the small Gippsland dairying town where I lived from the age of three. I remember following my mother around, watching her daily tasks. Monday was for me the intriguing day and for her the most gruelling. In the washhouse, a building that stood apart, the large vat known simply as the copper had to be filled with cold water, the fire beneath had to be lit, and into the water were piled – and prodded down with a wooden pole – the first load of white sheets. As the copper came to the boil the rising cloud of steam heralded the hard work in which I wished to take part. The hot and steaming items were lifted from the copper and rinsed with cold water in a wooden trough and then put by hand through the revolving rollers of the wringer. Nearby were chunky bags of blue, rich in colour, with which white shirts were made whiter. In the open air, at the long wire clothesline, I was allowed to hand up the wooden pegs with which sheets and shirts were fastened to the wire. Soon the rows of items were flapping – if the wind was blowing – before another load came to the boil inside the washhouse. Still to come was the task of ironing all the clothes, for this was before the era of drip-dry.

The house had no hot-water service. Late on Saturday afternoon the water was boiled in the copper and carried in buckets to the iron bath where each one of us had a turn at bathing. All over Australia, children were being scrubbed in readiness for Sunday, when they dressed in their best clothes.

As children we went to church once each Sunday – never twice – and also to Sunday school. Without being told so, we learnt that the hallmark of Methodism was congregational singing – strong and fervent. I sometimes overheard my mother say, after she returned from an event held in the church or hall of a rival denomination, that its people 'just didn't know how to sing'. When I was young, my favourite hymn was 'Jesus Is My Shepherd, Wiping Every Tear'. I have not heard it for fifty years. Like many others I was also captivated by the hymn 'When He Cometh, When He Cometh, to Lay Down His Jewels'. I liked the pictorial hymns. We knew no pop songs but something of their magic was present in the hymns we sang. They were taught to us in Sunday school, which in the country towns was usually held in the afternoon.

Once there was a revivalist mission – the only one I remember at any of my father's churches. The visiting evangelist taught the young to sing 'Wide, Wide as the Ocean, High as the Heavens Above', and other songs which were collectively known as 'rousing numbers'. Reciting these choruses from memory, I am not certain whether I have assigned them their exact opening words. A child does not always hear words correctly. Hundreds of hymns, many by Charles Wesley, made such an impression on me that if, today, I hear the first two bars of a recording of one of them played unannounced on the radio, I know which hymn it is to be.

In those years the grassy green hills separated us from the outside world. I knew nothing of what went on in Melbourne or Sydney. If I had heard of Canberra – which was then pronounced as Can-berra (to rhyme with error) – it was not often. I am unsure whether I had yet heard of Don Bradman the famous cricketer or Oppy the champion cyclist who late in his life was my friend. I was probably too young to know that in 1937 Japanese soldiers were advancing into China and the Germans were rearming and preparing again to go to war.

When playing games in the yard we often made aeroplane noises just as we made car noises. Engines then were loud, and made distinctive and noisy sounds that a clever child could imitate. At playtime we sometimes pretended to be Sir Charles Kingsford Smith, flying our own planes with our arms outstretched as wings. He had died in an accident near Burma in 1935 but his feats were legendary. Significantly I had never been close to an aircraft and knew, during the first eleven years of my life, nobody who had flown in one. Their overhead noise, however, was haunting.

At a certain hour on most days we heard a small aircraft fly overhead and were told that it was carrying the daily cargo of airmail and a few passengers from Melbourne to Tasmania. As I had only a faint idea of where Tasmania was, it could have been flying to Ethiopia for all I knew. One day news reached the town that the De Havilland plane flying the relatively new route between Tasmania and Melbourne was missing. A pilot and eleven passengers were aboard. For a few days we looked up in the sky, expecting that somehow the missing plane might reappear and that we might be the ones who discovered it. Presumably it crashed into the sea, and no wreckage was found. It was one of Australia's major air disasters of that era.

My brother John was technically skilled for his age and curious about machines; he spent many hours at the railway station watching the shunting of steam trains. One morning in our street Joan and I were seated in the back of the parked car, while John – aged about eight – sat at the steering wheel. To show us his skill he released the handbrake. As the car rested on a slight rise it began to roll backwards. Turning all his attention to steering the car he succeeded miraculously – for he was too small to use the rear-vision mirror – in steering the car safely past a cross-street. Conscious that the car was gathering speed and that the hill behind him was descending rather steeply, he made the bright decision to give a strong turn of the wheel and guide the car backwards into an embankment. The car halted and shuddered, and was barely scratched. As spectators Joan and I felt more a sense of astonishment than danger.

One hour's drive away, and close to the sea, was the black-coal town of Wonthaggi. In February 1937 an underground explosion trapped a group of miners, and none was found alive. That drama did not fire our imagination in quite the same way as the disappearance of the aircraft.

Methodists were known for their 'tea meetings', held usually in warmer months. Families each brought a plate of cooked food or homemade cakes and sandwiches and – unless they were too poor – a silver coin for the collection plate. In the local hall the feast was then laid out on trestle tables overlaid with white tablecloths. It was a rural version of the smorgasbord. Nobody, however, could begin eating the huge meal until a hymn was sung to the tune of 'All People that on Earth

Do Dwell'. The opening line was announced – 'Be seated at our table, Lord' – and those who were not standing at once stood up. Fervently it was sung, all the words being known to the adults by heart. Smallish children did not join in: we did not know the words but we moved our lips, pretending to sing.

The excitement, when the last line of the last verse was concluded, was almost feverlike, for at that moment – or soon after – the food tables were invaded. Then followed one of the most delicious hours of childhood. The feast ended with cups of tea, the water having been boiled in a large copper sitting over a wood fire blazing outside the hall. The evening closed with a short message from the preacher. Sometime after sunset the procession of horses and buggies and jinkers and a few second-hand cars would set out for the various farms, but we were among the last to leave. The lights of the departing vehicles, bobbing slightly as they climbed the nearest hill, were memorable.

Our house was a calling point. On weekdays farming people would call at our house for a long conversation or just for help. They were sad, or lonely or almost penniless, or eagerly giving something of themselves. A few brought, as gifts, a small cardboard box full of field mushrooms, or a dozen eggs packed in straw, a bunch of flowers, a box of plums or loquats, or homemade jam and chutney. When I was old enough to read the handwritten labels on the jam, I realised, to my amazement, the existence of adults who could not spell.

When we heard a knock at the back door of our weatherboard house we rushed to be the first to open it. At times, standing on the doormat, a neighbour would hold out as a gift a pair of rabbits, freshly skinned. A local farmer would call with a snake that he had arranged like a trophy on his car crank-handle; the same iron handle had been used to kill the snake. Every so often an old woman used to arrive with a clean cloth covering a basket of homemade butter, 200 grams (half a pound) of which she sold to us. Her butter did not taste as well as factory butter, but it was bought mainly to help her. We learnt that her husband had been killed decades ago, when a giant tree fell across the road on which he was travelling in his horse-drawn jinker. In living memory the district had been dense forest and fern gullies; and death as a result of a falling tree was not rare.

The calls on our family for help were frequent during this last phase of the Great Depression. In the course of a week many unemployed men knocked at the back door, looking for odd jobs, a free meal or a packet of sandwiches. Some, being bolder, wanted money. My father, like the neighbours, would often ask them to do a task – digging the garden or chopping the firewood.

In Leongatha our car at first was a second-hand Whippet of the 1920s, to be replaced by a larger 1928 Chevrolet. With a soft hood and running boards standing high off the ground the car had a starting button that did not always work. The engine then had to be started manually by the driver who, standing in front of the radiator, turned round the metal crank-handle with a firm grip of his hand – a difficult operation that sometimes could break a wrist. The car's cellophane-like windows could be removed from the doors in hot weather. At night its tail-light could be switched on only by the driver climbing from the car and turning on the light. The Chev was large enough to seat the growing family; and, when we were about to go on holiday to a seaside resort, we could stow a lot of luggage on each running board. Just before the journey was about to commence, John and I would rush to the car and occupy the window seats in the back, leaving our uncomplaining sweet-natured sister to occupy the middle seat; the youngest brother Ellis travelled with the parents in the front. To claim a car seat as my own I shouted, in the fashion of the time, 'I bag that seat!' In our assertiveness we were always 'bagging' this and that.

As cars rarely travelled above 60 kilometres an hour, and often at a mere 30 kilometres, a trip to Melbourne – allowing for one punctured tyre and a boiling radiator and a long stop for lunch – was a prolonged event. As it was summertime, a brown canvas bag full of drinking water was carried, the bag being tied to the front of the car so that the rush of air kept it cool.

My interest in cars, thanks to my brother, was intense. I knew nearly every make of car on the road – except perhaps the luxurious models that had no reason to appear in a dairying district. Along the country road I could identify the approaching Dodges and Lincolns, the Talbots and Rugbys, Nashes and Austins, Vauxhalls and Morrises, Oldsmobiles, Hupmobiles, Essexes and many other kinds of cars, mostly possessing a soft cloth roof, headlights like large eyes on short stalks, and radiator caps through which, on a hot afternoon, the steam from the overheated engine hissed. The shining brass radiator cap was often the clue to the make of a car, whether the Buick touring sedan or the four-door Pontiac. The engine noises were loud compared to today's purring sounds. When the gears were changed the noise of each gear had its own music; and boys could even imitate the sounds of varying 'makes' of cars running in different gears. When I was driving an imaginary car, which was often, I loudly imitated what I thought were the correct engine noises.

The box-shaped Model T Ford was the popular car; but maybe half of the farmers, owning no car, sat in a horse-drawn buggy or two-wheeled jinker when they drove to town on their weekly visit. It was their hope, one day, to buy a car. A miracle-like event in the town was the arrival of what was called 'the motor show'. In 1936, after the Depression was over, a local car dealer arranged for a variety of brand-new cars and trucks to come to the town in convoy in the hope that buyers would be tempted. On the long-awaited day, once the school lessons were over, we rushed, all panting, to the main street to see the display. For us it was a glimpse of the twenty-first century. One car was a spotless white, a colour unsuited to the mud flanking most Gippsland roads in winter.

I associate an early sense of beauty with those country roads. The hills were green and shapely, with the dark ribbon of bitumen curving around them. I was transfixed by stretches of roadscape near Ruby and Jumbunna, with the narrow highway sometimes shining under the headlights when wet with rain. Only the highways were sealed, and the bitumen was used sparingly so that a car had to move from the hard surface to the gravel or grass in order to pass another car.

One day in 1934 the rains poured. On the following day we were driven – the car was then an Overland – to see a river in flood. Driving around a bend of the road we suddenly saw that the wooden road bridge had been swept away. When the car halted I looked downstream and saw the bridge, wedged against tall riverside gum trees. Years later, when I hosted a television series on Australian history, I recalled that scene, so momentous and awesome to a four-year-old.

When in summer we were driving in the countryside, the sight of a snake gliding across the bitumen, especially a black snake, was spellbinding. It was rumoured that a snake, when driven over by the wheels of a car, could be forcibly flipped through the open windows of the car and deposited at the passengers' feet. On a hot day – when all the lightweight windows of the car were removed to provide a draught of air – I feared that one would somehow land on the floor of our car.

At home was a small vegetable garden, in which Dad let me use a patch of unused soil for my own roads. I learnt to mix dirt and water in the right proportions and to lay the wet mud on the ground, smoothing it with the back of the spade so that when dry it resembled a ribbon of bitumen highway. In Gippsland a road was meaningless without farms, and so I created tiny farms with wooden would-be fences from sticks of equal length. To serve as cows, I scavenged the small round car batteries and placed them around my crudely fenced miniature paddocks. I excavated dams and poured in water; but they were no sooner filled than the water disappeared in the soft soil. For some years my ambition was to become a farmer and milk cows.

Meanwhile I was almost old enough to take an interest in but not yet able to understand what our father did for a living, nor why he did it. For more than half a century he was to keep a record of each Sunday service he presided over. He also recorded the biblical words he chose as the basis of his sermon, and the four hymns that were sung by the congregation. On most Sundays he conducted at least three services, in three different places. I did not realise how systematic he was until I saw, after his death, the notebooks in which these devotional details were recorded in ink, week after week, decade after decade. Possibly he had a fear of delivering a sermon that his congregation had heard from him a few months previously: more likely he wished to keep a true record of what he regarded as his trusteeship as a worker in the Lord's vineyard. Handling statistics with pleasure, he knew the number of every one of the thousand and more hymns in the Methodist hymnbook. He knew too the precise chapter and verse in which thousands of verses could be found in the Bible.

He remembered the numberplates of hundreds of cars owned by people whom he knew. Sometimes he would pass a car travelling along the road, notice its numberplate, and remark that it was the car once owned by an acquaintance in a certain country town. That was in the era when cars travelled so slowly that it was easy to read their numberplates.

Keeping a large library, Dad spent more on books than he really could afford. As a preacher he was thoughtful and perhaps slightly mystical in his later decades. He often spoke of heaven but rarely of hell. Preparing sermons carefully during the week, and basing them on texts chosen from the Bible after much deliberation, he carried into the pulpit a neat summary of what he wished to say. Listeners gained the impression that the sermon was largely delivered off the cuff. Most sentences were created on the spur of the moment but the main thoughts and the sequence in which they were expressed were carefully thought out in advance.

When he preached he did not play to the gallery. While he knew that many congregations liked human-interest anecdotes snipped from that week's news or from the reported doings of living celebrities, he did not present that kind of newsworthy sermon. He mainly preached the Bible, applying its message to the trials and triumphs of the lives of the people who sat listening. He must have timed his sermons, because they rarely were too long (except for little children) and never too short. Hearing or half-hearing him on nearly every Sunday of the first fourteen years of my life – Methodist babies were taken regularly into church to soak up the spirit – I almost took him for granted, not realising until later how skilled he was at what he viewed as his duty and privilege: the preaching of the Word.

At the small west Victorian town of Jeparit, he was to have one of his long-remembered moments as a preacher. For several decades the Menzies family, then storekeepers, were stalwarts of the local Methodist church, there being no Presbyterian one. Some thirty years later one of their sons, Robert Gordon Menzies, as Liberal prime minister of Australia, accepted an invitation to revisit his boyhood town and church, and my father was invited to return and preach in the same church that morning. 'Bob' Menzies in his commanding way stood up and read aloud a psalm from the Bible, and later my father gave the sermon, but they probably did not shake hands, for Menzies and his wife Pattie had to hurry away to another engagement as soon as the service had ended. Months later in Melbourne, when by chance they were at the same social event, Menzies recognised my father and walked over and graciously congratulated him on his preaching and the theme of the sermon. My father, who probably tended to be a Labor sympathiser, could never forget that kind and spontaneous gesture.

In a country town the minister's contacts were overwhelmingly with his flock. If visitors stayed at our house, they were usually Methodists, arriving on what was called 'a deputation'. When our parents did business in the town – buying meat or groceries, or taking our boots for repair – they usually did it with a Methodist. This was natural. Their income came from these same people, by way of the collection plate handed around in church, and they tried to repay a little of it. If two Methodist families operated a draper's shop or a milk round in the town my mother divided the business between the two, with a slight preference for the cheaper one. When bad luck befell Methodists, our mother would help. The coming of the passenger train from Melbourne was a major event; and one morning, just as the locomotive was leaving the railway station, a waiting woman fell on the tracks and her legs were severed. Her son came to our house to stay.

These tightly knit congregations have largely vanished. They are no longer viewed very sympathetically in the media and sections of some universities, but the years will return when their merits – along with the defects – will be seen more clearly. With personal disaster and adversity they coped bravely.

On the day I began school my mum was in hospital, having her fourth child – our brother Ellis. It was an unusual Christian name, and John thought it sounded slightly like 'Alice', but the name was precious to Mum. Ever since she was a young teacher she had been close friends with Ellis Bankin, an adventurous and likeable lad originally from the Ballarat district. He had punctuated his young years as a rural teacher with a trip overseas, and he must have corresponded with Mum – she loved letters– and so Dad perhaps was perturbed slightly when the name Ellis was given to our newborn brother. The choice of Clifford as the baby's second name presumably was a successful form of appeasement.

The name Ellis was dramatically revived seven months later when the headlines announced that Ellis Bankin was missing in the far outback. On his Triumph motorbike he had made remarkable rides during school holidays and, heavily loaded with small cans of water, he even crossed a desert at a time of year when only camels could survive. On 13 January 1936 he was last seen alive at Ernabella mission, far south of Alice Springs. The search for him filled the headlines. Eventually his corpse was found beside his motorbike, its fuel tank empty. Uluru – not yet a tourist destination – was almost within sight. The news of his death in the desert caused a stir as well as sadness in our house and was for long a topic of discussion with visitors. That was the first time I heard that Australia possessed deserts.

Meanwhile Mum had prepared me for school, teaching me all kinds of useful knowledge. Nervously, at the age of five-and-a-quarter, I set out. To school was an easy walk, and my brother John kept an eye on me as we crossed the main street and the bridge over the railway line. At the end of the school day, and the sound of the school bell, he divulged an exciting way of walking home. We hurried towards a wide swamp, an adventure that actually took us in the wrong direction. To avoid the shallow pools of water we jumped from tussock to tussock and from one patch of high ground to another. If we were alert, our feet splashed in the water only five or six times. Though we wore stiff boots – a typical Gippsland boy wore boots – they did not prevent us from arriving home on many afternoons with damp feet. We paid a price. First was John's friend, Ben Stephenson, who caught rheumatic fever, followed by John who became very ill, while I had a shorter illness. John went to stay with our grandparents in Melbourne for a month, safe from the temptation of the swamp. At that time the fear was high that the fever would permanently weaken his heart but he is still alive in Sydney, aged ninety.

Sometimes a local doctor, Horace Pern, came to see us, with his leather bag of instruments and potions, and his sense of fun. An urgent call for his help came when, preparing to ride my tricycle, I enthusiastically blindfolded myself with a piece of hessian. I was playing the game of being invisible. Pedalling rapidly, I could not see ahead. Suddenly I bumped into a fence, and the iron handlebar pierced my face a fraction of an inch below the right eye. Dr Pern gave his opinion, anxiously awaited. He simply said that I was fortunate. Not long afterwards, he fell ill and died. I was surprised to see his officer's cap – he had served at Gallipoli and in France – perched on the coffin as his funeral procession was assembling.

There were arresting events in our town of a thousand or so people. One such event reached the national headlines, though I did not read those headlines, the daily paper having been carefully concealed from us while the event was being played out. Attending our church was an English family named Rushmer. I sometimes played with their daughter June, and once we hunted together for lost golf balls on the sides of the local fairways. In our ignorance we used to fetch the balls and throw them back to the nearest golfer.

One day in December 1935 she was missing. Her body was found; the sadness and the excitement were intense. Detectives arrived and 'had a door knock around the town'. Soon an arrest was made, and a woman – she regularly sold us home-laid eggs – came running into our house: 'They've cotched him, they've cotched him,' she cried. The strange pronouncing of words was then common: later the television and radio were to transform pronunciation and grammar across the country.

The arrested murderer, Arnold Sodeman, lived just around the corner and we slightly knew his family. He confessed to police he had murdered other girls, in Melbourne and Inverloch, some years previously.

June, who was about six months older than me, went to our school and Sunday school. Accordingly our mum, soon after the death was announced, called on Mrs Rushmer with a freshly-baked cake and a posy of flowers. In the country, hand-picked flowers were more expressive than words.

At the funeral in the crowded church, one of the dead girl's little friends began to call out her name, repeating loudly, 'I want to see Junie', and Mum took the crying girl to our house, next door, and read her a 'happy-ending story'. Meanwhile we children, released from school, formed a guard of honour in the main street and, standing in a neat line, waited restlessly. Eventually we glimpsed the approaching black hearse, covered with flowers. To my surprise my father was sitting up in the front of either the hearse or the following car. I did not realise that one of his duties was to conduct funerals.

Much of the news about this tragedy was not spoken of in our presence, for fear of frightening us. Years later when I was studying at university I learnt that Sodeman's trial – he was sentenced to death by hanging – was a landmark in Australian legal history. The troubling question of whether he was insane led to two famous High Court judges, Sir John Latham and Sir Owen Dixon, taking opposite sides. The murderer's unsuccessful attempt to appeal against the death penalty appears in the records of the High Court under the title of *Sodeman v. The King*. Meanwhile the Rushmer family, newish migrants, returned to England where Mrs Rushmer was still living half a century later.

When I think of Leongatha, I hear children chanting, for in classroom we chanted together for much of the day. We chanted our multiplication tables, and we chanted spelling and geography. There was a special rhythm to each chant: 'Two times two are four, three times three are nine'. These eternal mathematical truths were recited at a different pace to such vital geographical facts as 'Melbourne on the Yarra, London on the Thames'. Other facts we chanted with equal seriousness. There was a sense of belonging when we recited together in voices that were not too loud but far from soft. One teacher, Miss Dungan, deserved more respect than we gave her. Behind her back she was called Miss Dunnycan. The town was not sewered, and the excreta from each household was carried from the outhouse or dunny in a large tar-coated drum that was called 'the dunnycan'.

Our grandfather Lanyon once visited us for Christmas. He had set out from Melbourne on the train, a journey of more than two hours, and we were waiting at the station half an hour before he was due. To our surprise, when the train came to a halt, he stepped from the passenger carriage and, offering us a cheerful greeting, hurried to the rear of the train where he collected his bicycle from the guard's van. The episode puzzled us: why had he not ridden his bicycle all the way, instead of travelling in the train? We did not realise that Melbourne was about 130 kilometres away.

With a fourth child to look after, Mum worked even harder. As was the custom of the day, Dad did not help around the house, but his life was strenuous and he was always on call. Much of his time was spent in visiting the sick and the well, in conducting church meetings or in preparing his sermons for the Sunday – and these duties probably needed about seventy hours a week – he also dug and weeded the garden, grew the vegetables, clipped the hedges and chopped the firewood, a large amount of which was consumed in the kitchen stove where all our meals were cooked or in the fireplace that warmed the sitting room.

Our meals, eaten in the kitchen unless visitors were expected, were simple. At breakfast we ate hot porridge – breakfast cereals were too expensive for a large family – and on each plate of steaming porridge was poured a little milk and more sugar. Occasionally, in place of sugar, a spoon of golden syrup – a richly coloured treacle – was trickled onto the porridge. On our slices of toast we usually spread dripping, which was the fat saved from the roasting of meat, and a little salt. We loved hot toast and dripping, but it has been banished from Australian menus by a mixture of prosperity and a rising fear of heart attacks.

Although we lived close to dairy farms we ate little butter – it was expensive. Even for cooking cakes and biscuits, butter was rarely used. I remember that one swagman, to whom my mother gave sandwiches, threw them away at the front gate because the bread holding the meat was either unbuttered or merely flicked with butter. My mother was vexed by his contemptuous behaviour because she always gave strangers the same food as we ate. On days when we ourselves ate butter we obeyed the family rule that you could eat toast with butter or toast with jam but not both together. This frugal rule was observed in countless households.

The midday meal was hot, and known as 'dinner'. It concluded with a hot pudding or – in summertime – junket or custard or stewed fruits: Mum had shelves full of fruit that she had bottled herself. The evening meal, called 'tea', was lighter but could be formal if visitors arrived. Every church visitor to the town was accommodated in our house. For their benefit, butter was put on the table, and perhaps eggs were cooked at breakfast.

Potatoes, pumpkins, other fresh vegetables and bread dominated our diet. We also ate mutton as well as the cheaper butcher's meats – lamb's fry and kidneys which I loved, and brains which I loathed. Poultry was eaten at one meal of the year, Christmas dinner, the chosen fowl having lost its head on the chopping block in the woodyard on the previous day.

After each meal the dishes were washed in the kitchen sink. From an early age we children took turns in using a light tea towel to dry the dishes. To wash dishes and cooking utensils, hot water was poured from the black kettle kept standing on the top of the wood stove. The hot water for the tea – we drank no coffee – came from the same kettle. Like most families we had no hot-water tank or service, and so we washed our face and hands in the morning in a basin of cold water. Maybe on very cold mornings the water came from the kettle. The constant instruction to us was to 'wash behind the ears', which suggests that we usually did not.

When I ran home from school – or the swamp – I would find Mum making jam or baking biscuits and cakes in large quantities, or darning holes in socks and jumpers. She owned no vacuum cleaner, no refrigerator, no clothes dryer, no electric stove nor gas stove, and none of the other household aids now considered to be essential. She did, however, possess the Singer sewing machine which she pedalled, enabling her to manufacture the kind of dresses and pinafores that many people bought ready-made in the shops.

Whenever the family moved to a new district she – and we – had to make friends afresh. It was a bonus if a woman she had known as a teenager or as a young teacher moved to our town. The unexpected arrival in Leongatha of Alma Joshua, the wife of a young clerk at the local Bank of Australasia, was a happy day, and Alma would sometimes come in her best clothes for afternoon tea; and when we ran home from school – we ran the last 50 metres – and heard her voice or that of her littlest children we knew we could help ourselves to the remains of the cakes and sandwiches still sitting on the pretty china plates assembled for the occasion. Mrs Joshua, who possessed vivacity and human warmth, was a Catholic. In a smallish town it was unusual, in the era of sectarian rivalry, for the wife of a Methodist minister to have a close friend who was a Catholic. Her husband Bob had been a student at Wesley College and was an Anglican. During the Second World War, in North Africa, his bravery won him the Military Cross. Later he supported the nationalisation of all the trading banks – perhaps because he himself had worked for a bank. Even later, as a

Labor member of the lower house in the federal parliament, he became the first leader of the breakaway Democratic Labor Party, a minority party that helped Sir Robert Menzies to remain as prime minister for a record period.

I cannot remember listening to a radio broadcast when very young. If we did possess a radio it was inadequate, and picked up distant stations only after darkness set in, by which time – except in summer – we were almost ready to be tucked into bed.

In one room of the house stood a player piano, its polished wood gleaming in the firelight. On some Sunday evenings, the church service being over, young people would be invited in to chat and laugh, and to sing hymns around the piano. Sometimes I heard them singing and woke up for a few minutes. Of course they had to be given supper, and Mum was sensible enough to leave the supper dishes in the sink and wash them next morning.

A special vocabulary was part of our childhood. We lived in a house called the parsonage whereas the manse was the Presbyterian residence and the vicarage was the Anglican. A Methodist minister was always said to be *stationed* at his church. The word is no longer in common speech but was a resonant one in our house. It signified that to be a Methodist minister was to travel on a lifelong train that never stopped at the same station twice. Ministers, when they were young and unmarried, were transferred to another town every one or two years; but after they were formally ordained they were transferred every three or four years. I was to attend four different schools before I was twelve.

In April 1937 it was time to leave Leongatha. Our destination was chosen by 'the stationing committee', which met at Wesley Church in Melbourne. It publicly announced a first 'reading', at which all the ministers about to move were tentatively assigned a new church. As appeals or expressions of unease sometimes came from the minister himself, indirectly from his wife, or from the congregation to which he was to be assigned, the serious complaints and protests were met as much as possible in the later 'readings' which were printed in the news columns of all the major newspapers. That year the final reading, anxiously awaited, transferred us to Newtown, an old suburb of Geelong.

There were farewell sermons and much shaking of hands at the numerous wayside churches where Dad regularly preached. In Leongatha an evening 'public social' was held, speeches were made, and a gift was handed to my father to recognise what was hailed as 'an entirely successful ministry' by the local newspaper. 'A cheque', it added, 'was also presented to Mrs Blainey by the ladies of the church as an evidence of their love and esteem, and suitable gifts were made to the four little folk of the family.' What we, the little folk, received I cannot remember; but the cheques were sufficient to buy a large mantle radio-set.

I have rarely seen the town since leaving in 1937, but half a century later I was invited to launch a financial appeal for the Leongatha and Korumburra hospitals. After the speech I was presented with a painting on a gumleaf – the painting was of a wooden building, the pioneering Lyre Bird Mound Church, in which Dad had apparently preached. Later, during afternoon tea, older farmers from the hill country came up to say how much their family appreciated our parents' ministry to them. One recalled that his blind father loved the game of chess, playing it by touch and feel, but could find nobody else with whom to play in that hardworking district. Dad, in response, learnt how to play chess seriously so that he could play a game with the blind farmer.

3

BY CORIO BAY

Geelong was hustling and bustling in the eyes of those arriving from small towns. Street-trams turned sharply around the corners, even passing our house. In the early mornings a regiment of workmen cycled towards the Ford motor factory, the fertiliser works and the new wheat silos in one direction and the woollen mills in the other. Their bikes occupied so much of the road that the few cars could barely pass them. There was an urgency in the way some people, when pedalling, rang their little bells fixed to the handlebars.

Sunday in a small country town was quiet, but in Geelong the numerous church bells pealed, though our church in Newtown owned no bell. In front of most churches a noticeboard announced to passers-by who would preach that day, at 11 a.m. or at 7 p.m., and which particular text from the Bible would inspire the sermon.

By Saturday night, the noticeboards were lined with texts from Corinthians, Romans and Revelation, as if these would persuade people to abandon their own church and visit another.

From the verandah of our house on the slopes of Pakington Street we glimpsed the bay and the rugged You Yangs. The hoot of cargo steamships was sometimes heard when the wind blew our way. Along streets near the wharves many Scandinavian and a few Indian sailors sometimes strolled, while a few young people from the Pacific island of Nauru always were studying in the town: Geelong had close links with that phosphate island close to the equator.

John, Joan and I were enrolled at Newtown, a state school about a kilometre from our home. Miss Mockridge, who presided over the younger classes – she lived to be 100 – looked at our reports and concluded that Joan and I should be advanced a grade. John was already three grades above me. Year after year, we were each among the youngest in our classes or forms. In my crowded classroom maybe seventy students were taught by the one teacher; and the keener students were enlisted to help those who lagged in their lessons.

At Newtown State School the female teachers seemed more animated than the male ones, some of whom were returned soldiers and perhaps affected by their experience of war. One languid good-natured man opened our gates of knowledge in the morning and wearily closed them well before the day was over. In one year the most rewarding lesson was in gardening. A few of us were allowed to turn on the tap at the top of the schoolyard and let the water flow down the irrigation channel we dug in the soil. The garden sometimes blossomed.

It is easy to forget how vulnerable we were. In the street or in a shop an adult could rebuke us sternly and sometimes unjustly: adults had more moral and punitive authority than they have today. Even in the school's playground an older bully could snatch our bag of marbles or small bundle of football cards and run away, knowing if he was big that he might never be pursued.

On the whole we must have liked school. During one year I did not miss a single day of attendance, even sacrificing the chance to visit the distant city of Ballarat in the family car. That afternoon, however, I trudged home to the empty house and wished that I had missed school.

In wet weather, at recess time, groups of boys assembled in what was called the shelter shed where they gloried in a game called 'hoppo bumpo'. The custom was to fold one's arms, hop forward on one leg, and try to bump over a rival boy who had hopped forward from the other side of the shed. At playtime in winter a makeshift football was produced from somewhere, and the game of kick-to-kick prevailed. As leather footballs were expensive, a small, cylinder-shaped 'football' was made from a rolled-up newspaper. Imitating our heroes in the Geelong Football Club we would swagger around, making important gestures with the paper ball in hand, and taking an inordinate time before we kicked it.

In the year we moved to Geelong, I first watched its team play football – the game of Australian Rules of course – at the old Corio Oval, not far from the bay. A few years ago I went there; and to my surprise the football ground in the hollow below the Botanic Gardens had completely vanished, leaving no sign of the two grandstands, the steep embankments where the spectators stood, or even the oval itself. That they have vanished does not really matter, because I see the scene vividly.

My first visit was on a dull winter day and I went with my father. Setting out late we could hear the intermittent roars of the crowd as we came closer to the Corio Oval. Walking past the rows of parked cars, we paid our silver coin to enter the ground, and walked up the earthen embankment. Suddenly, as we neared the top, the green grass and the thirty-six players in bright colours came into sight. Instantly I thought it was a magical scene. Geelong was playing South Melbourne and the navy blue and white of the Geelong footballers' guernseys and socks contrasted strongly with the red and white of the opponents. The bright colours and the painting-like quality of the scene captured my imagination.

Back in Leongatha we had sometimes watched the local team but knew nothing about big-time football. I did not even know the names of most of the big league teams in Victoria. When suddenly we were confronted on the embankment of the Corio Oval by the sound and sight of people roaring their support for Geelong, I did not even know whether I should be on their side. For an hour or so I was inclined to support the opposing team, its colours being brighter, but by the end of the game I was a Geelong supporter and have remained so.

In the course of that year I became totally infected with the local enthusiasm for football, and by the time the 1938 season commenced I was determined to see as many as possible of the nine games that were played at Corio Oval in that year. Dad bought a membership ticket that entitled him to sit in the smallish grandstand and to take several children with him; and from the flat wooden benches I could see the marshes and the bay. I could smell the burning wood that, at little makeshift stalls behind the grandstand, boiled the water that heated the saveloys. From the footballers' change rooms below came wafting the smell of eucalyptus. The cheap universal medicine, eucalyptus oil was used to rub down the arms, legs and backs of footballers and also, in the form of a few drops soaked in white sugar, as a magical cure for our coughs and colds.

If we arrived early at the oval, we could see the last of the players arriving individually, with their footballing clothes packed in their small Gladstone bag. An afternoon at the football was a special outing; and numerous spectators dressed for the occasion in their Sunday suit – their only suit – and wore that wide-brimmed grey felt hat without which a man, in those days, was considered ill dressed.

Nowadays barrackers like to wrap themselves in their team's colours. Before the Second World War, however, virtually nobody except the footballers wore the team's colours. I did not once see a Geelong flag or banner carried by a spectator to the football ground. I knew no child who owned even a scarf in Geelong's colours of navy blue and white. In fact young boys were inclined to see the scarf as 'sissy' and to be worn only by girls.

As boys we longed to wear a Geelong guernsey, but they could not be bought at the clothing shops, and in any case would have been too expensive for most families. A few mothers, however, were coaxed into converting worn-out school jumpers into football guernseys, and to affix a number to the back. Sadly those home-stitched jumpers did not look remotely like a football guernsey, for in those days the real one had a collar. Seeing the coloured beanies, scarves, flags and jumpers of a modern football-going family, whether poor or rich, makes you recall the frugal era when new items of clothing were expensive. Maybe most of the nation's children in the 1930s wore second-hand clothes.

The team mementos that I did possess were precious. Small cards, larger than the present credit card, they displayed on one side the photo of a footballer, either in black and white or full colour, while the other side provided details of his footballing skills. Originally they had come in packets of cigarettes, one card to each packet, and were known as cigarette cards. By the 1930s they were issued with tiny packets of chocolate and also with slim packets of chewing gum, which was then the juvenile fad. Somehow I acquired 200 or more of these cigarette cards from the wife of a returned soldier. She explained that her boys, growing up, no longer collected them.

I divided the cards into the twelve teams of the Victorian Football League and treasured them. My brother and I even devised a game in which the cards lay in an oval-shaped section of the carpet in the best room (only the best room had a carpet) with players of one team in their set positions resting alongside players of the other team. A round marble served as the football; and the player cards kicked the ball towards their own goal. I kept a notebook in which the final scores of each match were recorded. When I was the umpire and the sole court of appeal, the Geelong team did well in this imaginary code of football.

When the Geelong team was playing in Melbourne, and the match was important enough to attract a radio station, I prepared to listen to the large 'wireless' in the sitting room – and operated my own scoreboard. In those days a game of football usually started at 2.45 p.m., so that people who worked in the morning could have time to go home, change out of their working clothes, and then proceed to the football ground. When the time for the radio broadcast came near I was in a state of tension, hoping that the sound of the broadcast would be clear and that Geelong would win. The football 'match of the day' on ABC Radio was introduced by a military band playing a Strauss tune, and the band was allowed to play uninterruptedly for a minute or more before the announcer on duty advised us that 'we are now crossing' to so-and-so ground to hear a broadcast of the match. The idea of playing classical music as a prelude to the broadcast of a popular football match would now be seen as highbrow.

I kept the scores not only on my homemade scoreboard but in my memory. Long afterwards I knew by heart the quarter-time scores, half-time scores and final scores of every match in which Geelong had played when I was a boy. Nowadays when I return from a Geelong football match, I write the final scores in my diary, knowing that otherwise I might forget them.

Soon I devised private games that imitated football. When walking on my own along Aberdeen Street to school each morning – members of our family all left home at separate times – I would play an imaginary match of football. Cars travelling one way served as scores for Geelong, and cars travelling in the opposite direction served as scores for, say, Collingwood. If the car was a pre-1930 model it only counted as one point whereas the latest Ford or Willys counted as a goal which equalled six points. Likewise, when I entered church on Sunday morning just before eleven o'clock, I looked at the board that listed the numbers of the four hymns to be sung. To me they were, when translated, forecasts for the football scores on the following Saturday.

Not until later years did I realise that my father, in attending the football, was carrying out his pastoral duties though he also enjoyed the game. His church had footballing links and he thought it his duty to take an interest in whatever attracted the members of his flock. The most famous footballing family in the history of Geelong were the Rankins, and they belonged to our local Methodist church. Teddy Rankin, as some called him, is said to have been the inventor, in a match against Fitzroy, of that sensible custom, when running with the ball on a wet day, of not bouncing it on the sodden ground but of leaning down and briefly touching the grass with it. His ingenious solution became a tradition of the game. One of his sons, Cliff, captained and coached Geelong to its first premiership in nearly four decades, and Bert was the champion goal kicker in the league.

Ted Rankin, his footballing days long past, sang each Sunday with his wife in the church choir, which stood in a high gallery looking straight down on the faces of the congregation. Alongside Ted in the choir stood his youngest son, Doug, who at that time was a promising Geelong forward.

Almost next to our house, in a side street, lived a fair-haired boy named Jimmy Knight. He was so slender that he might not be selected today in a senior football team but he was quick and courageous and very fit. He became a rover for Geelong just before the Second World War. On some Saturdays soon after lunch we saw him set out for the Corio Oval with his Gladstone bag. Often he said 'Good day' to us which we counted a privilege. Once he agreed to take to his team's training room my new red-backed autograph album; and a week or so later he returned with the autographs of all the Geelong players. When Japan entered the war he enlisted in Australia's air force and, serving at Goodenough Island in New Guinea in October 1943, he crashed his plane and was killed. Four decades later, after I praised him in an article in Melbourne's evening *Herald*, his sister wrote me a letter of reminiscence.

Only once did we attend a football match in Melbourne, though that city was barely 70 kilometres away. We attended the 1940 grand final between Melbourne and Richmond, and the crowd was so large that those of us who were young could see almost nothing until the last quarter when the crowd began to disperse. Hitler controlled nearly all of Europe, and yet here was a huge crowd behaving as if it were peacetime, and as if the real enemy was the umpire. Sixty years later I was invited to a large dinner in honour of some of Melbourne's premiership teams of the past, with Ron Barassi speaking for the 1960 team and Percy Beames for the 1940 team. Being a football historian

I was invited to speak on behalf of the 1900 team because all its players were dead. Later, around the table, I listened with fascination to the three surviving players of the 1940 team discussing the ups and downs of their grand final. In the course of the evening I learnt more about that match of long ago than I had seen as a submerged spectator.

In the provincial cities the churches were the focus for social and sporting activities. When the younger boys of our church decided to field a cricket team, Ted Rankin borrowed much-used stumps, bats, pads and ball from Geelong College, where he was the head groundsman, and entered us in the under-age section of the Protestant cricket association. We played our first match on a matting pitch, and our opponents came from a small farming village called Stonehaven. Being young, we failed to realise that the two umpires would not make certain decisions unless we first appealed to them by shouting, 'How's that?' So the umpires remained silent through all kinds of near-fatal errors by the opposing side, until Rankin advised us to appeal in loud voices. Our match, like scores of others, was reported in the *Geelong Advertiser* which listed the low scores that we each had made.

Next to the church was its own tennis court where we taught ourselves to play. In every sport we had to teach ourselves: there was no coaching. My brother John taught himself with high success and when very young could play a straight bat, bowl accurately, and kick a long drop kick. I had no sense of style, and did not learn how to imitate others. But at tennis for a time, maybe through sheer determination, I was skilled beyond my years.

One weekend the Australian tennis stars John Bromwich and Adrian Quist, along with Harry Hopman, came to Geelong to play exhibition games. It may have been just before they won the Davis Cup against the United States, and a big crowd was expected. The Geelong tennis chieftains decided to appoint ball boys, and though aged only eight or nine I was one of the boys selected, along with John, to fetch the balls and throw them back to the players. My parents told me to clean my tennis shoes – in those days they were painted by hand with the aid of an old toothbrush and a kind of white liquid. Spick and span I appeared at the tennis courts. A highlight for spectators was when Quist hit the ball so hard, in such an unexpected direction, that it almost knocked me to the ground. More memorable was the end of the tournament when I was presented with several shillings for my day's work.

The matinee at the cinema was a high point of the social calendar in suburban Australia, and groups of children, perhaps on a birthday outing, arrived in their neatest clothes and were ceremonially shown to their seats by an official and – if they were late – escorted to their seats by an usher shining a torch into the darkness. I felt only a small attraction to the cinema, unless the film was an adventure or firmly historical. On those few Saturdays when I was invited by friends to attend a 'movie' matinee at the West Geelong picture theatre, I usually resented the waste of the afternoon. One visit was part of the birthday of a friend of my sister. The main film starred Shirley Temple, displaying her curls and dimples, and performing her dances and songs with a pert cuteness. In 1938 she was Hollywood's top star but boys of my age disliked her. As I owned no watch, I thought the Shirley Temple film would never end.

The theatrical event of the year took place in our own house on the morning of 25 December. A Christmas tree, consisting of a green branch of a pine tree brought from the country on the previous day, was tied to the wall and topped with streamers and silver paper, and on the branches we placed a present for each member of the family, bought with our own money. At that time no family of our acquaintance erected a Christmas tree. It was our mother's belief, not our father's, that we always must have a Christmas tree. Curiously the Methodists, viewing the exuberant celebration of Christmas with distaste, did not honour the day with a special church service unless Christmas fell on a Sunday. Accordingly the whole day for us was usually free of duties.

The Newtown Methodist Church was rather stately, of yellow sandstone and white limestone, with two aisles separating the lines of ornate wooden pews. The minister's wife and family always sat on the left side, halfway down: that was presumably the tradition. Each Sunday morning one of the stewards or ushers, waiting at the front door to shake the hand of adult members of the congregation as they arrived, deemed it his duty to escort my mother and her four children down the aisle and show us to our regular seat. Methodism was proud of its friendliness, and the shaking of hands but not the kissing of faces was the custom at every opportunity, before and after divine service.

The sense of togetherness on which Methodists prided themselves was audible in the singing of hymns. A congregation was judged worthy according to whether its singing was 'hearty' – a ubiquitous word in Methodism – and not lukewarm. From an early age I joined eagerly in the singing.

My father preached in our church building about every second Sunday morning, for other churches nearby also demanded his attention. In his absence his fellow ministers or laymen conducted the service and delivered the sermon. One of the laymen was J. J. Peart who lived within sight of the church. A rural headmaster, long retired, his manner was stately, and his authority unchallenged. When he walked slowly down the wide carpeted aisle to his favourite pew with Mrs Peart at his side he resembled a reigning monarch. He had once been the headmaster of the goldfields school at Majorca where the Nicholas children were pupils; and after two of the Nicholas boys became the manufacturers of Aspro, the most popular patent medicine in all Australia, they sometimes gave money to Peart's favourite charities.

J. J. Peart was the first speaker who made me feel that a poet was worth admiring. He centred a few of his sermons on talented poets and hymn writers who were in their heyday when he himself had been a young teacher. He would recite religious verses composed by Christina Rossetti and Frances Ridley Havergal and link the verses to episodes in their lives. He largely controlled his strong emotions when speaking, and that made them the more powerful. For the closing hymn at our church he would occasionally, from the high pulpit, call on the congregation to sing with all its heart Miss Havergal's charming hymn 'Master, Speak! Thy Servant Heareth'. He would recite expressively the first verse, as the custom was, before the pipe-organist was allowed to play the opening. On the rare times I hear that hymn on the radio, I see him facing the congregation, an image of an elderly King George the Fifth, his face slightly radiant.

For most Australian children of that era, Sunday was a special day though it was seen as a day of duty as much as a holiday. I observed the atmosphere of Sunday morning, even at maybe the age of five. There was a silence in the streets, and almost everything was closed. It was different to the other days, and we were allowed to read in bed until a slightly later hour; and Mum and Dad by their attitude announced quietly that they were not completely in charge of us. I suspect that they both had imbibed the religious text that, in full colour, was printed in flowery style on pieces of cardboard framed on the walls of countless Australian sitting rooms or placed prominently on the kitchen mantelpiece: 'This is the day which The Lord hath made. Let us rejoice and be glad in it.'

When we awoke we saw our Sunday clothes laid out ready for us to wear. On such a morning I used to rub into my windblown hair a sweet-smelling yellowish oil called brilliantine, which almost kept it in place. To have your hair neatly parted, in a straight line down the side or right down the middle, was a high priority. On the previous evening we had to clean our shoes, rubbing the black polish into them and then shining the leather. My father, however, cleaned his shoes almost every day of his adult life – except Sunday when he gave them just a flick with a cloth. Another ritual of Sunday morning was an inspection of faces and behind ears by our mum. She presented each of us with pennies to place in the 'collection' plate passed around at a certain stage of divine service. Though we did not know it, we were helping to pay our father's own salary or his 'stipend', as it was called. A few years later our parents decided that we should be paid a larger sum of weekly pocket money, and that from that sixpence or ninepence we should personally set aside our own money for the collection plate. This indirectly served to diminish our dad's stipend.

The whole family was out of the house for much of Sunday. The custom, however, was that the back door should not be locked.

When Mum had a new baby, she carried it in her arms to church. Crying babies – so long as they did not cry continually – were welcomed in the congregation, though if they happened to bellow during the prayers or sermon they would be taken outside and patted on the back, rocked to and fro, and perhaps fed a little milk from the breast before being carried back into church.

Dad was fond of classical music and made financial sacrifices so that we could learn the piano. Miss Wyatt used to ride her bicycle with a stately posture down the hill to attend evening services in the Newtown church, and she taught the piano in an elegant house with verandahs fronting the wide Virginia Street. At about the age of nine I was enrolled as one of her piano students. Instructed to play the piano each morning at home, aided by the rhythm of a metronome she lent me, I found the piano practice a burden, and instead used the metronome to mark the time in some football game I had ingeniously contrived.

The highlight of Miss Wyatt's year was an afternoon gathering – almost a soiree – at her house where the young students in turn played the piano with the sheet music before them and plates of chocolate biscuits – then a luxury – arranged as a reward. I played her chosen piece and was also granted permission to play 'My Old Kentucky Home', one verse only. My parents, observing with their own ears that their money was being wasted, readily met my plea that the lessons should cease.

I was too young to show more than a flickering interest in history. When I was aged eight, Geelong celebrated its centenary, and children had to take a role in the civic rejoicing. At the Corio Oval, where in winter the Geelong team played in all its glory, a festival was arranged, and we were dressed as golliwogs and our faces were darkened with a sock-like black mask with holes for eyes. On the arena I heard for the first time Percy Grainger's jaunty tune 'Country Gardens'. Of popular music I knew almost nothing – moreover that tune was not yet so popular as it later became.

Sometimes I would ride down to the nearest wharf to see deep-sea ships coming and going. Many coastal freighters, grimy or rusty, used the wooden piers close to the main streets. Each afternoon at 4 p.m. the tiny SS *Edina*, said to be one of the oldest steamships in the world, for she was built in 1854, set out with passengers for Portarlington and Melbourne. The one-way fare was a mere two shillings and the signboard on the wharf was cautionary, always announcing that she would sail 'circumstances permitting'. The port had its seasons and as I loitered around the wharves, watching and listening, I realised that there was a regular season for the overseas wool ships which mainly used the Yarra Street pier and another for the overseas grain ships which often tied up at Cunningham Street pier.

On some Sunday afternoons, Mum would walk us down to the port with Ellis, then the youngest child, sitting in a pusher. It was exciting to examine the stern of a ship and see, above the propeller, the painted name of its home port. Yokohama or West Hartlepool, when painted in white on a half-rusty strip of iron, seemed exotic. Sunday was a kind of open day in the overseas ships berthed alongside the piers; no loading of cargo took place, and an officer, more neatly dressed than on weekdays, might be on duty at the top of the gangway. Visits by parents and their young children were often welcomed, and we would walk carefully up the steep gangway and from the deck look over the side of the ship to the water that seemed so far below and, if we were lucky, be shown the captain's quarters or the wireless operator's room. In Japanese ships the officers, usually dressed in white, spoke no English but were notably friendly.

One weekday afternoon, holding my bike and dawdling at the piers, I watched the grubby coastal ship SS *Saros* taking in her heavy cables from the wharf and being towed into the shipping channel of the bay, and a day or two later I read in the newspaper, to my astonishment, that she had been wrecked somewhere beyond Wilson's Promontory. After the interstate ship *Orungal* was wrecked on a reef close to the headland at Barwon Heads, I cycled to see the strange sight of a stranded ship onto which the waves were breaking. At home one wall held a coloured map of the British Empire, alias the world, on which were drawn the main sea lanes; and when I heard that a departing ship was about to sail to a foreign port I would ride home and inspect the route it was likely to follow.

The family suffered one serious mishap at Geelong. Dad, perhaps through overwork, caught measles and then rheumatic fever and had to lie on his back and keep his head firmly on the same pillow for eight weeks. On Sundays members of the congregation poured into the house to visit him and wish him well. 'The Geelong ministers stood in to a man,' he recalled. We crowded into his room to share Christmas dinner in 1940.

An exciting event of my childhood now seems trivial, but then fell like a gift from heaven. It involved Grandpa Lanyon, whom I must now introduce properly. Henry Maynard Lanyon was his full name but he called himself Maynard, the name coming from his grandmother – one of the three Misses Maynard who, Protestants by religion and seamstresses by trade, had emigrated as teenagers from Wexford in Ireland in the early 1840s. On the other hand, the Lanyons were Cornish. Our grandfather, the son of a Cornish-born farmer, had been reared on a wheat farm on the north-western plains of Victoria near Boort. Eventually he became a teacher and moved around Victoria, becoming the head of larger and larger schools. While he usually wore an orthodox grey suit and a grey felt hat, he favoured what was called the batwing collar which meant that he wore no tie. He displayed what my mother called the longish 'Lanyon nose'. He was the only one of our relatives whom we met in nearly every year of our childhood, and we rejoiced in his visits.

I did not yet know how public-spirited he was. When the new language called Esperanto became the rage – an artificial East European language that was intended to end all verbal misunderstandings and even to terminate all wars – he embraced it. He taught my mother and her brothers and sisters how to read and write it. Not long before the First World War, he was spending a large sum in posting picture cards, with Esperanto messages written by his own children, to penfriends in Vienna, Prague, Berlin, Warsaw and other Central European cities where the new language was being hailed by many professional families as the saviour of humankind. Dozens of his penfriends must have died in the First World War.

In 1917 when victory in the war was not yet in sight, he addressed a manifesto, printed in Esperanto, to selected soldiers of the warring nations and even to President Wilson of the United States, outlining his plans to end the war and to prevent future wars. He advocated not only a United Nations organisation but also the creation of a strong international army and navy to intervene for the sake of peace. These steps, if successful, would be followed by a general disarmament around the world. A printed version of his manifesto was widely discussed in Australian newspapers. His was a long-range plan; he did not wish to halt the recruiting of more Australian soldiers for the depleted armies in France and Belgium.

On controversial topics of the day his interest was intense. A wall of his house displayed a framed certificate proclaiming that he had voted at the referendum held in 1899 to decide whether Victoria should enter the proposed Commonwealth of Australia. When a few years later the federal parliament, meeting temporarily in Melbourne, had to decide which was the best site for the new capital city, it could not make up its mind and toyed with a dozen sites in south-eastern New South Wales. One summer, my grandfather set out on his pushbike to inspect nearly all the sites, travelling hundreds of kilometres along hilly gravel roads He carried his few possessions on his bike and, if I understood him correctly, regularly posted his stained shirts and underclothes back to his wife who was living in Corryong in north-eastern Victoria. When he reached a town with a draper's shop he bought a few more shirts and pairs of socks. This procedure relied on a hardworking wife.

When young he rode a motorbike; but an accident permanently stiffened one of his arms, and even the act of putting on an overcoat became awkward. He then travelled everywhere by train until, at about the age of sixty, he bought a streamlined Plymouth. This American car miraculously appeared outside our house in Geelong during a school vacation. Grandpa asked whether any of us would like to travel with him on the day-long journey to Bendigo, and the two oldest were selected. So one fine Saturday morning in May 1938, we joined this enthusiastic driver, my brother John in the front seat and I in the back.

At a speed that would have shocked our mother, we were soon charging along the road towards Ballarat. We boys knew enough about cars, our father being a very safe driver, to realise that we were travelling with Jehu.* It only enhanced the outing. In no time we were in East Ballarat where old Aunt Polly was providing hot tea and

* Jehu, leader of the army in Biblical Israel, was noted for his 'pell-mell style of chariot driving'.

cake while her silent husband, much older, sat by the fire, a black iron poker in his hand. A few hours later our fast car left for the gold city of Bendigo. This was the first time I had ever seen signs of goldmining; and in paddocks alongside the highway were mullock dumps of clay or stone, many of them fresh, the search for gold having been revived during the Depression of the 1930s.

We reached the outskirts of Bendigo soon after sunset. Our favourite Jehu, his one useful arm tugging at the steering wheel, eventually reached his own mother's house in the suburb of Quarry Hill. After we had rung the doorbell and waited for what seemed an hour she came to the front door. In a kindly way she instructed us, to our juvenile astonishment, to put the horses in the stables before we came inside. Her memory was failing, and she assumed that we had come in a horse-drawn vehicle. After all, she herself had travelled over much of the western half of Victoria when roads were unmade and the horse was king.

Once inside her rambling house, my brother and I were not in the least interested in questioning her about her slow dray journey, long ago, to become one of the first white women in a new farming district. Instead we longed to know who had won the football, for Geelong was playing at Richmond. From her wireless, after much tuning in, we heard the final scores.

The next day passed with a visit to the Quarry Hill church and all kinds of short excursions in the bright-green car. On the third day we left for home. As we sped along the narrow bitumen road towards the spa town of Daylesford we were full of merriment, until Grandpa picked up a swagman who had hailed the car. Thereafter, to our resentment, the two became absorbed in adult conversation. Our wonderful journey was almost over.

Grandpa neither smoked nor drank but had a craving for confectionery. Wherever he travelled he carried a white paper bag containing boiled lollies, acid drops, aniseed balls, humbugs and other tooth-breaking sweets. On the occasions we met he would take us on long strolls, handing out sweets, telling us simple jokes. His way of laughing was eccentric; and when his enjoyment of a joke was about to fade he could prolong the laughter for a few more syllables. On meeting a stranger, his common mode of address was 'My good man!' A child was sometimes greeted as 'My little man!' Unlike some of the stern, unbending teachers of that era, he was fond of children.

He taught us how to play chess, long before we had the patience that was demanded by that slow-moving game. When we visited him in Melbourne the chessboard was brought out, too early for my liking, in his darkish ground-floor study. There he kept a pleasing library including heavy volumes called *The Historians' History of the World* which he read assiduously. Their prose was too oratorical to appeal to the young but his reverent attitude to the books was noticeable. He especially liked statistics about Australia, and he presented to me at an absurdly early age his copy of the 1935 edition of the *Official Year Book of the Commonwealth* with its thousand pages of statistics in fine print, along with the odd press clipping that he had pasted on the appropriate page.

Knowing much about history, Grandpa helped to infect me. Like most people then, his knowledge of Australia's history came less from books than from the reminiscences of relatives and acquaintances. That line of contact conveyed him back to the 1840s with ease but in the convict era he showed no interest: the convicts primarily belonged to New South Wales and Tasmania whereas he was a Victorian. He accepted an invitation to write and print a history of his local Methodist church in time for its fiftieth birthday in 1933; and when several decades later I read his book I belatedly realised his restless talent. The topic of his history was narrow but was enlivened by his numerous asides and his high ideals: 'Why are we Australians just now waking up to the needs of our own aborigines? Why do we still inflict on our children the barbarism of English spelling, and the difficulties of our system of writing? Why do we keep up the language barrier between nations when there is a way out?' His way out was, of course, Esperanto.

In this book he chattered on, praising the cheerful morning greeting from a neighbour, the prose of the King James Bible, and the hymns which 'set the warm blood flowing'. He celebrated Australia's brilliant skies and wide spaces which, he hoped, would give rise to 'a spiritual individuality' that no other nation could express. He rejoiced in 'the glory of the clouds, the splendour of the sun, and the sweet quiet beauty of the moon'.

His wife Mabel was not often seen in the fast green car. Thin, neat, and practical she was always busy. Her thoroughness was evident even in her way of eating: she methodically chewed every morsel of food. A feeling of duty hovered over her during nearly every waking hour, and she did good works in every town she lived in, but there was a natural kindness mixed with the sense of duty. Though she had not received much formal education she read widely and seriously.

After she moved from the country to the Melbourne suburb of Box Hill she became active in this and that worthy organisation. The various missions to the Aborigines, Fijians and Papuans received money from her purse and also coins she collected from others. Becoming prominent in the local branch of the United Australia Party – the dominant conservative party – she baked scones, poured cups of tea, handed out how-to-vote cards on election day, wrote out the minutes of meetings, handed out petitions for indignant and passive citizens to sign, and put together the bouquet to be presented to the wife of the visiting speaker. When she died unexpectedly in 1942, R. G. Menzies reportedly said that her death was a blow to his political party which by then was in the doldrums nationally, though not in the suburban electorate where she had laboured.

Mum taught us to be independent. In many ways she was less protective of us than was our father, but more encouraging when we took risks.

In Geelong we were encouraged to earn pocket money. Along the narrow street running at the side of our house was a large bread-bakery and its team of delivery horses. It does not seem entirely hygienic for the stables and the sweet-smelling bakehouse to have been side by side, but the health inspector ensured that the stables were freshly hosed. Sometimes I took a wheelbarrow or a billycart there and in the vegetable-growing season I would deliver manure to backyard gardens of neighbours for a small fee. I also collected sauce bottles, jam jars and soft-drink bottles and sold them to a man who came round with his horse and flat-topped cart, calling out 'Bottle-o' in a high voice. As Dad did not like us to collect beer bottles – he was an ardent teetotaller – that eliminated one source of revenue.

I longed to be allowed to sell newspapers at busy intersections, after school. There was something exciting about this frontline activity. All the time the boys shouted aloud, 'Herald, Herald', and jostled potential customers or thrust the newspaper almost into their face. A tip occasionally was pressed into the hands of the newsboy. 'Keep the change' was one of the swashbuckling sayings of the era. As street newsboys were cheeky, many parents thought that their own sons would be 'keeping bad company' if they joined those selling newspapers on the street corners. It was considered more appropriate to be riding a bike and delivering newspapers to selected houses in street after street – a form of delivery called a paper round. In this lonely task there was little chance of mixing with the rough and tough and learning bad language. Nothing more distinguished that era than the determination of large numbers of parents and teachers to prohibit or frown on swearing and bad grammar and their confidence in denouncing it, when confronted by swearing in a public place or in the presence of women. It was astonishing that the son of a nonconformist clergyman, Bob Hawke, did much when prime minister to make swearing seem respectable; but then he, as a social rebel, was rebelling against a taboo that must have been imposed on him as a child.

At the age of ten I inherited an afternoon paper round from my brother John, delivering papers to a zone of narrow streets in West Geelong on each weekday or on the much busier Saturday. My employer, Mr Chapman, rented a shop close to the railway station; and my first task was to collect the heavy parcels of newly printed newspapers that had been tossed onto the main railway platform from the guard's van at the rear of the Melbourne express. I picked up the parcels, some heavy and some light, and carried them to my bike and, after precariously arranging them on the handlebar, pedalled swiftly to Mr Chapman's shop. On Saturday evenings my arrival was anxiously awaited, for already the shop was half-filled with customers eager for the latest news. Chapman pulled out his knife and swiftly cut the whitish rope that bound together the various bundles. Placing some *Herald*s on his counter and selling them to the waiting customers, he carefully counted the other copies before handing bundles to me and the various other newsboys to deliver. Then I rode along the narrow streets of my 'round', placing the papers at the front gate or door of the regular customers. In winter the evening papers were distributed after dark. Fortunately they were light in weight, for a shortage of newsprint was thinning the large-sheet *Herald* down to a mere sixteen or so pages.

As newsboys we each on our bike carried a few spare newspapers in case a passer-by wished to buy a copy. Every now and then we would shout our wares, calling 'Herald Sporting Globe!' as if it were one rather than two newspapers. *The Herald* then cost one-and-a-half pence, and some male customers handed over twopence and said, with a burst of generosity, 'Keep the change.'

On Saturday nights, I also delivered copies of the pink-coloured *Sporting Globe* which printed vivid descriptions of that day's league football matches, maybe to three-quarter time, with the final scores appearing in a column kept vacant on the front page and known as the 'Stop Press'. Most readers turned to this column before they read the headlines. The phrase 'stop press', no longer used, indicated that the actual printing of the newspapers had been stopped so that the latest piece of news could be added. It was one of the exciting phrases in the language during the dark months of the war, and in that little corner of the front page were the latest snippets about the bombing of London or – if no news had arrived 'by British Official Wireless' in the past few hours – lesser items of news from the front line.

In the winter of 1940 the war was at a crucial stage, and on some evenings many residents would be waiting at their front gate for their copy of *The Herald*. It announced dramatic events: the German troops entering Paris, the collapse of Belgium, Italy becoming our enemy, and the latest aerial battles in which ninety or more German planes were reportedly shot down from the British sky. There was even talk that

Hitler would invade Britain any day. The headlines often selected the good news, and it was my understanding that the Germans were losing the war. I did not realise that so many people were waiting for me at their front gates largely because they were fearful that the Germans would win the war.

I followed the disasters and the occasional triumphs of the Allied side in the European war every day except Sunday, when newspapers were prohibited by law. My fascination with the war in France became so intense that I tried to recreate it in a shaded corner of our side garden. In sandy soil where nothing seemed to grow, I began to dig a line of miniature trenches facing each other. No deeper than a forefinger, and paralleled by sloping sticks that I intended as tank-traps, the trenches were an imitation of what I thought was happening on the fighting fronts in Europe. Trenches were more the hallmark of the First World War than of the Second. In the early months of a new war it is the previous war that is likely to inhabit the imagination.

4

BALLARAT

Ballarat, to which we moved at Easter 1941, was unlike the towns we knew. The streets seemed eccentric, and one of the narrowest suddenly widened into a broad boulevard of spires and towers, shops and statues – the long Sturt Street. A canopy of old English trees shaded many streets while in the near distance could be seen a blue semicircle of timbered hills, distinctively Australian. After a year I vaguely felt that the nobler buildings and archways, cobblestone workyards, numerous spires and towers, were all trying to speak, but remained silent. Puzzling too were the pyramid-shaped mullock dumps, leftovers from the goldmines. I knew little about the history of Ballarat, and we were taught none at school, but in subtle ways I was becoming conscious of history without quite knowing what it was.

Our weatherboard house, furnished by the people of the church, lay on the narrow strip between the lake and the old cemetery, where dead miners and soldiers of the Eureka Stockade were buried. One of my Cornish great-grandfathers lay there, in the same grave as his brother who was killed in an underground accident in about 1861. The goldfields history that I first learnt consisted of anecdotes about or by relatives. I did not yet realise that my four great-grandfathers and four great-grandmothers had all lived on the early goldfields.

Almost as soon as we poured through the front door of our new home in Burnbank Street, a heavy knock on the back door was heard. It was a milkman carrying his big silvery metal can from which he ladled out milk, sold by the pint. A little later a second milkman arrived seeking our custom.

John and I went to Ballarat High – he was two years ahead of me. Originally an agricultural high school, it was proud to possess 40 acres, mostly pasture turned into sporting ovals, as well as a new and open-air swimming pool. In all Australia few schools possessed their own swimming pool. Not once, however, did we swim in the much-admired pool: after a fatal accident it had been closed.

The first-year students did not attend the big school but were housed in a few schoolrooms in Pleasant Street called 'The Branch'. Mr Hobba presided there. Of Cornish ancestry (as I now realise), with that slightly dark complexion and impish grin common to many of his kin, he was an utterly professional teacher. Hobba in his young days had taught at Benalla High where one of his talented students was Dr 'Weary' Dunlop, who was about to become a war hero in Malaysia and Thailand.

Recently the reports for students in my class were shown to me. To see them after all these years was like surreptitiously reading a private letter over somebody's shoulder. The marks for each of the ten subjects were set out in neat writing, presumably that of Mr Hobba. Probably because I enrolled late in the school term, I performed feebly at the first-term examinations. For science I was awarded 22 marks out of 100, for algebra 25, for geography 48, for history 50. Mr Hobba looked on this performance with more toleration than he should have: 'Working well. Making satisfactory progress.' In the next term I seem to have recovered strongly, and my marks even for science jumped to the 80s.

We were fortunate to live within three minutes' walk of the lake where in summer we could swim from a tiny beach or jump into deeper water from a jetty. At a bargain price I bought from a friend a roughly made iron canoe, painted a rusty brown and just large enough to seat a small person. In rough weather it was dangerous to venture out, but normally I went far from the shore, eventually paddling the canoe past every mud bank, reed bed and tiny island. I was invited to join the Sea Scouts who met weekly in a steep-roofed shed overhanging the lake, but to my disappointment they spent much of their time in the tying of nautical knots.

America's cultural and economic influence (I now realise) was becoming strong. Whereas the popular radio serial of my childhood was *Dad and Dave*, which was emphatically Australian, it was sponsored by the makers of that most American of products, Wrigley's chewing gum. American films were popular; and of the mere five or six films I saw in the first ten years of my life, most were from Hollywood. The cars that my father drove – Model T Ford, Overland, Chevrolet and DeSoto – were American though far from new. I had not yet set eyes on that American delight, a bottle of Coca-Cola. Britain decisively flavoured our political, economic and social life, but in 1942 for the first time I set eyes on an American person, a soldier in uniform.

We were to take a fortnight's annual holiday at the seaside at Point Lonsdale, but the house was not vacant until February when the school year was about to begin. One warm Sunday – it must have been early in February – we were playing on the beach, close to the narrow entrance to Port Phillip Heads when, out to sea, the smoke of approaching ships could be seen. Through the narrow entrance to the bay steamed a procession of grey ships, their decks crowded with soldiers. We could actually see the whites of their faces. Mum soon found out, from gossip on the beach or a word passed on from the nearby lighthouse, that it was an American convoy of troops, one of the first to reach wartime Australia. Unknown to us, our parents were emotionally moved by the sight.

Japan had bombed Pearl Harbor less than two months previously; the war for Australia and our allies had slipped from bad to worse; and the Japanese forces were sweeping through the Indonesian archipelago towards our coast. Now, in response, 'The Yanks are coming', as the popular song announced. Ballarat was selected as a temporary staging camp, and thousands of American soldiers arrived by train, and for a few weeks they were billeted in private houses around the city. To our disappointment our house was not chosen.

So many foreigners had not been seen in Ballarat since the gold rushes. Moreover the American privates were dressed like our officers and had dollars to burn and were happy to buy trinkets from enterprising children. Emboldened by tales of success I waited outside the American army camp where I tried to sell a small brass kangaroo, worth just a few pence. I offered it to an American soldier. He said, 'Thanks, buddy,' put it in his big pocket and walked away.

*

Darwin and the ships in its harbour were heavily bombed by Japanese raids on 19 February 1942. The newspapers, censored by the government in Canberra, minimised the deaths and the damage. Many Australians continued to fear that their country would be invaded, though children were largely protected from the fear: indeed they protected themselves, for their outlook on the world tends to be optimistic. Early in the year, lessons were halted at many Victorian high schools, at least for the boys, and nearly all hands were employed in digging air-raid trenches. We brought our fathers' picks, shovels or spades to the school and dug long trenches to a depth of about a metre and a half. The earth and clay tossed aside by the shovels gave the trenches an additional height. They were zigzag in shape, presumably so that a Japanese aircraft flying above in a straight line and firing a machine gun would hit only a fraction of the children sheltering there. The digging of the trenches was exciting; a sense of team spirit came from somewhere, and many of us were disappointed when the task was completed and we had to go back to the classrooms and full-time lessons. Once the winter set in, the trenches quickly filled with rainwater.

While the war was in this dangerous phase, I was allowed – at the age of twelve – to make a long journey on my own. It was arranged that I should go to Melbourne to stay with my grandparents during the May vacation. At the railway station the Friday afternoon train was soon packed, and even the corridors were congested with kitbags and standing passengers, most of whom were soldiers and airmen on leave. It was dark long before the steam train entered Melbourne's suburbs, and there the streets seemed ghostly, for the streetlights and bicycle lights were faint, and residents had been ordered to show as few house lights as possible so that any patrolling Japanese aircraft would not detect the presence of a large city. Even the headlights of the few cars waiting at the level crossings were dimmed by a metal mask that allowed only a narrow beam of light to extrude.

At Spencer Street station, Grandpa Lanyon was waiting with his welcoming grin. Next morning dawned the happiest of days. Travelling to the city in the suburban train from Box Hill we walked to the big library in Swanston Street. It was breathtaking to see the shelves rising high, tens of thousands of books groping towards the tall dome, and to hear the silence. Not even a whisper was tolerated by the stern attendants.

For an early lunch we went to busy Bourke Street where the G. J. Coles cafeteria was the vogue. Customers formed a line and, each carrying a tray, walked past the glass cases and selected a hot meat pie here, a plate of jellied fruit there, and maybe a lamington though that delicacy was fading away because coconut – once imported from New Guinea – was becoming scarce. Then we went in the tram to the football match at the Punt Road Oval where Richmond was playing Melbourne. It was the first footballing appearance for several years of the decorated war pilot 'Bluey' Truscott, who had just returned from the aerial combats in Europe where he had won the Distinguished Flying Cross and Bar. Now he ran onto the ground, conspicuous with his reddish hair and chubby physique, and from time to time he chased the ball. Sometimes it was generously pushed his way, and the neutral patriots in the crowd along with the Melbourne barrackers shouted their approval. He did not play football again. He was killed when his fighter aircraft crashed near the coast of Western Australia.

I assume that I was sent on that wartime holiday in order to relieve the workload on Mum. Two months later, on 31 July 1942, she gave birth to Donald: he was a long way behind the rest of the family, for John was now fourteen, I was twelve, Joan had just turned eleven, and Ellis was seven. When Mum was in hospital, people of the congregation looked after us. For a few memorable days I stayed with the Bryants, and I used the room of their only son who was serving in the air force. Etty Bryant was stout and warm-hearted while her husband Elijah, a maker of leather boots, was light in build and reflective in mood. In the kitchen Etty, her sleeves rolled up, served him bacon and eggs from an immaculate frying pan on the black-polished wood-burning stove. She allowed me the luxury of fried eggs too.

The nation, both home and away, was waging war with an intensity unimagined just one year previously. More and more people went to work in munitions factories or the armed forces. Petrol was already scarce, clothing was rationed, and everyone had to use a government ration book and deliver a few of its coupons in order to buy sugar, meat, butter and tea. The ration books were guarded closely even when the shopkeeper took them in his hand and with scissors cut out the required number of coupons. At times firewood and even freshly skinned rabbits became scarce, because trucks lacked the petrol with which to traverse long country roads.

The small monthly ration of tea was a hardship. People were always calling at our house, and a cup of tea was given to them almost as a ritual. The ration soon ran out, but Mum discovered in a magazine a recipe for making tea out of wheat. If sugar was spooned into the hot cup – and most people in those days added sugar – the wheaten tea was palatable at least to children. For a time we drank more wheaten tea than Indian tea.

At this stage of the war, every family was encouraged to produce their own vegetables and even eggs, for that would save the petrol consumed by trucks carting produce to markets and shops. My mother said she would buy what I grew, and so in a section of garden, almost in the shadow of the church wall, I planted beans, potatoes, pumpkins and whatever else would grow easily in the summer.

As eggs became scarcer I boldly entered the egg industry. The *Ballarat Courier* advertised that six laying hens were for sale in the vicinity of the Eureka Stockade, and I rode my bike to the house and examined the hens, about which I knew nothing. Paying out the money, I rode home on my bike with the hens in a large hessian sack on my back, the owner having tied their feet. Five were white leghorns, while the other, mottled red and brown, was pronounced by one expert to be a Rhode Island Red. The local grocer, Harry Lingham, sold me bran and pollard which I mixed with water for their breakfast, and loose wheat which I sprinkled on the earth floor of their shed for supper. At the height of the season they daily laid six eggs, one of which was brown. As a poultry boy this was my contribution to the war effort.

As labour became scarcer, a door-to-door salesman hired me as his offsider. He made his living by buying fruit and vegetables at the wholesale market, loading the boxes of bananas and cauliflowers and so on in the back of his panel van, and driving round a circuit of suburban homes. Throughout Saturday, and occasionally on weeknights, I was Mr Smith's helper. He went first to the back door and collected an order from the housewife, pencilling the details in his notebook. Back at the van he weighed the fruit, then put them unwrapped in a large cane basket, which I carried to the house. Sometimes I had to arrange the produce on the kitchen table, or in the washhouse or bathroom adjacent to the back door. Always I collected the money and handed back any change. He was extremely trusting.

Meanwhile he drove on to the next house, sometimes 800 metres away, and collected another order. I followed on my bike, with the leather moneybag hanging from my shoulder and the empty basket on the handlebar. Sometimes he was busy flirting in a light-hearted way with the housewife – he was in his thirties and his ruddy face radiated vitality and goodwill – and I might sit for the next half-hour on the tray of the van, waiting for him to reappear. When waiting I was allowed to eat all the fruit I wished. I also received a payment in shillings which at the end of the day he took from the leather moneybag and counted.

On the fruit round, I met my first author, Nathan Spielvogel. He had been known for his travel books, one of which – an overseas tour – was called *A Gumsucker on the Tramp*. In his retirement he lived in a side street near our home and looked after the old synagogue in East Ballarat and presided over the local circle of history enthusiasts. Nearly always it was a housewife who presided over the purchases of fruit and vegetables, but Mr Spielvogel was the exception, and in a benign way he would tell me to arrange his new-bought apples and oranges in a bowl sitting near a backyard window before he paid me the money. The tradesmen, of whom I was one, always called at the back door.

The fruiterer taught me economics. When cutting the Turk's-cap pumpkin with a long knife or weighing the pears – he placed 'weights' on his slightly rusty hand-scales – he would talk about prices. It was he who told me whether eggs were in short supply, as often they were, and what price I should charge my mother. He told me how to reply to customers who complained about the prices. So I pointed out that Professor D. B. Copland, the wartime price commissioner, fixed the price of everything, even bananas; and accordingly if a Ballarat customer complained that our large oranges were each twopence, whereas a city friend was paying only one-and-a-half pence,

I explained that we were allowed to charge country prices. When I came to know Professor Copland two decades later I assured him that at one time I was his obedient servant.

On the eve of one Easter there arrived a parcel. It contained hundreds of postcards written in Esperanto and originally posted to Grandpa Lanyon and his family from countries in Central Europe. Mostly written just before the First World War, the cards displayed on one side a hand-coloured photograph of a street scene in Prague, Zurich or other cities. The blank side of the card usually began with the words 'Cara samidiano', meaning dear friend, but it was the postage stamps in the right-hand corner that attracted me. Most depicted the head of a monarch but one mauve twopenny Tasmania stamp showed snow on the mountain high above Hobart.

That Christmas, I received as a present an album covered in mock leather, with letters of gold proclaiming that it was the Premier Globe Stamp Album. Spacious white pages, consisting of a chessboard of squares in which used stamps could be stuck, were assigned to nearly every land from Abyssinia to Zululand. Weeks of my spare time were spent in licking small hinges and fixing my stamps to the appropriate page. Puzzling were the German stamps issued in the early 1920s when inflation was out of hand, one coloured stamp alone costing 4 million marks. I knew nothing about inflation but I was learning geography.

After school I sometimes rode my bike to the library owned by the Mechanics' Institute; the ornate building had once been the stock exchange. It sometimes gave off a musty smell consisting perhaps of fresh clag, stale leather and dampish paper. Gaining courage enough to dawdle there, I began to read purposefully, my early favourites being the travel books. Possessing an intense longing to see the world, I used to climb onto the high iron roof of our weatherboard house and sit on the topmost ridge. There I could see the timbered Great Dividing Range, on the other side of which were the plains that led all the way to those northern shores of the continent that were sometimes being bombed by Japanese planes.

One day in summer, resolving to travel as far as possible to the north, I rode along the narrow bitumen road stretching past brown paddocks towards the gold town of Clunes. A strong tailwind blew me there. I spent hours butting into the headwind in order to make the return journey of 32 kilometres. On reaching home, I announced that I had more or less seen the world.

In school I was lacklustre in manual activities such as drawing. At woodworking, which was called sloyd, I spent hours making a small wooden teapot-stand, an item that was once in every house. My stand had a slight wobble when placed on the kitchen table. At unskilled tasks I was more competitive. When we had to dig the air-raid trenches I was called upon to take a sharp spade and straighten their sides.

In schoolyard games such as marbles and tipcat, I became a lesser star. The dangerous game of tipcat must already have been banned in most Australian schools but was tolerated at Ballarat High because so much space was available in its playgrounds. The 'cat' was a thin oblong piece of wood, with each end shaped by a knife or chisel to a sharp point. The player carried a stick, hit the sharp end of the cat so that it flew into the air, and then thumped the airborne cat as far away as possible. The risk was painfully high of a sharp wooden point of the flying object hitting the face of at least one spectator.

With so much grassland surrounding the school, nearly everyone could play sport. My brother John was a fine drop kick and stab kick but I was not: I could pursue the ball well but I had a most unconventional way of kicking. I counted myself lucky when in 1942 I sat as nineteenth man, meaning the spare reserve, on the boundary line at the Redan oval in a match against another school. I was neatly attired in the sea-green football jumper of our school, with thick white laces tying up the football boots I had borrowed, but in those days the nineteenth man did not play unless there was an injury. In the following year my friend Rex Hollioake gave me half a minute of glory. At a time when even in senior football a player would use a handball only as a means of escaping from trouble, Rex was capable of using it creatively. Once when I was standing alone he unselfishly punched the ball to me – he still recalls the occasion – and I kicked a goal. His sporting career was to be in Ballarat but two of his nephews were to play cricket for England. Half a century later I was to become the first chancellor of the new University of Ballarat – now called the Federation University – and it gave me such pleasure to see Rex sitting at the same long table as the members of the governing council.

When young I loved mental arithmetic and literary subjects such as English and history. In the third year of high school a young teacher, A. L. Moore, taught us history and literature with flair. He had an eye for students whom he thought were eager, and he encouraged some of us without saying anything that could positively be called encouraging: the skilled teachers don't necessarily need to offer incentives because their whole manner and spirit are an incentive. I delivered fruit to the back door of Les Moore's lakeside house on Saturday mornings, where usually I met his charming wife, and so I knew more about his home and family than he realised. Later he went to Canberra where, as private secretary to R. G. Menzies, and then as the deputy head of the prime minister's department, his talent was appreciated.

As a twelve-year-old in Ballarat my knowledge of history earned me a rare prize. On commercial radio a popular peak-hour program was called *The Battle of the Sexes*. A quiz contested by teams of men and women, it offered a reward – not often awarded – to listeners who could prove, in writing, that the quizmaster of the show was in error. One night in 1942 a question asked of the rival teams focused on the birth or death of Muhammad and whether it took place in Medina or Mecca. One team gave its answer, which was accepted as correct by the judge. I wrote a letter pointing out his error. In the following week *The Battle of the Sexes* announced that 'Master G. Blainey of Ballarat' had exposed an error in the previous week's quiz. My prize, a postal note worth £5, was sufficient to buy a second-hand bike. For a few days my success was widely talked about in Ballarat where the radio program always attracted a large audience.

Sundays revolved around church. We went to the Christian Endeavour meeting – for the very young – in the early morning, to church itself at eleven, and to the Sunday school in mid-afternoon. Miss Ross supplied the Christian component of the Christian Endeavour. Her family looked after the railway gates at the end of our street. Wearing large surgical boots, she limped her way each Sunday from the railway gates to the church with some difficulty, a Bible and hymnbook in hand. She could not always maintain order, strong-willed as she was. We were unmanageable.

One of her favourite hymns was 'Build on the Rock, and Not Upon the Sands'. When the singers reached the lines that announced that the house would stand firm even 'when the earthquake shook', Harold Troon and Edgar Bartrop and I would climb on to the seats and then jump, landing with a thud on the wooden floor at the very moment when the song reached the word 'shook'. This was an era before spontaneity and self-expression were encouraged in the young.

The church where we gathered at eleven o'clock was nearly always full. Built in the previous century by that sect called the Primitive Methodists, it was austere inside. A high pulpit was set against the back wall, and just below sat the large choir which had rehearsed its anthems during the previous week. There was no pipe organ but a strong cabinet organ for which the air was supplied from a vertical pump worked by hand. The boy who worked the pump, Ivan Sweatman – his older brother was soon to die as a prisoner of the Japanese – was paid a small sum each month. When he went on summer holidays I took over his task. The bobbing head of the pump boy, as he pressed hard with both hands on the handle, could clearly be seen by the congregation.

The windows of the church held not an inch of stained glass. There was no symbolic cross, and not a hint of an altar nor – God forbid – a candle. But the singing of the congregation was hearty; and sometimes on a hot summer evening when we and neighbouring friends were playing in our house next door – for we did not go to evening church – we heard the robust singing, the doors and windows of the church being ajar or open.

A commanding member of the congregation was Johnny Lavars, whose jaw seemed to be of iron and whose grey hair was cut unusually short. Though one of his legs was stiff, probably from a mining accident, he walked with conspicuous dignity when handing out the collection plate. Serving also as a caretaker of the church's properties, he needed to give only one glance to scare away a trespasser. In conversation he spoke loudly, as if addressing a distant audience. He was accustomed to addressing outdoor audiences, for in 1901 he had been president of the local branch of the Amalgamated Miners' Association when it was among the largest trade unions in Australia. He was one of the few citizens who in these wartime years was active in honouring the uprising of goldminers at the Eureka Stockade in 1854. I assume he was a relic of the old Primitive Methodists, who had built our Burnbank Street church and had also been influential in England where they were founders of its Labour Party.

In Ballarat the Methodists owned more churches than the Catholics and Anglicans combined, and their ministers regularly preached in each other's pulpits. The most frequent such visitor to our church was the Reverend Arthur Lelean who was in charge of nearby Pleasant Street – nearly every Methodist church in the city was named after a street and not a saint. As a missionary in Fiji he had been a founder of a powerful farmers' movement. Today Lelean would be called a faith healer though that description was not quite appropriate. Plucking from his pocket a round metal object rather like an empty pocket watch and running it over the fully clothed body of someone who was sick or lame, he made his diagnosis according to the ticking sound or the way the watch 'oscillated' on its cord. At least that was how I understood the technique of this tall, bald and gracious man. He did not ask for money. Not claiming to possess a detailed medical knowledge, he usually was happy to direct his patients to the appropriate doctor though he and the medical profession were not natural allies. For those patients who had no time for real doctors he had his own pet nostrums, recommending that they should bathe their aching limbs in borax. That medieval medicine, the green dandelion leaf, was another of his favourite cures, and occasionally at home Mum would experiment with a dandelion sandwich.

Lelean with his trusted, ticking watch case was sometimes taken to a parched paddock and implored to tell the farmer where a well or bore should be sunk in search of water. In money he personally had no interest. He had a touch of the saint, and many people who called on him felt that they were 'in the presence of a man of God'.

Slowly the news of what were called 'his gifts', along with the report or rumour of miracle cures and uncanny diagnoses, spread across the countryside. So many people came to consult him – the tally exceeded 12 000 by 1951 – that he had less time for his religious duties, some of which fell to my father.

Dad was also pastor of another flock at the wooden Jubilee Church, still standing on the Wendouree shores of the lake. In the front row of its congregation sat a stooped, deaf old man called Sampson Selman. One evening during the darkest chapter of the war he knocked at our front door. I was the one who opened it. He announced that he wanted to see Dad on a matter of grave importance. He added that he wanted to discuss 'that man Hilter'. He meant Hitler, of course.

The fortunes of the war in the Pacific slowly began to favour Australia and our allies. The Japanese forces that invaded New Guinea were repelled on the Kokoda Track. In May 1942, on the ocean far east of Cairns and Townsville, the aircraft carriers, warships and troopships of the Japanese invasion force on their way to Port Moresby were halted and turned back in the Battle of the Coral Sea. The danger of an air attack on a major Australian city was receding. Though in 1942 tiny Japanese submarines did sneak into Sydney Harbour, and a

Japanese seaplane – unknown to us – flew over the industrial suburbs of Melbourne, the enemy seemed far away. Most of our school air-raid trenches, having become a breeding place for mosquitoes, were filled in during the following summer.

Meanwhile more and more people were called up for war service or to work in munitions and other factories. In the church halls there were farewell concerts and socials, which we were allowed to attend, though quietly leaving for home before they were over. There were speeches and presentations, perhaps a song or hymn by the church choir, an 'item' or two from a solo singer or even a mouth-organ player, and a recitation of a serious or comic poem. A wallet enclosing a few banknotes, a Methodist hymnbook, a fountain pen or a biscuit barrel were popular gifts for the young men and women departing. Months later word might come back that one of them had been wounded or killed.

As labour and petrol became scarcer, all kinds of activities were halted – even senior football. The shops reflected the scarcities. Toffees, musk sticks, chewing gum and other sweets were hard to find. Homemade sweets became popular, but they were not very plentiful, for sugar was rationed.

A keen reader of newspapers, I graduated from the sporting pages to the war pages and more slowly to the political pages which I innocently saw as another version of a sporting contest. In the winter of 1943, a federal election was approaching. Ballarat took an abnormal interest in national politics, because local boys held the centre of the stage. John Curtin, who was born in the nearby town of Creswick, was the prime minister; and Robert Menzies, who had temporarily ceased to lead the Opposition but was its most celebrated member, came of Ballarat parents and for some years had attended schools in the city. There was even an ardent communist candidate, E. J. Rowe, the president of the Ballarat Trades Hall, and his speeches on the local radio (where a brass band usually played the rousing 'Internationale' at his request) were listened to with less unease than hitherto, for Russia and Australia had become allies in the war against Hitler.

I found myself reading the election pages in the newspapers. When the names of all the federal candidates throughout Australia were published, I read the long lists and noted all the parties, familiar or strange, that put forward candidates. Curtin thought the Ballarat seat, then held by Labor, was so important that he came by train to speak; Menzies spoke at another packed evening meeting. Against the candidates representing the two main parties stood a third candidate, Gordon Irish, a railwayman. We knew him – he was an earnest teacher at our Sunday school. Calling himself a 'Christian Independent', he must have been the only candidate in Australia who issued how-to-vote instructions under the proclamation 'Thus saith the Lord'. Teenagers from the church, too young to be voters, were enlisted in his team handing out the how-to-vote cards on election day, from eight in the morning to eight at night. On the far side of Ballarat my brother John handed out cards for Bill Roff, a popular plumber who was the conservative candidate. On the Saturday of the election, I climbed onto the house roof and for hours watched the people arriving to vote in the adjacent Sunday-school hall, which was a major polling booth.

Across the nation Labor won the election by a huge majority. In the following fortnight, my desire to recreate competitive events being quite unslaked, I wrote in an old ledger a list of all the electorates in the House of Representatives and all the contesting candidates. Then I conducted a federal election. In my mind's eye I went round Australia organising and casting votes. Actually the votes for each candidate were determined by my throwing a dice four times, the first throw giving the voting tally in thousands, and the second throw in hundreds. This meant that many of the results were surprising. I forget whether I devised a way of distributing preferences in close contests.

A few teachers must have noticed my new-found zeal for public affairs, though the war itself was not discussed in the classroom. Accordingly on the eve of the school's speech night, a teacher chose two appropriate books as the prize I was to receive. *One World* was a bestselling travel book by Wendell Wilkie who was to stand against Franklin D. Roosevelt in the coming presidential election in the United States. The other was a memoir by a captain of the German navy, Franz von Rintelen, who during the First World War had gone to the United States as a spy. It was odd that so German a story should be on sale in a wartime Ballarat bookshop, but the German captain had written his book in the early 1930s, in the hope that there would be no further wars.

The speech night was held in the barnlike Alfred Hall, perhaps the largest weatherboard hall in Australia and standing astride a creek. In our green guernseys and freshly washed shirts, we sat in our well-scrubbed ranks, girls and boys. Parents came in hordes, and dignitaries sat on the lofty platform. Millie Peacock, who had been the first woman in Victoria to win a seat in parliament, was wrapped in a large fur as if she were a pet tabby-cat, and beamed at the procession of quick-walking prize-winners, to each of whom she offered homely words of praise. I still possess the two books Lady Peacock handed to me. Printed on brownish, chaff-flecked wartime paper they are enriched by the bookplate pasted in the front, and the copperplate signature of the headmaster, G. A. Simcock. His initials G.A.S. yielded his nickname.

*

I did not return to the school. Several months earlier a minor item in the newspaper announced that the estate of a dead man was financing an unusual scholarship. He was Howard Hitchcock, who in life had been the owner of a Geelong emporium. The original sponsor of the construction of the Great Ocean Road, he had also provided the money that two or more decades previously enabled John Brownlee, who played the cornet in a Geelong brass band, to go overseas for the tuition that launched him on his famous career in opera. This new princely schoolboy scholarship, named after Hitchcock, was open only to sons of Methodist ministers. Moreover they had to be aged about thirteen, and they had to live more than 30 miles (48 kilometres) from Melbourne.

I showed the news item to my parents. They suspected that I had a strong chance of winning but were not openly enthusiastic. For me to go away, to live in a different and less religious environment, to be in the company of boys who presumably would have more money than I could possess, must have worried them. Nonetheless they gave their tentative consent. They bought me a railway ticket and I went on my own to Melbourne the day before the scholarship exam. It was conducted at Scotch College in Hawthorn, and sitting slightly mesmerised in its baronial hall I answered the exam papers. It was soon my impression that I could win the scholarship because there was only one other competitor! A few weeks later my father received a letter saying that I had indeed won.

The scholarship, perhaps the most benevolent in the land, enabled the winner to be a boarder at Wesley College without paying fees of any kind. There was even an allowance for textbooks, train fares to and from Melbourne, and weekly pocket money. My parents, with five children to feed and frequent public and private calls on their own purses, foresaw hidden expenses that they doubted they could meet. A year or two earlier my father had experienced a minor financial crisis, and had been forced to sell the family's most valued possession, our fine German player piano. Naturally he was wary of incurring debt.

A few days after the arrival of the letter announcing my success, a Ballarat neighbour stopped to yarn with my father who was weeding the front garden. Enquiring after the family, he learnt that I had just been offered the scholarship. My father added that it would probably be unwise to accept the offer, as additional expenses would inevitably arise at the school, and he might be unable to meet them. Once the neighbour heard the news he walked the hundred or so steps up the hill to his house, and returning with a valuable banknote in his hand, presented it to my father.

J. F. Kittson, the neighbour, had won the Military Medal on the Western Front in the First World War and was the head of a rural butter factory and one of the directors of an institution of which the town was proud, the Ballarat Banking Company. His gift to Dad was doubly generous because he and his wife Minnie had once been prominent in our church but had walked out, along with friends, after a dispute – maybe theological, maybe personal – split the congregation some years before our arrival. The Kittsons thereafter had 'worshipped' with another Methodist congregation. I now realise how gracious was his offer, strictly anonymous, to help the pastor of the very church from which, in earlier years, he had publicly parted.

My father promptly wrote to Wesley College to accept the Howard Hitchcock Scholarship in my behalf. Of this gift from the neighbour I was, sensibly, told nothing. I owe him a deep debt.

5

BIDDY, FIDO AND TOSH

Using his scarce ration of petrol, Mr Kittson drove my father and me to Melbourne. It was in mid-February 1944, a hot northerly was blowing, and as we passed through the small township of Melton the brown clouds of dust obscured the main street. Once inside the city I thought the St Kilda Road with its avenues of green trees, and the school itself with its tall poplars and that green oval known as the 'Front Turf', were an oasis; the school was completely new to me. We briefly met the headmaster, I was shown a dormitory where I was allotted one of four beds, and then Dad went to catch the evening train to Ballarat.

The school held a powerful sense of tradition: never before had I felt part of a tradition that I could comprehend. It could be sensed and felt each weekday morning at twenty minutes to nine, when the senior school assembled in the Adamson Hall. Its walls held dark wooden honour boards, on which long columns of initials and surnames printed in gold, and usually running to the high ceiling, recorded the names of Wesley boys killed in war, along with the captains of football and rowing and cricket and athletics, and winners of scholarly prizes extending back to the start of the school in 1866. I could readily pick out a few familiar names: a recent prime minister, a winner of the Victoria Cross, star cricketers and footballers, and well-known professors. As I grew a little older I came to recognise more and more names.

The morning assemblies held in that hall were presided over by Neil Harcourt MacNeil, a headmaster of grave appearance even when not dressed in his black flowing gown. Each Friday morning, in a sombre and resonant voice, he read the long lists of names of the old boys killed in the two world wars, each name beginning with the year he had entered the school. Presumably he had known some of those people killed in the First World War, when he himself had won the Military Cross. Every few weeks a new name joined the list of the dead. The name was not announced as a new entry: it just slipped into its rightful place in the roll call. A few of those killed were the older brothers of boys still at school. I suppose we all privately wondered on rare occasions whether the day would come when our name was read out.

General George Vasey, an old boy of the school, came as guest of honour to one assembly. The first general I had seen, his khaki uniform with its vivid patches of colour was a splendid sight. It was easy to glimpse why he was popular with the Australian forces fighting in the north. After hearing him for twenty minutes we felt that we almost knew him. In the following year he was killed in an air crash near Cairns. Thirty years later I sat on a committee with the general's younger brother Gilbert Vasey, who told me that he had lost a brother in each of the world wars.

The sense of tradition stirred me. The boarding house I liked, and its feeling of solidarity. Though far outnumbered by day boys, the boarders – numbering eighty or so – felt that they were the heart of the school. It was still the era of the nickname: everybody must have one. The resident masters who lived in the boarding house included Plug (who was Mr Kennedy, the housemaster), Tiger Pete (a kindly and inwardly wounded First World War veteran), Milky, Narse, Brandy-Faced Jack, Hopalong and Joe Blow. Among the boys were Creamo Crust – he had very white hair – and Gandhi, whose father was an Australian doctor in India. There was Donga Dave who came from Wodonga, and Do who was named after his extravagant 'hair-do', and Peewee and Pegs. And Eigentlich which was the German for 'actually' and given to a fast runner from the Wimmera who began his sentences with the English version of that word. Many of the names were plays on words. As General Blamey was the best known Australian soldier, I was called General which was later shortened to Ral, by which name occasionally I am still called.

We ate at long tables in the dining room with its magnificent carved European sideboard at one end. Porridge, shepherd's pie, roast mutton and beef, stews, hot puddings, banana or apple fritters, and hot cups of weak tea were there in plenty. On each table at breakfast was placed a square of butter – the tea, sugar, butter and several other foodstuffs were still rationed by the government – and a boy cut it with a knife into an equal number of small oblong pieces: he himself had to take the last piece – an incentive for him to be fair. The meals pleased most of us though somebody from a very wealthy family might have been disappointed.

As labour was scarce, the boarders had to do most of those tasks that in peacetime had been carried out by maids, gardeners, cleaners and other servants. We made our own beds and helped to operate the washing machines in the big spotless kitchen: a washing machine was a luxury and rare in our own homes. In the evening, our help might be called upon if a major cricket match was to be played on the Front Turf next day. The groundsman, an Englishman named Frank, normally supervised the draught horse and the heavy iron roller that flattened the cricket pitch; but if heavy rain had made the wicket too soft we would be summoned to replace the horse and pull the roller. The horse, which lived within walking distance of the school, was a particular favourite with those boarders who came from the wheat belt where teams of sturdy Clydesdales prevailed.

Before long, I knew the names of the country towns where most of the boarders lived. This strange mosaic of geography is still in my head, and if by chance I meet any of the former boarders I can say instinctively, 'And how's Culgoa?' – or Dimboola, Nullawil, Warracknabeal, Charlton, Yanac, Orbost, Corinella and thirty other townships or rural crossroads as well as towns interstate. Peter Nixon came from Orbost, Sid Muir-Smith and Alan Dixon from Dimboola, the two Morrisseys came from Ingham in north Queensland. In no time we knew each other's hometowns. And there was also Sheep Hills, a tiny Wimmera township that had been the long-time home of Old George, the handyman in the boarding house. Slightly stooped by a life of hard work, he walked with a swaying gait as he carried a mop and a bucket of warm water, halting every so often to tend his tobacco pipe. He longed to yarn about old times, and droughts, bumper harvests and his succession of sheepdogs. He could remember when the very first fences were laid across the plains near his childhood home. Unknowingly he taught me rural history.

The year was divided into three terms, and the end of each was a day of elation for many boys. Suitcases were packed before breakfast. At morning assembly the traditional hymn began with the line 'Lord, dismiss us with Thy blessing', with a final verse farewelling 'all who here shall meet no more'. After the last lesson of the afternoon we each carried our suitcase to the St Kilda Road tram and went to the city railway stations. Nobody caught a taxi. In my first year nobody went home by aircraft or an interstate train because long-distance travel required a permit which was not easily secured.

Near the top of my class at Ballarat, I fell behind at this new school. While I was one of the youngest in the class, I did not yet realise the quiet ambition that permeated many boys. The desire to excel seemed to stem from a minority of the boys and their parents more than the staff. I doubt whether I even heard the work ethic specifically extolled by any teacher until Major Jack Kroger, who had been captured by the Germans in North Africa, returned in 1945 as a master in the boarding house. The most warm-hearted of men, he had sympathy with failure as well as success, but he also believed that we all had a potential that we could pursue by sheer willpower. He especially praised the hard work of the wartime Swiss, with whom he had lived after escaping across the mountains from enemy territory in north Italy.

In my opening term in 1944 the only subjects in which I stood near the top were history and 'Divinity' which was really religious history. In the two mathematics I fell far below the average. At the end of the first term I finished, overall, in twenty-sixth place in a class of thirty-four. In the winter term, working harder, I finished ninth. 'A marked advance', wrote the headmaster in my report book. There had been a long way to advance.

The senior teacher of history encouraged me. Arthur E. Gwillim came from the Victorian goldfields near Taradale, the son of a Welsh-born mining manager. He could be courtier-like in his manner, but his mind was his own and his opinions were in no danger of being blown inside out by the latest popular gust. Walking in quick short steps this shortish, portly, elderly man exuded mental energy and quick perception. Combining geniality with authority, he doffed his hat to all and sundry in the street. He was also our deputy headmaster. Though his face was oblong his facial features were sharp. Noticeably his small topknot of hair stood up like the crest of a helmet. He made it his business to know the name of every boy – only surnames were used in the school – and something of their background. In his eyes I was Ballarat. As he thought well of Ballarat, I was the gainer.

His teaching methods would not find their way into a modern teaching manual. He would select a book, Professor Ernest Scott's *Short History of Australia* being his favourite, and let it guide our lessons. Requesting each boy in turn to read aloud a paragraph or two from Scott's blue-coloured book, he benignly corrected their mispronunciations of people and places; and then, when they had finished their reading, add his own reminiscence of the person or place. Now in his early sixties, Gwillim had heard the speeches of most of the leading politicians of his generation, and could create a lively verbal portrait of Alfred Deakin and George Reid and other long-dead prime ministers of whom he approved. A Latin scholar, familiar with an earlier empire that was as influential as the British Empire now was, he imparted his perspective on the long sweep of history.

Gwillim devoted months to the history of India, South Africa and other British colonies. Capturing his zest, I would wake at sunrise and read in bed one of the library's books about the Boer War. His head was a nest of quotations, especially from Shakespeare, and he would pluck one at the appropriate moment. When the forty-minute lesson was over, and we were ready to go to our next classroom, he would recite with the voice of a major general those lines from *Macbeth*: 'Stand not upon the order of your going, But go at once.' His son, always referred to as 'my son Jack', was away at the war, and the father treated many of us as if we were adopted sons.

Known as 'Fido', Gwillim in his eccentric way was an impressive teacher. He had enthusiasm and a willingness to teach us to write clearly. The handwritten essays we submitted he marked diligently, adding a few tasty morsels of information as well as corrections of grammar and spelling.

Only one woman taught us. Named Edith Barrett Eastaugh, her nickname was Biddy. My first sight of her, so straight-backed, left me apprehensive, but I cautiously became fond of her. She taught German and Latin; and as I arrived with no knowledge of German and was at least one year behind the other students, I relied on her help. After school she generously gave me additional lessons in the hope that I would catch up. When my father heard that I was studying German he posted to me a large German–English dictionary set out in quaint Gothic type: he had used it as a boy in Bendigo. I learnt many German words that caught my fancy, though they were not in the syllabus, but my grammar did not match my vocabulary. In my two years with her I learnt just enough to save me years later when I crossed Siberia in an all-Russian train where nobody else spoke English but one spoke German.

Probably in her mid-fifties, Biddy wore a long dress with long sleeves: her arms too were long. She once rolled up her sleeves an inch or two to display to us her wrists. One wrist, her tennis wrist, was thicker than the other. That delicate display was the closest she came to bohemianism in our presence. Personally she was affectionate to those few boys she came to know well, and I think I was among her favourites. She did not say she liked you but instead would say how much she admired your neat handwriting or praise you in other ways that were beyond reproof.

In our final year, Biddy would reminisce to a few of us, though her sense of duty allowed her only a few minutes for such a frivolous pastime. When very young she had taught at the old South Melbourne College, under the leadership of the poet J. Bernard O'Hara; and when that college of prize-winners was taken over by Wesley during the First World War she came as part of the purchase. To us the picture of propriety, she had once been on affectionate terms with many writers and artists. After leaving school I bought in a second-hand bookshop a volume on the popular poet C. J. Dennis, which reprinted a photograph of a bohemian gathering at a holiday house in the Dandenong Ranges. There sat Biddy, much younger in looks, her hair black, her gown and white topcoat spread far down, and her face maybe a little wistful. She once told us that she had helped to give the hill town of Kallista its name – the word was classical Greek.

Arthur Angell Phillips, the other bohemian in the school, taught me English and literature. Strictly speaking he did not teach everyone: he taught only those who were willing to listen. Pacing up and down the long and low platform in the front of the classroom, he spoke in an emphatic and slightly rasping voice, his hands in his grey flannel pockets: a lonely and sensitive rambler. He fixed his eyes on the floor as he walked, the edge of the platform being a hazard; and he glanced upwards only so that he could maintain order, which he usually did, though at times his margin of victory was narrow. Nonetheless he liked to hear the more impudent or brighter interjections – not that many came his way – and he even relished a minor disturbance in the room, for that gave him an opportunity to score with his tongue. His weapons were wit and mild sarcasm. When he marked essays, which he did conscientiously with a round script, his comments were forthright.

When I arrived at Wesley at the age of thirteen, I wrote a prose style that to my eyes seemed rather sophisticated. Slightly antiquated and florid, it was not suited to the mid-twentieth century. In the margin of one of my essays, in his owl-like writing, Phillips added the simple word 'flabby'. Reluctantly I began, with some relapses, to follow his advice. In the most senior form, where he also taught a subject called English Expression – compulsory at the public examinations – he singled out the weaknesses in our prose, for this was his last chance to reform us. On my first essay for that year, a comparison of the reporting in the *Age* and the *Argus* newspapers, he wrote sternly: 'Material very good; but the style does not come off.'

He was painstaking in reading each essay, so long as it did not exceed the word limit he imposed. Occasionally he would pencil on the margin: 'not quite the right word'. The surplus adjectives in my writing he deleted, and every overstated argument he queried. My emphatic arguments would provoke the comment: 'Over dogmatic'. By the middle of the year he was winning his battle. At the end of one essay, worth 16 out of 20 – a high mark by his standard – he noted: 'A fairly terse economic style best suits your type of thinking.' In my last essay for the year, a discussion of the rocket range proposed for the lonely interior of South Australia, he awarded me 18 out of 20 and wrote pithily: 'more effective than your florid style'. Since then I have tried to write tightly, using no more words than are necessary – though not always successfully.

I understood A. A. Phillips' views on writing after once skimming his essay on the literary critic and newspaper commentator

Professor Walter Murdoch. Now also remembered as the uncle of Rupert Murdoch, the media magnate, Walter in his heyday was known nationally for the essay he contributed to each Saturday afternoon's Melbourne *Herald*. Phillips was to the point: 'Murdoch doesn't have a style: he simply writes very well. His meaning is declared with an unemphatic firmness and an infallible clarity.'

In a school whose headmaster revered punctuality, Phillips tended to be a rebel. To be fair to him, he arrived only two minutes late. He would have seen punctuality as a dereliction of duty – duty to himself and to his thoughts. His late arrival in the morning was forgivable because, in that era when the electric razor was unknown, he had trouble in shaving his face with the sharp blades in vogue. His newly shaven face might be marked by a strip of sticking plaster, a dab of cottonwool, a torn piece of cigarette paper, or streaks of styptic pencil applied to stem the blood. His upper lip was spared, for he wore a moustache, neatly clipped. It was slightly stained with nicotine; he liked to take one last puff at a cigarette before he entered the classroom.

Of partly Jewish background – the painter Phillips Fox was a relative – Mr Phillips was a cartoonist's joy with his lean and slightly sad face, his curved nose, his eager eyes and – if he woke up late – his accidental shaving gashes. His first task on entering the classroom was to wipe from the blackboard those cartoons of his face drawn in chalk by John Stafford and other wayward boys a few minutes earlier. Behind his back we called him 'Tosh', that being a word with which he himself dismissed statements that he deemed to be worthless. I don't know what he thought of us, except that he probably viewed us on the whole with as much affection as dismay. His influence on those willing to be influenced was profound.

An all-round teacher, he coached me in the Under 15 cricket and football teams. He umpired football wearing a strange harlequin jersey that he probably acquired during his time at Oxford. His training instructions occupied barely a minute, and at times he seemed absorbed more in his own thoughts than in the game of which he was in charge. And yet he was observant of each boy and their personality while on the field. In the 1920s when he was a very young schoolmaster he must have observed how a boy called Harold Holt played football on the school's oval; and forty years later, when Holt was prime minister, Phillips summed up his character by saying that he was an able back pocket, that being a defensive position in Australian Rules football.

In nearly every cultural activity A. A. Phillips was our leader. He supervised the school's large and handsomely printed magazine called *The Chronicle* which I edited for three terms; he ran lunchtime and evening debates in which I took part; he managed the school library which was impressive by the standards of the era; and he produced the school's annual play. At a time when the English departments in most universities neglected Australian authors, Phillips promoted their plays and poetry. At school he even staged a new play, *The Fire on the Snow*, written by the poet who conducted the literary page known as the 'red page' of the weekly Sydney *Bulletin*, and was therefore one of the few influential literary critics in the land. This young literary lion came down from Sydney to view what must have been the first performance of his new play. That afternoon, from an upstairs window, I was curious to set eyes on this slight, dark-haired man who, I was told, was Douglas Stewart. A quarter-century later we sat regularly on the committee of the Commonwealth Literary Fund where we became allies and friends.

It seemed a waste of talent that 'Tosh' Phillips should teach reluctant boys, for he was one of the more astute critics in the land.

It was he who coined one of the most quotable of Australian phrases, *the cultural cringe*, which Paul Keating as prime minister was to employ vigorously more than one generation later. The 'cultural cringe' referred to an old-time Australian tendency to bow down in the presence of English culture. The day was to come when many Australians tended to 'cringe' slightly in the presence of the multicultural.

In 1985 – when he was in his mid-eighties – I heard word that Phillips was in a big hospital in Malvern, and rapidly failing. I found his room, and he climbed out of bed and put on a colourful dressing gown, the scene bringing to mind his old harlequin jersey. For half an hour he was spirited in conversation. Then he told me that he had cancer, adding, after a pause, 'It's incurable.' The words were said without fear or self-pity. I thought suddenly of all he had given to us.

He had not long to live. He apparently suggested that I should speak at his funeral, and on the day of his death his wish was passed on to me. I paid him tribute in the school chapel – a building he had rarely, if ever, entered.

I must return to 1944 and the Christmas vacation, when I spent my last weeks in Ballarat. My father's four years were almost over, and the Methodist tradition insisted that he must move on. I enjoyed that last summer, having a deep affection for Ballarat. During the previous year I had added 3 inches in height and was now 5 feet 8 inches (173 centimetres), as I noted in my pocketbook diary for 1945. Being – since the age of seven – one of the youngest in each class, I had also been one of the smaller; and now at the age of fourteen I was catching up.

That was a summer of incessant swimming: in the lake at Ballarat, in rock holes of the Wimmera River, and on the beach at Point Lonsdale where the family stayed for almost a fortnight about Christmas time. I could swim long distances in the lake at Ballarat and in the big swimming hole at the nearby gold town of Creswick. One afternoon, in a display of showing off, I swam 2300 metres. It was a hot summer of dust storms, some of which blackened the sky, and it turned out to be almost the end of about half a century of relative dryness in the south-east quarter of the continent.

On Monday morning, 5 February 1945, just before eight o'clock, I took my suitcase aboard the train at the railway station, knowing that I would not live in Ballarat again. My parents were preparing to move to Melbourne two months later where my father was posted to a church in Thornbury, about 10 kilometres from the city. One of the closely settled northern suburbs, in today's terminology it was perhaps more like a 'western' suburb. The high-roofed brick church stood conspicuously on a ridge, with no other large buildings nearby, and so in clear weather it could be seen from the Heatley grandstand at the Carlton football ground. It was called the Prince of Wales Park Methodist Church, though no park was in sight: it was simply the flowery name given to a new neighbourhood by a developer of property late in the previous century.

My father relished the move to 'The Park', as they called it. The congregation was strong, the people were warm-hearted, and in spirit they reminded him of the corner of the Bendigo goldfield in which he had grown up. At The Park nearly everyone barracked for either Collingwood or Fitzroy, from which inner suburbs they or their parents had migrated. Under my father's guidance they formed a church football club, with Billy Libbis, a former Collingwood and Melbourne star, as coach. The day would come when the suburb was repopulated; and The Park is now a Greek Orthodox church.

I remained a boarder at the school – the rules of the scholarship so required – and went out to The Park in the double-decker bus to spend the vacations. The suburb had advantages. Whenever I wished, I could travel in the double-decker which stopped not far from the Public Library (now called the State Library) in Swanston Street. There in a large room where I was the youngest reader by far, old Australian newspapers gripped me. I suppose, without knowing it, I was becoming a historian.

6

AND THEN THE BOMB FELL

War was the all-absorbing event. We, however, did not study it in class; the wars we studied were those of the eighteenth century. The war against Japan and Germany was not even discussed in the humble ranks of the cadet corps in which I learnt to carry a rifle and bayonet. Several of the boarders had been much affected by the war but did not talk about it. In my first year the senior boy in my dormitory was Johnny Adams whose father, a planter in New Guinea, had been taken prisoner by the invading Japanese and died before the war was over. In my second year I became friendly with Jim Greenhill whose brother, earlier a boarder, lost his life in the air war over Europe.

One Sunday I went in a suburban tram to visit my father's father, Samuel Blainey. To my surprise my grandpa began to talk eagerly about Asian places where the war had recently been fought. Now in his early seventies, and suffering from Paget's disease, he talked of his years working in Eaglehawk's goldmines and then as a skilled engine driver on the Great Boulder Mine in Kalgoorlie, before explaining how he left behind his young family so that he could travel in a cargo ship from Sydney by way of Darwin and Java to the Malay port of Malacca. After riding in a covered bullock dray for sixty hours, and boating down a fast river, he reached the Chinese-owned mine of which he was to become the engineer. He hired a Chinese cook and a Malay 'bhoy', learnt to speak Malay, observed the various whims and talents of his employees from the Punjab, Canton and the Malay highlands and – unless they did something outrageous – thought that they were all equal in the eyes of God.

Speaking about his own sufferings from what he called 'fever and ague', he described the tropical terrain in which Australian soldiers had faced the Japanese just two years ago. I could almost see the rough roads – he sketched them in the air with his forefinger – along which Australian soldiers had retreated. When I asked about Singapore, now under Japanese occupation, he recalled the tension in the city when he was there in 1904, in the very month when the Russian naval fleet was steaming past to take part in the great naval battle of the Russo-Japanese war. He gave me, as a record of his time in 'the East', a neatly folded copy of the *Straits Times* newspaper, which I eagerly scanned on the returning tram.

Not until half a century later did I learn that his side of our family had another link with Asia. Long after the typical British migrants of the nineteenth century settled in Australia they lost all or nearly all touch with their relatives 'at home'. My grandfather must have vaguely known but did not mention to me that his first cousin, Frederick Thomas, had been professor of Sanskrit at Oxford and – according to the English *Dictionary of National Biography* – was an expert on Buddhism and Jainism and the discoverer and decipherer of 'a hitherto unknown language of the Sino-Tibetan borderland' which he christened as 'Nam'. Of humble background – the son of a colliery clerk and of Miss Frances Blainey – Professor Thomas was then living in retirement in Oxfordshire, full of academic honours, but isolated socially by the intense deafness from which my grandfather, as we talked, also suffered severely. By chance in the early 1990s my wife and I were to meet the Thomas families, living on the border of England and Wales, where to our surprise we found that we were almost on the same wavelength.

Meanwhile in the newspapers in 1944 I followed the war on the Russian front, the heavy bombing of German cities, the fighting in New Guinea, the Allied invasion of Italy and the landing on the beaches of Normandy. Therefore the outbreak of peace in Europe in May 1945 was not really a surprise. As our headmaster, like many others, saw no reason to grant a holiday for the victorious ending of the war against Hitler, we attended our normal lessons, in an air of muted excitement.

The war with Japan was still being waged. When exactly it would end was a topic of daily debate, but we did not know – even the Allied leaders did not know – that victory was near. On Tuesday 7 August 1945 the dramatic dropping of the first atomic bomb on Hiroshima promised to shorten the war. The first news of the bomb appeared in the late afternoon newspaper, and I walked to the nearest newsagent and bought a copy. Even we could see that it was like no other weapon in the history of the world. Though smoke prevented the United States' airmen from seeing how much the Japanese city was damaged, they expected that virtually everybody living there would die. In fact the casualties, while terrible, were not on such a scale. What was clear from the newspaper was that the atomic bomb was small in size but mighty in power compared to the orthodox 'blockbuster' bombs that had fallen on German and Japanese cities during the massive air raids of recent months.

The first atomic bomb – made from the mysterious uranium – persuaded one scientist in London that atomic energy would peacefully transform the workday world. His prediction was that it would lead to the closing of all coalmines: their fuel would no longer be needed. The impression given by the first patchy reports wired from London and Washington was that a bright light was shining on the whole world. Some high officials even prophesied that once this war ended there might be no more war, for the United States, in possessing such a weapon, could threaten to wipe out an enemy in the space of minutes.

I kept a daily diary – one of those tiny booklets bought for a few pence at the newsagent – and in the tiny white space set out for each day I was just able to cram in a few words about the war and our school's activities.

> Tuesday 7 August: Atomic bomb used against Japan. Ordinary school day.
> Wednesday 8 August: Worked hard most of the day.
> Thursday 9 August: Exams started with Latin in the morning – hard paper. Swotted in the afternoon and at night. Sunny day.

The war went on. Would the Japanese islands have to be invaded – a dangerous venture – before their emperor and his admirals and generals would accept defeat?

> Tuesday 14 August: False rumour of peace in evening. Goal and distance kicking.

These kicking contests were held annually on the Front Turf after school, to see which one of us could kick a football the straightest and the furthest. The footballs were not put aside even for one minute by a rumour that the war was over. On this same grass, scores of boys who were killed in the two world wars had once sent their neat punt kicks and drop kicks or wobbly old propeller kicks. We were naturally so absorbed in our activities that there was no sense of the symbolism of what we were doing. It was the last day of world wars that, for a time, had seemed likely to wreck civilisation.

> Wednesday 15 August: Peace! News came through at 9.30 a.m. Public holiday but I did Economics and History exams.

We were so busy with exams that the state of the world meant very little. After the evening meal I walked with friends to Albert Park Lake where searchlights played on the clouds overhead and rockets and fireworks were let off – civilian fireworks had not been available for much of the war. We then walked in the darkness to the Shrine of Remembrance, where from the high ground a few searchlights could be seen above the darkish city. 'City crowded and people went mad' – so I wrote in my diary. I must have learnt that from the radio and newspapers, for no trams were running and we did not reach the city.

The outbreak of peace was almost an anticlimax. A new alarm bell rang. Even before the devastation in Hiroshima and Nagasaki was fully known, the effects of the atomic bomb were brought home to Australians. Black-and-white maps, pointing to the hazards, appeared in newspapers. Thus, if the first atomic bomb had fallen at Swan Hill, 300 kilometres north of Melbourne, the ripples of the explosion might well have broken windows in rural South Australia. If the first bomb had landed on top of the Exhibition Building in Melbourne, which of the streets and buildings would have been smashed to pieces? A small hand-drawn map showed the zone of utter devastation – a mere trifle compared to that of later bombs. Curiously there was little sympathy for the Japanese civilians who had been killed instantly or fatally wounded by the two bombs. The sympathy rose as the enmity diminished.

Though I knew little about physics, I acquired the idea that these powerful bombs, after the Second World War was over, would multiply. Some day, they might blow up much of the inhabited world. Of course we now know that the Bomb – and ultimately it multiplied into the tens of thousands – remained unused during the remainder of the century. But in 1945 nobody could feel confident. Adults who had just lived through years of all-out warfare were not likely to accept the prediction that world wars belonged to the past.

Several weeks after the first atomic bombs had fallen on Japan, I felt more despondent than I have ever felt since. I disclosed my fears to nobody, though undoubtedly others felt the same. I imagined that the civilised world might be replaced by chaos. The sense of hopelessness was strongest during the vacation in the second half of August when I had time on my hands and no routine to absorb me. One day I went into the Public Library and, for the first of hundreds of times, asked in the big newspaper room whether they could retrieve – from the basement – a bound file of a Melbourne newspaper of the late 1930s. After it arrived, I buried myself in the football pages, reading about matches played in 1937 and 1938, when I was mesmerised by football. For a few days the world seemed secure.

My anxieties faded. I half-expected a nuclear war to commence at some time, but I did not feel that I would be a victim. Even when the omens became less favourable, I did not feel anxiety. During the Cuban missile crisis in 1962, when a crippling war between the United States and the Soviet Union seemed possible, I felt inwardly secure. I do not mean that my feeling of safety was based on logic. Rather I had been inoculated in 1945 by the experiencing of one deep episode of shock and fear.

After the end of the Second World War, like many older and wiser people, I pinned my hopes on the new United Nations organisation rather than on American, British and Australian arms. I did not realise that the United Nations was likely to inherit the disunity and indecision of its predecessor, the League of Nations.

In 1945, studying economics for the first time, I was nudged towards the left. Dick Belshaw, a Northern Irelander, taught economics. Formerly a high-school teacher in Korumburra, a town near Leongatha, he had known my father through – I assume – the masonic lodge, and he took a fatherly interest in me, handing me books of economic history that he hoped would sharpen my mind. With calmness and clarity, he discussed the laws of supply and demand and the realm of economic behaviour but also objected if they defied Christian ethics. He encouraged us to read the business and political pages of the daily newspapers and to announce in class what we thought of the news. He might not be seen today as a moderate but in 1945, when left-wing views were almost at their peak in the world, he kept his balance. His view was that the profit motive had its legitimate place in economic life. What was wrong was to enthrone it.

Most of the masters at our school were probably more sympathetic to the left than they would be ten years later. Utopianism tinted textbooks that we read. One temporary utopian was Charles E. W. Bean, the historian of Australia's armies in the First World War, and the author in 1943 of a yellow paperback that was on our syllabus for English expression. Entitled *War Aims of a Plain Australian*, it insisted that there must be a new order, which would arrive only with the help of a born-again Australian people.

Our headmaster, half conservative and half radical, produced his version of the same argument. Under such influences I wrote out my opinions in an essay I produced as a fifteen-year-old for A. A. Phillips, and he was so impressed that later he reprinted my opening paragraph in one of his bestselling textbooks. When the word went around the school that it was actually a passage taken from my essay, Phillips quickly pointed out that the prose style and the choice of words were mine, but that the argument I used had been plucked from the air we all breathed, and owed more than a little to the headmaster's line of thinking.

The library of the school, unknown to most of the parents, was stocked with the works of English Fabians, and I read in my spare time H. G. Wells and George Bernard Shaw. I admired, and still do, Shaw's prose style, his skill in mental combat, and his impudent cheerfulness when arguing or rebutting. One school prize I received in 1945 was his bestselling book *Everybody's Political What's What?*, which speak highly of Britain's leaders and educators. Shaw, who was in his eighty-eighth year when he wrote the last chapters, had the cheek to announce that he was 'a very ignorant old man' – an impression he had shown no intention of conveying during his forty-three earlier chapters. His intellect and fluent prose gave me pleasure even after the tenor of his arguments ceased to satisfy me. Long after he died, I went out of my way to see his house in rural England, not as a pilgrim but as an admirer.

For several years, if allowed to take the floor in school debates, I tended to voice arguments against several facets of capitalism while remaining wary of socialism as a theory. Of the morning papers I had little time for *The Argus* which, to my mind, too often criticised Ben Chifley's Labor government. I preferred the public ABC to commercial radio, so much so that I would have been pleased if commercial radio were tightly controlled. I have the idea that I might have been a utopian; but several essays I wrote for A. A. Phillips reveal that even then I did not believe in the 'perfectibility of human nature'.

For the subject called English Expression we were encouraged to write on the burning national and international questions of the hour. Phillips, like an alert referee, watched how we argued. While he sympathised with the left he denounced all shoddy arguments, even those of the left. When my line of attack was unrelenting he wrote on my workbook, 'Call your dog off, Mister'. When my handwritten prose demanded that the government should provide the public with 'a correct and unprejudiced news service', he wrote on the margin in pencil: 'How do you solve the problem that the Government is not an unprejudiced source of news?' He tried to induct us gently into the ways of the rough-and-tumble world.

The more alert students, stirred by the federal election about to be held in 1946, decided to run their own public election. My friend and classroom rival S. E. K. Hulme was chosen as the Liberal candidate, and made an eloquent speech in the half-filled hall. Phil Symons, a Jewish boy possessing a touch of red in his hair and a mental balance far beyond his years, spoke as an independent. The school's boarding house, usually a nest of rural conservatism, produced the two radicals. Ted Sikk, a Hobart boy of Estonian descent, spoke purportedly as a communist, and I spoke purportedly as the Labor candidate. Being friends – we still are – Ted and I carved up our territory so that we would achieve the maximum effect. We also paid a trifling sum to print a large advertisement in support of our views (such as they were) in a magazine that was privately typed and published by one of the boys, Harry Payne, and largely devoted to stamp-collecting. Our expensive advertising campaign was a waste. In the final count Ted and I, though we imagined we spoke persuasively, polled a very small number of votes. Most of the audience were in favour of private enterprise. They were no doubt disappointed when, soon after our own mock election, the Australian Labor Party under Ben Chifley won a massive majority at the federal election.

I must have been quite independent, for my age. My temptation was to go into intellectual pockets or areas that were largely unoccupied. As I preferred to be on my own in some debates, I was tempted to take unpopular sides. In my last year the form master, the tall 'Stumpy' Hughes who had been a soldier in the First World War, expressed in my first-term report the seeming contradiction that I was high up in the school, and a prefect too, but well known for expressing 'his provocative views on social questions'. He told me, privately of course, that he agreed with many of those views.

As the world within the last one-third of a century had experienced the worst economic depression ever recorded and the two worst wars in history, a sense of impending doom was only to be expected. While it lasted, it darkened many discussions about the future. Parts of an editorial I wrote early in 1947 for the school magazine, *The Chronicle*, reflected this widespread belief that drastic steps must be taken to win the peace:

> The problems of the peace are just as difficult as the problems of war. Great armadas and armies are just as expensive as the solving of great social and economic problems.
>
> Germany and Russia understood this and the success with which they overcame their immense difficulties in the decade before the war can be attributed to their co-ordinated utilisation of all their national resources. They demanded sacrifices of the people, and while we may bitterly oppose the lack of individual liberty in these nations, we are forced to admit that the economic strength of these powers was increased to a hitherto unprecedented extent.
>
> What impresses us as the essential feature of the pre-war dictatorships – equal sacrifice – is the essential quality most lacking in democratic countries to-day. Australia is no exception. Before the war this deficiency was only too frequently obvious. Instead of demanding equal responsibility for the defence of the country we left it to a few enthusiasts, who comprised the militia, and so we were unprepared until Munich rudely awoke us. Instead of organising a campaign to combat soil erosion and bush fires, a few unorganised volunteers were expected successfully to combat the menace.

Occasionally the attempt was made to woo me as a potential ringleader of worthy causes. The Reverend C. O. Leigh Cook, the school's chaplain, could see I was independent and thought that I would influence other boys if I made the decision to become a formal member of the Methodist Church. I liked him, and liked to argue with him, but was not attracted by his request. My mind was made up the moment he asked me. Curiously I remember the exact spot in the front cloisters where he made his plea, but not the reasons that I gave for my refusal. I remained intensely interested in religion and in no way perturbed that my family belonged to a sect that some intellectuals laughed at, calling them 'wowsers'.

The countryside attracted me more than the cities. I liked, especially from the age of thirteen, the Australian landscape in all its variety. Something of the painter was in me, though I was bereft of painting skills. My attraction to the landscape was not fed by Streeton, Roberts, Buvelot and other Victorian painters who profoundly influenced national attitudes and visual tastes. Though Ballarat owned one of the country's best collections of Australian landscape paintings I cannot remember entering its gallery as a schoolboy. In Melbourne I rarely visited the National Gallery, which was then housed in the same building as the library: it was the library I frequented. My affection for the Australian landscape came more from family influences – my mother was a romantic – and from prose and poetry.

Early in 1945 during a week of the summer vacation my schoolfriend Alan Dixon invited me to the town of Dimboola. The day-long journey from Ballarat, with the steam train stopping at nearly all stations, showed the parched plains in drought. I lapped up the variety of scenes: the elbowy gum trees throwing their shade, the bleached white grass, the shimmer and mirages on the plains, the post-and-rail fences, the sandy beds of the empty creeks that the train crossed, and the clusters of rural folk standing at the level crossings and – thirsty for news – calling aloud for that day's newspaper to be thrown from the window. From Dimboola, on a few afternoons, we rode bikes along the plains, the stubble of the wheat harvest being visible everywhere, and not a bird to be heard while the heat lasted. When we halted in the shade of the wayside Lutheran churches, I found that I could read several of the German sentences on the headstones of the churchyard graves. It was the nearest I had been to travelling overseas.

During one winter vacation, I went to Gembrook where my aunt Lorna and my uncle Bill – just back from the war – grew seed potatoes on the steep hills. Bill's father lived in the small town nearby, and with his long beard and his command of foreign languages he was seen as an eccentric. Much of each day he spent in his personal library which he had slowly accumulated at second-hand bookshops in Melbourne. At 6.30 on many Saturday mornings he had caught the Puffing Billy train to Ferntree Gully, changing to the broad-gauge train and so reaching Melbourne for his day's browsing and buying. After spending no more than a few shillings he would place his second-hand books in a large jute bag and carry it to St Paul's Cathedral where, seated in a pew, he read until the train was about to leave.

On reaching Gembrook I found my uncle Bill (whose real name was Genseric) ploughing with the help of two Clydesdale horses. Instantly I liked the rich smell of the earth and the smooth lumps of soil turned to one side by the steel blade of the plough. My first task was to walk along the furrow behind the slow plough and pick up the potatoes that the forks of the potato diggers had overlooked during the recent harvest. Placing the potatoes in a bucket, I regularly emptied them into a large bag standing upright at the end of the furrow. Bill and Lorna, though battling to establish themselves on the farm, generously paid me. Their steep paddocks were almost on the edge of the native forest, which stretched far beyond the eye. You could push your way through thick scrub in several directions for at least 200 kilometres without striking a town. Exactly sixty years later Lorna and Bill, by then close to ninety years old, were still working their hill farm with virtually no outside help, though they had wisely switched from potatoes to cattle. I spoke at his funeral: he was somebody special, as was Lorna.

During one of the long vacations, just before Christmas, I went to Chapman's orchard in the Dandenong Ranges, where fruit pickers were urgently needed and well paid. The ripening cherries would soon rot, or be pecked by birds. 'Joe' Joss and I cooked breakfast in a simple hut and then, clambering up and down the high stepladders, picked cherries and placed them in a shoulder bag. A fellow picker, lean and stooped, was close to eighty. I should have questioned him more, for he had experienced one of the exciting moments in our nation's history: the West Australian gold rushes of 1892. On a day of high heat, when a hefty wind was shaking our stepladders, he said to me, 'Here comes the willy-willy.' Memories of Coolgardie filled his mind; and he spoke feelingly of the white tents being sprinkled with red dust, and the handbells rung by the Coolgardie traders when they sold, at a high price, their gallons of slightly salty drinking water.

Another uncle who was short of labour asked me to work on his farm during the two weeks' vacation which in those days fell always in August. I prepared, one Saturday, to ride my bike 160 or more kilometres from a northern suburb of Melbourne, all my possessions in an old Gladstone bag sitting on the handlebar. Leaving at a quarter to seven, I made a wrong turn near the Maribyrnong munitions factory and was slow to reach the Geelong road, by which time one of those cold south-westerlies was blowing. At times the winter wind, rushing across the stony plains, almost halted my bike. Fortunately there was not a drop of rain, and the traffic on the road was sparse. I pressed on, passing through Geelong in mid-afternoon and reaching the Barrabool Hills just when the wind eased. Though weary, I felt strangely elated at the sight of the soft winter light playing on the green curves of the hills.

The bike had no headlight – or the light wasn't working – and so it was difficult to see the surface of the road when darkness arrived. The moon was either not shining or was faint. The cars on the main highway were few – perhaps one in every twenty minutes – and so their headlights only briefly showed the way ahead. Then I heard, not far away, rowdy voices coming from a shed at the Winchelsea football ground. The football match was long finished, and a small band of players and supporters was singing the ditty 'Roll Me Over, in the Clover'.

For a long time I waited on the railway station until the Warrnambool express arrived, its headlight flaring. Placing my bike in the guard's van I travelled to Colac. As I pedalled out of that town, pitch-darkness descended. When at last I reached what I assumed was the side road leading towards my uncle's house, perhaps a quarter of an hour away, I had to climb the tall signpost to read the printed signs. Meanwhile my uncle Cecil and aunt Rose, waiting and waiting, had turned on the light at their weatherboard house in Cororooke's main street – indeed its only street! On their front door I knocked at a quarter to eleven.

I saw, next morning, the rich colours of the volcanic soil, freshly ploughed, and the green hills and the scattered lakes. In the following days I drove a tractor over that chocolate soil, sometimes pulling a disc and sometimes a 'smooge' that flattened the furrows of the paddocks where the potatoes and onions were to be planted. Flocks of seagulls followed me, pouncing on the upturned soil. It was one of the most English of landscapes – or rather Irish, for they owned most of the farms. They were full of conviviality and eager to argue. I had not previously met groups of people of Catholic and Irish descent.

My uncle leased paddocks rather than owned them, and also used his tractor to plough for other farmers. He was nervous about the risk of the tractor knocking me over. The strong engine was started by turning the heavy crank-handle, and occasionally an arm or wrist was broken in the process. Moreover the tractor, if not in neutral gear, might lurch forward and knock you over while you were trying to crank it. So at first he came to the paddock where I was to plough, carefully started the engine for me, and then drove his old van to another job. I had to keep the tractor's engine idling all day – even when I halted to eat my lunch – because I had promised not to crank it on my own. When it was nightfall I would park the tractor under a tree, turn off the petrol and shut down the engine, place old bags over the radiator so that the engine would be started easily on the next morning, and then ride my bike to the house. If, however, I had finished the work I would drive the tractor to that farm where the next job was waiting. Nobody worried whether a sixteen-year-old on the open road held a driving licence.

Employed full time by my uncle was a young Seventh-day Adventist labourer who lived in a portable hut. Named George, he plucked fun from simple events. When our van passed a few road menders who had stopped for a smoke-oh he would laugh loudly if he saw, alongside them, a printed sign proclaiming 'Men at Work'. Leaning out the car window he would shout out, 'Why don't you pull your sign down?' The road menders knew George and, while shaking a fist at him, took his words in good spirit.

After my ploughing was completed, I hoped to ride back to Melbourne in the one day. Cycling across the undulating plains with the windbreaks of sugar gums, I could see the You Yangs long before lunchtime. With the same westerly that had obstructed me a fortnight earlier, I travelled the 160 kilometres with ridiculous ease.

Next year I came back to Colac's volcanic hills. I was ploughing there during the school vacation of August 1947 just after the prime minister Ben Chifley announced out of the blue that his government would nationalise the private trading banks. The public consternation ran deep. Even in the equalitarian mood of the time Chifley was viewed widely as pushing social reform to the extreme. In contrast my uncle was usually in favour of private enterprise. Indeed, before he took up farming, he had worked for the stockbroking firm of J. B. Were whose chief, Staniforth Ricketson, was one of the small band of Melburnians who helped Robert Gordon Menzies to found what became the main conservative party of the 1930s. My uncle, like hundreds of others around Colac, was aghast at the idea of an all-powerful government bank decreeing who should or should not receive a loan.

One night we drove into Colac where a public hall was packed with protesting citizens. The spontaneous speeches from the floor compounded the air of indignation. I was stirred by the calls of the small farmers and shopkeepers for economic freedom – calls for which I would once have felt small sympathy.

Around this time Menzies came to our school to speak to a morning assembly. He was then leader of the Opposition, his most influential years ahead of him. Being an old boy of the school he was allowed to speak at length, and his melodious voice was mesmerising. He made no attempt to praise the virtues of private enterprise: he assumed his audience was already converted. Instead he spoke on the wonders of tradition, evoking his visits to Britain which, in the recent reign of Winston Churchill, had been the world's fortress of freedom. In stately prose, Menzies spoke about the House of Commons and other ancient buildings, many of which had been damaged by Hitler's bombs, and touched on the ten or more weekends he had spent as

Churchill's guest in his home, Chequers. This was the first time that I heard someone painting a vivid, breathing picture of European civilisation. As he stood on the platform, towering over us, his pauses seemed almost as eloquent as his words. He was the most arresting speaker I had heard up to that time, though I did not accept all of his political views.

One day our sheltered world was temporarily shaken. Our headmaster, Neil MacNeil, dropped dead. His presence was commanding even on his last day. MacNeil had a strong jaw, eyes that could be cold or kind, and one of those short cramped moustaches which in the interwar years were probably favoured even more in Britain than in Germany. Rarely did he laugh: more common was a benign but somewhat stiff expression of amusement. When he walked briskly along the windy front cloisters – his gown flowing behind him, and a black mortarboard in his hand – he gave the impression that he owned the school. At the weekend his wife Jean went walking with him, though often a step or two behind. She was good-looking, gracious and cultured. They had no children.

He had grown up in Melbourne, the son of a Presbyterian evangelist who died when young. Reaching Balliol College in Oxford as a Rhodes scholar, just when the First World War broke out, he went to war with the Highland Light Infantry. On a battlefield, at Loos in September 1915, his 'conspicuous gallantry' won him the Military Cross, and later he was flying above the battlefields, an early war pilot. After completing his degree at Oxford and doing good works in Poland he returned to become, at a tender age, the first headmaster of the Knox Grammar School in Sydney. Almost two decades later, he was recruited by Wesley when it was believed by some critics to be slightly run-down and a captive of its past. A headmaster of a big school today is less visible, inside and outside the school, but MacNeil was never out of sight. He presided over the assembly of boys each morning, and on some evenings he strolled purposefully into the boarding house at about 7 p.m. and took part in the singing of the hymn that preceded the period of formal study. Whatever he did was draped in dignity and an engulfing sense of duty.

His speech was thrusting. When he spoke on education, the newspapers reported his views. He had the belief that everyone, rich and poor, should have a right to a sound education. He believed in the virtues of hard physical labour in the countryside for the thinkers as well as the doers. He regretted a decline of civic spirit in the people and a lack of political interest in their real welfare; that slums were permitted to exist in Australian cities shocked him. On juvenile behaviour he had distinct opinions, including an intense dislike for the boys' practice – then widespread – of putting their hands in their pockets as they walked. A few of his views were unexpected. He was an early Green when that word was unknown as a political noun. The organisation dear to him was Save the Forests, of which he was leader. Each year a group of boys, of whom I was not one, attended his forestry camps, for he believed that Australia would become a wilderness unless we began to tackle erosion and manage the floods and other ills of nature: he was a sire of the rural camps and campuses now owned by so many city schools.

His favourite sport was rowing – he had rowed for Oxford after the war – and he coached the Wesley first crew. Latin was his favourite subject. As the senior Latin students numbered only half-a-dozen, we saw his informal side, and admired or were startled by his attempts to be relaxed and friendly. Our daily procedure was to translate, in turn, a passage of Caesar or Virgil from the Latin into English; and once I chose the word saucer to describe what really was a stately sacrificial bowl. On hearing my mistake his merriment, while restrained for the sake of courtesy, was conspicuous. On the public platform he stood out as a defiant leader but as a teacher he could be patient and encouraging. I feel the urge to defend him when he is criticised by my older friends. His successor W. H. Frederick, a fine teacher, was relaxed and colloquial and convivial, but my preference (perhaps in retrospect only) was for MacNeil.

On Thursday 1 August 1946, MacNeil taught us Latin in the morning, as was his custom. He was the captain on the bridge, and no error of grammar escaped him. Just after lunchtime, all boys in the senior school were summoned to the Adamson Hall, without any idea why an assembly at such an unusual hour was convened. There for a few minutes we sat expectant and puzzled. 'Fido' Gwillim, being the senior master, climbed the steps leading to the platform and broke the news in a soft but magisterial voice. Most of us had had little experience of the death of someone close to us.

For the funeral on the Saturday morning we lined the footpath in Punt Road and watched the coffin being conveyed by boys from the chapel steps to the waiting hearse. Within a few minutes, life resumed its course. After lunch several of us went by tram and train to the old North Melbourne football oval to see Geelong play. On the way home I bought a copy of the evening newspaper and saw on the front page MacNeil's coffin being carried away.

Less than a fortnight later, 'Fido' Gwillim, who was the acting headmaster, fell ill. After a few days he too died. Attending his funeral in the school chapel and at the Springvale crematorium, I began almost immediately to write his obituary for the school *Chronicle*. It was my first venture in live, deadline journalism.

These two deaths, only a few months before the final public exams, did not harm the results of the sixth form. Wesley was not large, and it was in no way a cramming school, but its results at the public examinations that year were impressive. For my part I was lucky enough to share the Victorian government's prize or 'exhibition' for the main history subject, and also to win an exhibition as an all-rounder.

In another sense I was not quite so lucky. Being only sixteen, I was deemed by some as perhaps too young to go to university. For the next year I remained at school, taking on a few new subjects and busying myself as captain of the boarding house and a prefect. A lot of the intellectual excitement had passed.

Partly through A. A. Phillips' subtle influence, I had been veering more to the left in politics. There had been few signs of that veering, so far as I remember, in my first year at the school, and by my fourth and final year it had almost vanished. When I set out for university I was already on the middle of the political road at a time when the road travelled by most of the arts students still had a camber to the left.

7

THE ROAD TO EVERYWHERE

I had a burning desire to see Sydney. In our nation's short history, it seemed almost as pivotal as Rome was to Italy's long history. To visit the shining harbour now seems a humble ambition, but most Victorians of that time saw no prospect of travelling overseas, and therefore a short planned visit to Sydney was like a tour of Europe today.

My friend Alan Dixon and I made plans for the journey. Along the way we intended to camp in deserted sheds, in country railway stations, or in the open air. Even that frugal expedition required money for food and extras, and a room during a few days in Sydney – if we managed to reach it. We could not afford the railway fare, and therefore had to hitchhike, but we knew that few cars and trucks would be on the roads, petrol still being rationed. Early in February 1948 on the spur of the moment we decided to earn the travel money at Mildura where the grape-picking season was about to begin.

My load consisted of a small army rucksack on the top of which was rolled an old grey blanket sewn up in the shape of a sleeping bag. There was also a thin waterproof groundsheet, once belonging to the army. We would now be called backpackers, but our light makeshift luggage would be scorned if seen by a modern Swede or German.

The iron rule of hitchhiking was that you could only begin to hitch a ride from the passing traffic once you had reached a main road on the outskirts of a town. On our first afternoon we caught the tram from Melbourne to Essendon Airport, which was then an outer suburb, and walked across rocky paddocks until we reached the Bendigo road. On the way we passed two tiger snakes lying in the sun.

Sitting on the floor of a big covered truck we reached the outskirts of Bendigo just after dark. The truck carried two other hitchhikers who suggested we stay in their parents' house, close to the highway at Kangaroo Flat. Once a grand residence, it showed bare floorboards with only a stick or two of furniture in some of the larger rooms. The family had what were then called 'racing connections' but at the humbler end of the scale. The frayed interior was aglow with hospitality. On the wood-burning stove a meal of fish was soon fried, the hosts laughing all the time. After the meal we were shown to one of the vacant rooms. At breakfast the stove was again alight, and bacon and eggs were sizzling. No payment was expected. I offered to chop firewood: they wouldn't hear of it.

Next day we went through Bendigo but by the late afternoon we had barely covered another 100 kilometres. Hitchhiking was a slow way of travelling. Most rural people in that era of petrol rationing drove trucks and vans, some of them loaded with firewood or animal skins, and were going only to the next town. Moreover, the further away from Melbourne, the sparser was the traffic on the roads. Nonetheless about one in every two drivers stopped, either to enquire where we were heading or to offer a ride. 'I'm not going far,' was their opening remark, 'but hop in.' Not often encountering strangers, they were eager to talk.

That day we waited on the outskirts of the wheat town of Charlton until after sunset, but there was no northbound traffic. The town was too far away to justify walking there to buy food, and we ate our only supplies – a tin of that cheap and popular pulverised meat called 'camp pie' – and slept on the verandah of the golf clubhouse. The floor was hard, the night surprisingly cold, and by morning I felt very hungry.

We soon were beside the road again. An empty furniture van slowed down. We ran alongside and jumped in the back. Two hitchhikers were already there, making their way from a hydro-electricity construction camp in Tasmania to Mildura for the grape picking. After an hour or so the van halted in the main street of Wycheproof and we went with the driver into a Greek or Italian cafe for breakfast. We had bacon and eggs, with bread and butter and hot tea and those thin red slices of cooked beetroot that were the common decoration on dinner plates in country cafes. This was probably only the second time in my life that I had eaten a meal in a cafe or restaurant.

The big van churned clouds of dust whenever its wheels left the narrow bitumen, and we were caked brown on reaching Mildura late that afternoon. Mildura seemed as exotic as Arabia. Buying the local newspaper, we found advertisements calling for grape pickers, and went to a public telephone and rang a grape grower. He said he was grateful to have two new pickers, no matter how unskilled they were. 'I'll be over as quick as I can,' he said. Old Rob drove us along the curving sandy roads near Red Cliffs, with the grapevines standing on both sides and irrigation channels crossing here and there. A soldier from the First World War, he quickly pitched a bell tent for us and set up camp stretchers with mosquito nets. Driving us to the nearest general store for provisions, he introduced us to everybody as if we had just fallen from heaven.

Work began at 7.30 in the morning. We worked mainly on our knees, picking grapes that would then be dried into black currants. When the day became hot, occasionally reaching 38 degrees Celsius soon after noon, the local fruit pickers stopped work. At a place where the irrigation water flowed into a billabong we swam until two o'clock when the picking began again. At about six, the tractor and trailer came to collect the scores of iron buckets into which we had tossed our newly picked bunches of grapes.

We thought we were handsomely paid though we did work long hours. Some of the older pickers, however, were loud in their protests at the downy mildew affecting occasional grapevines and at the tax deducted from their pay. They said that after 4 p.m. they were working for Canberra. The complaint of a good-natured, fat woman known as 'Flo' was unchanging: 'I ain't going to work for old Chifley – no, or old Menzies either.' *Old*, a favourite word of condemnation, was also a word of mild affection, and two of the local fruit pickers were known as Old Charley and Old Bruno. There was also Old Len, who was drunk when he arrived and repentant when sober. 'Do the right thing!' was his favourite phrase.

In ten days we earned so much that, to the dismay of the owner, we prepared to begin the journey to Sydney. With our banknotes in our pockets we actually caught the bus into Mildura instead of hitchhiking, and bought the latest newspapers and a big bottle of lemonade. On the far side of the long bridge into New South Wales we began to hitch a ride. Our hope, utterly impractical, was to hitchhike directly across country to Sydney but the trucks and cars on those back roads were so few that after Balranald we had to veer south back into Victoria and travel up the Murray Valley Highway. On one day we needed nine separate lifts to travel from Swan Hill to Echuca, a mere 150 kilometres away, where we slept in the judge's box in the showgrounds.

Next morning, not bothering to light a fire and cook breakfast, we left early. Tramping through the town, we eventually reached the livestock saleyards, where droves of sheep kicked up the dust. A strange sight came nearer. I saw two elephants standing on the back of heavy trucks, and swaying a little. It was a travelling circus but not going exactly our way. After two hours of waiting, we hitched a commercial traveller in his neat car. He could take us only for 20 kilometres, but he presented us with something priceless. At a time when road maps were almost unprocurable he gave us his own, a coloured Ampol map covering all the main roads of the region. In one way it was little consolation, for there was hardly any traffic, but at least it persuaded us that we must go much closer to Melbourne in the hope of reaching the only road to Sydney that carried traffic.

We did not, for much of that day, move more than a few dozen kilometres. Our failure was so complete that in the half-asleep town of Nathalia, we actually paid to travel in a diesel rail-motor that would take us to a busier highway leading south to the big river town of Shepparton. Riding the last section on the back of a truck carrying drums of petrol we were in Shepparton before dark. Eventually another driver, waiting for a cargo of newly picked fruit, promised to take us to the Hume Highway, if we turned up at his truck at 11 p.m. It was loaded high with wooden packing cases of peaches, and we climbed to the top where, seated precariously, we set out with a noisy changing of gears. The moon was full, the old gum trees on the watercourses stood out in the light, and from our swaying grandstand the countryside seemed magical. A hill or two came into sight. We had been on the plains for a fortnight. When we reached the Hume Highway the moon had gone and the darkness was complete. We slept on the edge of the highway, ready to go north.

Morning came. Though it was the busiest long-distance highway in Australia we did not know whether it carried much traffic. Eventually a van took us all the way to Albury, its windscreen spattered with more and more squashed grasshoppers. After a meal we walked a few kilometres towards Sydney and waited and waited. The road was almost empty.

After four hours we could hear a large semitrailer coming towards us. We waved – or pointed our thumbs with a sweep of the right hand. The driver almost stopped, his noisy engine idling. 'Jump on the back,' he shouted. We did and quickly wedged our packs inside the spare wheels resting on the open tray. The truck bumped so much on the potholed sections of the road that we were in danger of being thrown off; there were no sides protecting us from a fall. The sealed surface was narrow, and in places the oncoming cars had to draw to one side while making way for us. On narrow bridges there was room only for our truck.

At Gundagai next morning, deciding we were not violent, the driver invited us to sit beside him in his roomy cabin. We responded by buying him breakfast – we were rich – at a little truckers' cafe sitting beside the monument to the Dog on the Tuckerbox. It was not yet a tourist stopping place but the cafe sold a shining metal matchbox holder with the verses printed on the back. I used it for years. In this secular land a relic from Gundagai was almost like a relic from Lourdes.

The driver was eager to reach Sydney before dark. Having no cargo he could put his foot on the accelerator and sometimes he must have travelled at 70 kilometres an hour. He made me nervous. About midday he was hurtling down a steep hill towards a narrow bridge when suddenly a car and a caravan seemed to emerge from nowhere and crawled across the bridge towards us. Our driver pumped his brakes with his foot and honked the horn. He was white in the face. I still carry the sense of impending doom. How the caravan managed to cross the bridge seconds ahead of our thundering arrival, I don't know. My eyes were closed – his too, I suspect.

In that green and eloquent countryside, the convict era was visible to me. Not far from the winding road were the stone ruins of homesteads and occasionally a roofless, crumbling hotel. Here and there stretched out the crooked branches of ancient trees which perhaps had carried their first apricots and pears when convicts and ticket-of-leave men were scything the long grass around them. This was virtually the road along which the first skinny flocks of sheep and then the first postman came overland from Sydney to Victoria. Here marched the troops – 'Foot, horse and artillery', as Professor Shann described them in the eloquent textbook of our day – despatched west to quell the anti-Chinese riots at Lambing Flat in 1861. Here passed the port-bound wagons stacked so high with square bales of wool that the top-heavy load swayed in the wind like a ship at sea. I imagined all this as we travelled. In the afternoon we crossed the range called the Razorback and later, from high ground, I was excited to glimpse ahead the tall harbourside buildings of Sydney.

A room at the YMCA (Young Men's Christian Association), which was just about the cheapest lodging house in Sydney, was four shillings a night. Sausage rolls and pies were cheap, and thirty bananas could be bought for just one shilling from sellers who shouted at the kerbside. In two days we saw almost everything listed in the simple tourist brochures of that era. The memorable moment was on the Manly ferry, rocking and bobbing on the edge of the ocean swell, with the sight of the rugged sandstone cliffs towering over the same unchanged harbour heads where the sails of the First Fleet had appeared in 1788.

Sydney could not quite meet my expectations, for they were too high. Moreover the air was sticky and steamy, the sky cloudy. The streets were a foreign land, and the hats of the school girls and boys were unusual, and some adult men wore neat white shorts and shirts as they walked to business. Sydney's magic, however, still affected us.

We had to set out for home, as the university term would soon begin. At first the travelling was snail-like, and we even accepted a ride for a few kilometres in the large box that served as the sidecar of a motorbike. Conveyed next by a motorist down the wrong road we had to walk after dark some 10 kilometres across country towards the town of Camden and the Hume Highway. On the road the sole of my shoe fell off. When we finally reached the highway we slept under a tree in a schoolyard. Next morning we hailed an approaching car, and it slowed down. An empty taxi, its driver – working on a government contract – wanted conversation on his journey back to Canberra. We were there by midday. On learning that the official camping ground was several kilometres away and that there was no such place as a cheap hotel we hid our packs and sleeping bags in a clump of bushes opposite the police station in Civic Square, which was then the commercial heart of the town. We spent the night hidden by bushes. Nearby a tap was ready to wash us in the morning.

Not a capital city but a capital town, and encircled by blue uninhabited hills, Canberra had little to offer the few visitors. Crossing the Molonglo River on a bridge whose wooden planks shook with the passing of each truck, we reached the white parliament house – the largest building in the town. There were no security officials; to enter was easier than entering an art gallery. We found the atmosphere captivating. The day's sitting of the House of Representatives was about to begin. The small visitors' gallery, with its close view of the seventy or so seated members, was empty until a small group arriving on a Bond's bus tour audibly gasped when R. G. Menzies, then the leader of the Opposition, strolled purposefully into the chamber.

In this era before television, unless you went to a night-time political meeting in a town hall, it was difficult to know what leading politicians were really like. Their photo might be in the newspaper, in black and white, or they could be seen in a newsreel cinema, but those cinemas were small and few, and only in a few cities. It was difficult for most of us to know a politician's height, manner of dress, the face when angry or pleased, and the gestures. Here was the nation's theatre, the stars all present, with no audience except a few journalists and the tens of thousands who listened eagerly to parliament on radio.

It was marvellous to see, so unexpectedly, so many people who were prominent in national life: little Billy Hughes who had become prime minister as long ago as 1915, sitting there like a small marsupial, his ears pricked up; the big J. T. Lang, who had been the revolutionary premier of New South Wales during the Great Depression, conveying an air of destiny though his destiny had passed; and Eddie Ward, Arty Fadden, 'Black Jack' McEwen, Arthur Calwell, young Kim Beazley Sr, Tommy White, and a circle of others celebrated in their day. Unmistakeable was Mrs Enid Lyons (even then known as

Dame Enid) who with Mrs Doris Blackburn was the only woman in the house. Looking motherly and very much at home, Dame Enid was then in some ways the most celebrated woman in the nation, for temporarily no Australian opera singer or film star could match her fame. Her fame had unusual ingredients. Married in Tasmania at the age of seventeen, the mother of eleven living children, the widow of a long-serving prime minister, an excellent speaker and broadcaster, and here she was, having celebrated her fiftieth birthday only the previous year. She wore a tweed suit, sat quietly, and had not a touch of swagger.

There with a very straight back stood Joseph Benedict Chifley, once a locomotive driver and now the dignified prime minister, and we heard his gravelly voice. On the roadside near Yass, several days later, we tried to hitch a lift from a black government car whose only passenger was easily recognised. At that time most cars travelled slowly, no windows were tinted, and it was easy to see a face inside. It was Chifley, sitting in the front seat, and returning to his hometown of Bathurst for the weekend.

That first day in Canberra was memorable. Debates were intense, for Australia more than ever before or after seemed on the road to socialism, and some members exulted and others feared. It was feared – or cheered – that all the private banks would be nationalised by Chifley's government. While many members of parliament had little formal education and pronounced certain words in a quaint way, they spoke with a force and conviction rarely heard today when, in a more educated parliament, many members read aloud speeches they themselves have not mainly prepared or written. To read a speech was forbidden in 1948.

In the early evening, when the politicians adjourned to dinner, we walked back to our camp in the bushes, our possessions still untouched.

After eating fish and chips near the Civic Centre we were enticed to return to parliament: perhaps this was the only night entertainment in the capital town. Now they were debating the tariff. Even that dullish subject seemed momentous. These were tense times in federal politics: indeed, a turning point in the nation's history. It was to be the last full year in which Labor held power until the inaugural Whitlam year of 1973, exactly one-quarter of a century ahead.

Next morning, after inspecting the Australian War Memorial and its outside exhibit of a midget Japanese submarine that had entered Sydney Harbour during the war, it was time to begin the short journey to Yass and the Sydney–Melbourne road. Hardly a car or truck was to be seen, and no driver offered us a lift. Just before sunset we managed to hitch a ride back to Canberra. Next day, rising early, we travelled with the postman to the village of Hall. There we had to wait so long that eventually we decided the only way to travel was to pay for a seat in the vehicle known as a 'service car'. Packed with passengers, it broke down just along the road. A mechanic eventually arrived and lifted up the bonnet. At last we reached Yass.

By nightfall we were travelling on a slow semitrailer loaded with new radio-sets and covered by a heavy tarpaulin, tightly roped. I sat on the very top, clinging to a rope. We were heading home.

8

GREAT IDEAS WERE ABLAZE

At the university, I felt slightly restricted. At 11 a.m. and 3.15 p.m. and those other times when students moved from one lecture theatre to another, the narrow walkways and corridors were as crowded as Asian city lanes. Students wheeling bicycles added to the congestion. Close to 9000 students were on the one campus, though many were part time and arrived late in the afternoon.

It was a surprise to be addressed in a new way. At school the masters had called us by our surname, and I was 'Blainey' – the name 'Geoff' they rarely used. At university, however, I was addressed almost invariably as Mr Blainey. To be so addressed at the age of seventeen was to be treated as if one was already an adult. This mode of address was welcome because it came from those who, wearing a black gown when they taught, spoke with authority. By the early 1960s when

I began to lecture at the University of Melbourne the gown was fast vanishing. Not once did I wear a gown when I lectured but always I wore a jacket and tie, even on a scorching day.

The women were few compared to men, and most studied arts. They were noticeable in the cafeteria in Union House and the library, which was a tall sandstone hall facing the old quadrangle. Short of seats, the crowded library was a major meeting place. Most male students dressed neatly, nearly all wore a tie, and most wore a sports coat while others wore suits. An American ex-serviceman studying law wore a fur-lined jacket: he was nicknamed 'Bear Skin', as if he were a trapper. Warm overcoats, especially old military coats, were widely worn in winter because numerous buildings were poorly heated.

A thousand or two students were ex-servicemen who received a grant of money enabling them to study full time. Without that subsidy most would have been farmers, tradesmen, bank clerks or teachers and would not have attended a university. This was a most imaginative subsidy of a cross-section of Australians, and it brought to our everyday discussions a layer of maturity and experience that the university had not previously known and might not know again for decades.

The biggest lecture theatres seemed like high grandstands to those coming straight from school. The moment when the lecturer in gown entered the theatre by a lower door could be dramatic. My first lecture on the first morning – in Latin – was delivered in a courteous manner by Mr George Gellie, back from the war. As lecturers had no access to a microphone they expected silence to prevail if their words were to be heard by all. Laughter was permitted, if it arose from the lecture. While the blackboard, written on with white chalk, was vital, other visual aids were rare. To attend lectures was then all-important, and students took notes with a fountain pen, writing as rapidly as possible.

Fortunately I studied ancient history under John O'Brien, a youngish man with a lean analytical mind. He spoke slowly, as if considering each word before uttering it. Occasionally we had to prevent our attention from wandering before his longer sentences were completed. He enjoyed nothing more than outlining an argument with some empathy, and then patiently pointing out its inconsistencies and deficiencies. A theory on why the Roman empire declined might come to Mr O'Brien's attention; and he would devote three or four lectures to an examination of its plausibility. A new theory was like a lump of ice that he held up to the sunlight. Then the ice melted away – so thorough were his methods. From him I gained little knowledge of the achievements, chronology and grandeur of Greek and Roman history, but some of us saw how we might become detectives and analysts of human behaviour.

Twice a week, straight after lunchtime, Mrs Kathleen Fitzpatrick lectured in British History – with capital letters. Then in her forties, she presided like a high priestess. A hush soon fell on the 300 or more students when with impeccable punctuality she entered the theatre. In the audience there was no whispering, for she insisted on a churchlike silence, maintaining it mainly with her eyes. She had high cheekbones and a handsome face, and her hairstyle appeared to be the creation of one of the city's fashionable hairdressers. According to my friend Lotte Nettl, our star lecturer was really a mix of style and restraint. Kathleen's eyelashes quivered at a tense point in her narrative, and her smile was spontaneous but after a second or two seemed slightly guarded. Most of her lectures, written in advance, she read slowly in an expressive voice. Between certain sentences her pauses were memorable. After each lecture her departure was impressive. Having placed her neat notes in her folder, she did not walk from the theatre but simply glided away.

Her audience usually consisted of first-year students, and we initially knew little about the British Isles at the time of the Spanish Armada and the Puritan revolution. She paid us the compliment of assuming that we knew more than we did. She did not, however, quite realise that religious topics which were historical and highly academic to her were still alive to many of her students. Reared as a Catholic and attracted to ceremonial, she was slightly averse – without ever saying so – to the evangelical intensity of the Puritans who were often the theme of her lectures. Moreover the Puritans had tried to close the theatres of England; one could almost hear the actor inside Kathleen Fitzpatrick crying aloud at their vandalism.

About this time Mrs Fitzpatrick was appointed an associate professor. She would have become a full professor had she been willing to move interstate. As it was, she was among the few senior women in the university.

At the end of my first year I hesitantly knocked at her door to ask whether she would write me a reference. A Melbourne newspaper had announced that it would select a young Australian to attend a youth forum in New York, and meanwhile it called on the applicants to provide a reference from a teacher. To my surprise and delight she said she would write on my behalf. Eventually the newspapers announced that I was one of the ten or so still in the contest for selection. I did not go to New York but received one bonus: Sir Keith Murdoch, then a giant but now remembered more as the father of Rupert, interviewed us one by one in his ample editorial office overlooking Flinders Street before dining with us all at the Oriental

Hotel, just around the corner. He was the first big businessman I had ever exchanged words with, and I was struck by the aura surrounding him even in the hotel.

About a year later I was captivated by a lecture given by Professor Fitzpatrick on an early Tasmanian governor, Sir John Franklin, about whom she was completing her first book. When it appeared in the university bookshop – it was too expensive for most students – I read its first chapter while standing near the counter. It began with the kind of grand opening she favoured in her lectures: 'The heart-shaped island of Tasmania hangs like a pendant'.

When she retired, before her time, to live in a house on a cliff overlooking the Southern Ocean near Lorne, she continued to write, though her output was not prolific. Of some of the political views I publicly expressed during her very last years she apparently did not approve though to me she said nothing. When in 1990 she died I was unable to attend the church for the funeral service in South Yarra but was free to pay respect at the brief Catholic ceremony, sparsely attended, at the graveside near the university. That afternoon the *Age* newspaper rang to ask whether I could write her obituary; and as I began to write, for the deadline was only a few hours ahead, I suddenly realised that she was a person of national significance though not yet known as such. So I began with the sentence: 'Kathleen Fitzpatrick, who was buried yesterday, was one of the few prominent women in public life in an era when no woman in Australia had yet become a judge, a premier, a head of a government department, a divine, a captain of industry or a professor.'

Intellectually the most exciting place at the university was the 'public lecture theatre' which stood near the clock tower. The theatre was like a spacious cave, with bench after bench of seats rising towards the roof. Here a politician or religious crusader would come by invitation to address lunchtime meetings; questions and short opposing speeches were permitted from the audience. Applause and hisses were normal but there was a tolerance that began to weaken a decade or two later in the major universities. Some days the audience was so large that knots of late arrivals would crowd the open doorways. Student leaders were eloquent in proposing their revolutionary hopes. In opposition, one of the most fluent speakers was Vincent Buckley, the Catholic poet, who in winter wrapped himself in his old blue air-force greatcoat.

When students took a break from lectures, many adjourned to the Union House. Membership of this club was compulsory, and we were proud to belong. At the long tables in its cafeteria, we drank tea or coffee, ate buns and pasties, and argued. A self-service cafeteria seems humdrum but was then a novelty. Elsewhere in the clubhouse, billiards could be played, as some all-day contestants found to their cost. 'Failed (Billiards)' was a pithy comment directed at students who failed in their university exams. A loungeroom was nearby for women, with another for men: the idea that they be combined belonged to the future. Upstairs was an art gallery with a collection of Streeton, Heysen and other painters that would have graced a smaller city such as Perth. At the far end of the building was the Union Theatre which was one of the most vigorous theatres in the land, at a time when local drama was temporarily at a lower ebb. And yet there were hundreds and hundreds of us who acted in at least one formal play, whether Shakespeare or Ben Jonson or G. B. Shaw, and on night after night the theatre was packed.

At the main entrance of the students' union, with its countless diamond-shaped panes of glass, was a marble sculpture. Carved at the turn of the century by the Melbourne artist Web Gilbert, and entitled *The Wheel of Life*, it depicted a Buddhist monk sitting on the banks of a shallow river. It had been carved for the lavish tomb of Mrs Springthorpe in the Kew Cemetery but, deemed to be unsuited for a Christian place of burial, it had found its way to our club.

My recollection of this building is tinged with the smell of shoe polish. In the basement we could blacken and polish our shoes, without charge. In those days even the teeth were cleaned no more diligently than the shoes. Nearly all Australia's shoes and boots were made within a few miles of the university – in Collingwood, Fitzroy and Clifton Hill where many students had lodgings.

In 1948, my first year at university, great ideas were ablaze. Momentous events were argued about. The rebelling Indonesians and the ruling Dutch signed a truce, thus heralding the end of the colonial era in South-East Asia. Almost at the same time two British colonies – Burma and Sri Lanka – became independent. In India the prophet and activist Gandhi, in his eightieth year, was assassinated. China was about to go communist. In Europe the battle between communism and democracy, or communism and capitalism, went on. Czechoslovakia, which had relative freedom, was seized by the communists. Berlin, the capital of the old Germany, was in danger of being severed from the West and divided into two. It was impossible to feel sure that the world's peace, ushered in three years ago, would last.

The church-owned residential colleges were more influential than at probably any other Australian university, though they accommodated no more than perhaps one in five of the university's full-time students. I lived in Queen's College, the Methodist college at the Carlton end of the university's grounds. Between Queen's and Ormond College was a large paddock where cows had once been kept. On the other side of Queen's stood Newman College, the exotic sandstone Catholic building designed by Walter Burley Griffin, the master planner of the city of Canberra. To walk along the side of the sports oval from Queen's to the main lecture rooms occupied a few minutes. Seven or eight minutes of walking in a slightly different direction was Lygon Street, a shopping place that was then more Jewish than Italian.

On the skyline of the city the university then stood high. The spire of Ormond College and the stone tower of Queen's could be seen from distant northern and western suburbs. Grand in their exterior, inside they were like old-fashioned rooming houses. A study, usually shared by two students, had its small 'grate' or fireplace where in winter we burned chopped firewood, carried in hessian bags on the shoulder up flights of stairs from the college woodheap; there was no lift nor elevator in the college.

Queen's had a cosy library at one end of a long corridor, and another library of dusty theological books in the upper tower. The chapel, at the end of another long corridor, was one of the prettiest in Melbourne, and late on summer evenings the sun sparkled on the stained glass. As thirty or so of the hundred residents were theological students in training for the Methodist ministry, a service in the chapel was held every weekday afternoon, and again on Sunday evening. There was a strong sense of belonging in Queen's, and the mix of students from many disciplines and several different countries – ranging from England and Mauritius to India and Malaya – sparked discussion.

Dr Raynor C. Johnson was master of the college. Self-effacing, slight in build, fitted with metal-framed spectacles that were more conspicuous than his thin moustache and receding chin, he carried a perpetual look of surprise. He appeared very distinguished when he wore his technicolour-dreamcoat gown from London University, but as a rule he dressed casually, his suit coat not necessarily matching his trousers, and his tie sometimes hanging inside out. A few new students wondered whether he was the college's handyman. Several, struggling with their heavy suitcases, were reported to have called on him to lend a hand.

While his oddly matched suit coat sometimes held several fountain pens and a propelling pencil, he often carried no paper. Outwardly he seemed disorganised but inwardly he was methodical and a skilled user of each hour. Though a Methodist he read aloud in the college chapel strange passages culled from Eastern prophets. An expert in his field of physics, he was increasingly attracted to spiritualism and extrasensory perception and wrote books on those themes, winning some international fame.

A prominent newcomer to Melbourne was invited, soon after he and his wife had settled in, to have afternoon tea with Dr Johnson; but on his arrival he learnt with some amazement (so he told me) that their host was late, having gone to St Kilda to exorcise a haunted house. Years later Johnson personally told me of his strenuous, scientifically inspired efforts to make contact with the dead. He confided that maybe about the time of the Second World War he had made a secret compact with his spiritualist friend Ambrose Pratt, the author of *The Lore of the Lyrebird* and *The Call of the Koala*. Under the compact one of them, when dead, should try to contact the other. Though Pratt had now been dead for some twenty years, Johnson said he was determined to contact him. For my part I had just returned from Mount Isa in Queensland where I knew that a mining lease owned long ago by Pratt was now one of the richest in Australia. I informed Johnson, who in some excitement promised to pass on this belated news to his dead friend, should contact ever be established.

'Sam' Johnson, as he was called, mainly allowed his college to run itself. Exceptionally tolerant, he closed his ears rather than hear gossip or mild slanders. Once or twice, when we were students, he was visibly vexed. One day he learnt that some Carlton men were grazing horses without permission on the paddock that lay between Queen's and Ormond colleges, and that one of the men was actually there. Johnson called on several of us to accompany him – to 'add moral authority', he said. The foxy-faced man in charge of the horses was taken aback when Johnson called out in his Yorkshire accent, 'Goot oot, goot oot!' The man certainly *got out*, taking his horses with him.

A succession of eager students of history lived in the college. Amongst the brightest was George Nadel, who had fled from Vienna to England in the late 1930s and arrived in Australia in the crowded ship *Dunera* as a wartime refugee. As one of the older undergraduates he was studying his final or third year in history when I was in my first year. Tallish with a slight stoop, of darkish complexion, he seemed to balance his pipe on his protruding lower lip as he spoke, speaking sometimes in a mysterious way. His eyes were falcon-like as he spoke but his look was often benign. His high state of alertness was slightly uncanny. He was partly of Jewish descent, but he took a keen interest in the sermons given in chapel. His knowledge of the sermons came partly by hearsay though sometimes he attended, a ragged black gown slung around him.

Each week George did not study for an exorbitant number of hours – he possessed a leisurely streak – but he quickly gutted the innards of those books he read. On any intellectual matter he held views, even if he did not have them when the matter was first raised.

Sometimes his opinions were not distinct to his listeners, for the grip of his teeth on his pipe could muffle part of a sentence. Moreover George – I hope it is not unfair to say so – was not always intent on making his views as clear as crystal. Bluff was one weapon in his impressive armoury: those who escaped from Hitler's Europe needed such weapons. For a time George was known as 'the dad', a nickname that suited him, for he seemed to lead most conversations in which he took part, even when he said little.

With all his talents he had his critics. Occasionally they were rowdy in his presence or slighting in his absence. He scornfully referred to them as 'gin-drinking boy scouts'. In the musical and dramatic life of the college his influence was pervasive. After chapel service on Sunday evening – it was not compulsory – many students would adjourn to Dr Johnson's lodge, where they sat on his carpet and drank a cup of hot tea while classical music was played. It was the era of the short-playing gramophone record, and sometimes George chose the records. During the mechanical interruptions when a record was turned over, he would deliver a slow and confidential comment on the music about to be played. Since he also was in the college's dramatic society at a time when it was one of the liveliest in Melbourne, many students felt, with some truth, that they were in the presence of a brilliant polymath.

One morning I heard on the radio that a well-known scholar of ancient history was visiting Melbourne. Harold Mattingly of the British Museum – a historian often cited by our lecturer as an expert on the Greek and Roman coins excavated in ancient Mediterranean towns – was aboard a passenger liner calling at Melbourne. It is a commentary on our isolation in that era that every British visitor of distinction was mentioned in the news. At breakfast in the dining hall I chanced to sit opposite George, whom I knew a little, and casually told him about the visitor. George was impressed. Find out, he instructed me in his benign way, the name of the pier where the ship is berthed. I found the answer – the wharf of each visiting ship was listed in the daily newspaper – and by mid-morning he and I were travelling seawards in the public bus.

At Port Melbourne we walked along the wooden pier towards the huge white liner; and George in his persuasive way informed the official guarding the gangway that we were calling on Mr Mattingly. Lo and behold, an 'Orient Line' or P&O steward in a white coat was summoned to escort us aboard. We followed him through the fascinating innards of the ship – I had not previously been in an ocean liner – to a wide wooden deck where Mr Mattingly, perhaps near his retiring age, was lounging in a deckchair. George introduced himself as a historian from the University of Melbourne and me as a first-year student. The waiter arranged more deckchairs and reappeared holding on high a tray with iced soft drinks for all.

The conversation, halting at first, gathered momentum. George enquired of the current excavations or research pursued by this and that British historian, and Mattingly answered fully. I can still hear him saying that 'young Richmond' (whoever young Richmond was) was making mighty progress. I was half mesmerised by the ship and the view of the blue bay but I could not help noticing the masterly way in which George guided the conversation and the equality with which he was accepted.

Mattingly revealed that he was here for only one day, being on his way to New Zealand, perhaps for family reasons. 'No,' he replied to George, he did not know anybody teaching history, let alone ancient history, in Melbourne. George therefore took possession of him, inviting him and his wife Marion to the university for afternoon tea. Actually the invitation was to George's small shared study in Queen's College where everything had to be rearranged and new furniture carried in for such a gathering. By mid-afternoon, when the Mattinglys stepped from their taxi, I had arranged tea cups, teapot and sugar bowl along with continental cakes and sandwiches which I had hurriedly bought, with George's money, in nearby Carlton. The Mattinglys had settled down in the cramped room, and the electric kettle was making a noise, when a knock was heard at the door. John O'Brien, the university's only lecturer in ancient history, had arrived by special invitation. George graciously introduced him to the Mattinglys. There was a faint hint, a word or two thrown into the air, that George, perhaps in an earlier phase of life, had enjoyed the company of the distinguished Harold Mattingly.

As George in a few days was to sit for his final exams in ancient and modern history, and as he spoke confidently with Mattingly about various theories, he scored highly in his examiner's mind. I now know how highly he scored. When later I came to know John O'Brien, that strange afternoon tea in Queen's College cropped up in the conversation. For the first time he learnt that George had met Mattingly by chance, and that their friendship was only four hours old when O'Brien entered the room. For my part I learnt how George, after returning from Port Melbourne pier, had rung O'Brien at his university office and invited him to come that afternoon and meet his distinguished guest. O'Brien was amazed how ably George conversed that day on some areas of ancient history.

An intellectual entrepreneur, George went on a scholarship to the new Australian National University in Canberra, and I did not meet him again. Within a couple of years he wrote a book, full of promise, and an article, 'Philosophy of History before Historicism', which won praise from the celebrated philosopher Karl R. Popper. In the United States, again on scholarships, he won his doctorate at Harvard and worked at the Princeton Institute for Advanced Study before he met an heiress. As expected, she married him. Living in England in some style he sadly did not reach old age.

Often we learnt more from our fellow students than from the lecturers. In the mid and late 1940s in Queen's, by chance, resided a succession of talented students of history, a large number for such a small college. In addition to George Nadel they included Owen Parnaby, John Bastin, Ken Inglis and Herb Feith. All were to be very successful academics. Colin Williams, a history and theology student who had left Queen's just before our time, was to be the celebrated Dean of Divinity at Yale in the year of the Black Panthers' trial, and Eric Osborn was to become well known in German universities for his research on early Christianity.

From several fellow students in the college I learnt to take lecture notes, not in an exercise book, but on single sheets of plain paper, thus gaining flexibility. I used quarto sheets of low-quality coloured paper, mostly green and yellow and pink, because they were cheaper than the white paper on which lines were printed. The opinion of the practical people – and they were right – was that notes should be taken on only one side of the sheet of paper. From Ken Inglis, an outstanding Melbourne High student who was one year ahead of me, I learnt how to file the notes in plain brown folders, one folder for each subject or theme. Such snippets of advice were vital for apprentices in the craft of history.

Soon I owned so many brown manila folders, mostly packed with handwritten notes, that I needed a filing cabinet. I went to the old

Chinese quarter in Little Lonsdale Street where tiny workshops made furniture to order. On a floor lined with planed wood and shavings, Sam Yick, the old and skinny master of the shop, wrote down my specifications for a wooden cabinet, about shoulder height, with four deep drawers capable of holding all my notes for several years to come. In broken English Mr Yick quoted the cost, writing the pounds and shillings on a stray sheet of paper. 'My plice!' he said proudly. The wooden filing cabinet arrived on the back of a truck a few weeks later, smelling of fresh glue. I still own it.

Alas, I picked up at least one working habit that made no sense. The writing of essays was the main task during the bulk of the year but some of the brightest students normally postponed the task. Though they had read widely and collected all the information they needed well in advance, they put off the actual writing of the essay until the last moment. I copied their habit and stayed up all night, writing my essays in longhand and then hurrying across to the university buildings next morning to hand them in right on the deadline.

There were weeks when downtown Melbourne, and not the university, seemed to be the hub of the universe. Acute was the sense of excitement when Laurence Olivier arrived with the Old Vic company to act in Melbourne. On another evening my friend S. E. K. Hulme revealed that he possessed a spare ticket for a classical concert in the Melbourne Town Hall; and we watched the conductor Klemperer hovering like an eagle above the orchestra, his arms moving like flapping wings. Arthur Huck, as theatre critic for the student newspaper, received two tickets to the opera *Eugene Onegin* and gave me one. I had not previously been inside an opera house; traditionally the Methodists much preferred oratorio to opera.

From the university you could actually walk with ease to at least six of the league football grounds – to North Melbourne and Carlton at one end and Richmond, Melbourne, Fitzroy and Collingwood at the other. At the Melbourne Cricket Ground, I saw most of the football finals each year; and my cup ran over when Geelong, after years in the wilderness, played two finals there in 1950. At Richmond, I saw the celebrated ruckman Jack Dyer, wearing knee bandages which were then unusual, run onto the field to play his last game. In the cemetery opposite Queen's College I watched a vast concourse of mourners, mostly the poor, virtually marching over the tombstones so that they could be close enough to hear the last rites read for the Fitzroy prize-fighter Archie Kemp who had been killed in the boxing ring in the West Melbourne stadium.

On Sundays in my first year I went to nearly every church in the city. In the little Swedenborgian church near St Patrick's Cathedral I sat with Henri Coutanceau, a French-speaking medical student from the island of Mauritius. I went to the Baptists, Lutherans and Presbyterians and of course the Independent Church with its elegant circular galleries from which one could look down on Gordon Powell who was one of the most eloquent Protestant preachers in the land. In the rooms of the Theosophical Society which had become, in its decline, a big property owner in Collins Street, I heard an astonishing address about a man who was swallowed by a fish in Port Phillip Bay. Alfred Deakin the prime minister was, when young, a follower of this sect but later joined the breakaway Australian Church, which I also visited once on a Sunday.

*

In my first year I drank no alcohol. Most university students of my age, whether female or male, did not drink; and if they did, it was only once or twice a year, and then by the half-glass. The aroma of beer, noticeable outside crowded hotels with open doors or windows, displeased me because it was stale and bitter. My ancestral background too was opposed to alcohol. All of my grandparents opposed it in any form, and my father as a teenager had been the secretary of, I think, the California Gully Tent of Rechabites, which sounds like a sissy society but – judging by the surviving photograph of them, rank after rank – was certainly not. Its members, whether young men or teenagers, had promised to abstain from alcohol so long as they lived; but Gallipoli and the Western Front must have weakened the resolve of some.

The smoking of tobacco was less frowned upon by my parents' friends. At the conclusion of Methodist services on Sundays, men but not women would light up a cigarette or pipe in the open air outside the church's front doors: some were men who would not allow more than a whiff of alcohol to pass their nostrils. At home my parents had no objection to tobacco and my brother John smoked by the time he was eighteen or nineteen.

I took my first smoke when I was waiting on the side of the road, in a western suburb of Melbourne, in the hope of hitching a ride towards Portland. I had bought a packet of ten 'Seahorses', knowing that a cigarette or two was a vote of thanks to a driver who gave me a ride, but now becoming bored with my long wait I decided to try one. It took me minutes to light the cigarette, for a strong northerly blew out each match. Finally alight, the cigarette smelt like a garbage tip on fire.

At Queen's College the drinking of alcohol was against the rules, though some cheerfully broke the rule. A few drank almost enough to make up for the many who didn't. On the other hand the smoking of tobacco was tacitly encouraged. The students' own organisation, called the Sports & Social Club, possessed a prewar entitlement to cigarettes; and nearly every evening at coffee time a student in charge of 'The Till', as it was called, sold quality cigarettes including Dunhill and Benson & Hedges which were virtually unpurchaseable at city tobacconists. When I went to my first professional work, at a copper field in western Tasmania, a ration of ready-rubbed tobacco – in the red State Express and the greenish Havelock pouches – was available for each employee. I learnt to roll my own cigarettes, often from aromatic pipe tobacco, and did so for twenty years.

Most students now eat various exotic meals in the course of a month, but for us a visit to a cafe serving exotic food was a luxury. Max O'Connor, a theological student with intense curiosity and a crabbed warm-heartedness, liked to dine out; and he suggested that a few of us visit the Old Vienna, a small and inexpensive restaurant in Russell Street where the waitresses wore ribbons and bows in what was assumed to be Austrian style. They also took in hand – a touch of class – the guests' overcoats and hung them on a rack. The Old Vienna served wiener schnitzel, veal being an exotic meat, and cold apple cider. Nearby in the Lingnan in Little Bourke Street I ate my first Chinese meal – dim sims followed by scallops in sweet-and-sour sauce and then fried bananas with a dollop of ice cream. The meal was so palatable that I invited my parents to have their first Chinese dinner. My surmise is that at this time only one in every 100 Australians had ever tasted a Chinese meal.

I had a burning desire to read outside the syllabus, and recently I came across a rough note of my reading during the last eight days of January

1949. One day I read the historian Macaulay's essay on the poet Goldsmith, and Carlyle's dramatic chapter on the death of Mirabeau, the French revolutionist. On another day I went to the Public Library and read the English periodical *New Statesman and Nation*, walked to the university to pay my fees for the coming term, and went home to read 100 pages of the autobiography of Neville Cardus, the cricket writer and music critic. Next day I was reading at the Northcote Public Library, followed by a day or two at the Public Library where I read three months of the daily *Argus* for 1885 and three months of *The Age* for 1890. I was surprised how much I could glean about the past from the classified advertisements. Buying a cheap copy of the 1944 *Who's Who in Australia* at a second-hand shop, I began to make lists of where people were born – I was learning Australian history my own way. I began to read Joseph Furphy's novel *Such Is Life*, finding the going heavy, and Ernestine Hill's *Great Australian Loneliness*.

For a month or so, keeping a daily diary in the kind of floppy notebook used then by shorthand reporters, I kept a check on my thoughts, such as they were. It surprises me to find that I was flirting with what is called economic rationalism and snuggling up to free trade, a doctrine that was out of favour in Australian academic circles. I favoured a reduction in Australia's import duties on foreign manufactured goods and hoped for a network of reciprocal treaties with Britain, Belgium and other manufacturing nations so that they would admit our wool, wheat and copper free of duty. I was temporarily straying from the gospel, shared by all political parties, that economic nationalism was in Australia's interests. I argued – if I could find anybody to argue with me – that internationalism was also in the world's interests. 'Greater interdependence in the world economy is a step towards peace,' I wrote. One quarter of a century later I dissected that peace argument, using world history as a laboratory, and abandoned it. Meanwhile I predicted that in time to come the old battle, fought over by the tariff protectionists and the free traders, would someday be resumed. I proved to be correct, but perhaps what came true was not a result of my logic but my guesswork or wishful thinking.

I was leaning more towards an ethic of personal responsibility rather than government responsibility – in short, I was deserting the team that I had so recently barracked for. Just at this time my uncle in Colac urgently wanted me to help in harvesting a crop of peas which previously must have been picked by hand. I drove the tractor that towed the header, or worked on the back of the header and unloaded the bags when they became full of peas. As there were frequent halts because of rain or mechanical troubles – the tractor smoked badly – we had a chance for argument. My uncle Cecil loved an argument about economics: what is more, he was a patient listener and his interruptions were rarely more than one sentence in length. I also harvested peas on a lakeside farm owned by another farmer named Harry who also liked to argue. His experience with the government's marketing of eggs and wheat had made him an opponent of excessive regulations. To our mutual disappointment, for we enjoyed arguing, we found we agreed.

It is difficult, in retrospect, to know why one's basic views change: it is difficult enough, at the very time they are turning, to know why they are making a somersault. Sometimes we slowly shuffle away from positions once tenaciously held, almost as if the mooring ropes become loose rather than some new idea arises.

At this time I also lost faith in some of my rather utopian ideas. I ceased to think that paradise could be created by a wise government –

partly because I came to the view that most human beings had a cussed and a contrary streak. We were capable of evil and mischief as well as trying to imitate the good and great.

In heading towards this more cautious view of human nature I was reflecting some of my serious reading during recent months: the study of English puritanism, the hearing of sermons on Sunday evening by the Rev. Dr Calvert Barber in the Queen's College chapel, and the occasional visits, sometimes with other students, to hear the preachers in a variety of city churches. I was affected by the somewhat gloomy New York theologian Reinhold Niebuhr, whom I read while holidaying in the Dandenong Ranges where occasionally my parents rented a house made up of old Melbourne cable trams. For many students then, serious books not on the syllabus were lighthouses; and perhaps they shone more than they do today.

By chance there fell into my hands a biography of Edmund Burke, the Irish orator who rebelled against the utopianism and violence displayed in the French Revolution. To his cautious assessment of human nature, I see that I gave tentative 'ticks' in one of my private notebooks. If I had not recently found the notebook I would have sworn I had never read Burke. On the whole I retained more optimism than pessimism about the world, whose future was so precarious during some years of the long Cold War.

9

FARMER FORD, 'MANNO' AND MAX

Our generation was lucky, for we did not encounter the global depression which had been predicted for the early postwar years. Instead, labour was so scarce that an eighteen-year-old could earn adult wages in many jobs. In the first of my long vacations I was a luggage handler for Trans Australia Airlines at Essendon Airport. Hauling a hand trolley carrying the passengers' suitcases from the newly landed aircraft to the small building that served as a terminal, I then returned with the suitcases of passengers booked on its outgoing flight. It was the era of the smaller Douglas aircraft and not many of these California-made planes came to Melbourne each day, thus providing us with many hours of idle time.

The two-engine Douglas DC-3 aircraft was small. Its cabin, just over 2 metres in width, seated only twenty-one passengers. After it landed and slowly taxied towards the shed that served as a passenger lounge, there was excitement among the small crowd of onlookers. 'Just imagine,' they exclaimed. 'Only three hours ago these people were in Sydney, and here they are!' Even we, standing around in our floppy white overalls, felt important.

Compared to daytime the night shift seemed endless. Only a few freight planes had to be loaded or unloaded. One midnight, Nadzab the foreman told me to sit near a parked plane, guard a coffin inside it, and ensure that nobody entered the cabin and removed the coffin. In the previous year a full coffin had reportedly been flown in the wrong plane to the wrong town on the eve of a funeral.

By working hard at unskilled jobs in the long vacations I could add to the income from scholarships. In the summer vacation the Commonwealth government paid train fares so that university students could go inland to help with the harvesting. In November 1949, Alan Dixon and I boarded the train for Bendigo and the northern plains where, we were told, a farmer would be waiting at the tiny railway station called Ultima. When our train pulled in we easily identified him. There he stood, not beside a truck but next to his horse and jinker. One of the district's youngest farm-owners he casually greeted us, adding that he was old-fashioned because, in the main farming tasks, he employed draught horses instead of a tractor.

After driving us along a track that zigzagged through the mallee scrub, he carried our suitcases to the spare bedroom in his weatherboard house, and introduced us to his young wife who gave us a splendid meal. Haymaking would start in half an hour, he said. With his horse-drawn reaper and binder he had already cut the hay and bound it into large sheaves which lay scattered across the dry paddock. Our job was to gather the sheaves and stand them up in the form of hundreds of self-supporting stooks, which in the hot sun were soon dry. Then came the day when the making of the huge haystack began, and we loaded the big horse-drawn wagon with sheaves, again and again returning for more. His haystack was his year's fuel, for hay and chaff were food for his huge horses.

John Ford, owner of the 1000-acre farm, shaped the rising haystack. While we stood on the wagon, seizing each bound sheaf with a pitchfork and tossing it up to him, he waited on top of the haystack and caught each flying sheaf with his fork and set it neatly in place. The stack crept so high that if he fell, he would break a leg. Now another pair of hands was needed for the procession of tasks, and the help of a neighbour was called for. Oldish and cheerful, he had his own way of earning a rest. Giving us a knowing wink he gently pricked the waiting horses with his pitchfork, thus prodding them into shuffling a few steps forward. For a few minutes, while the wagon was being returned to its correct place, the hard, arduous work of stack-making was halted and we rested and laughed and yarned.

Wiry and strong, John Ford loved a day of hard work. Working from sunrise until just before sunset, by the day's end we were almost exhausted. After a quick swim in the dam near the house we ate the hot meal prepared by Mrs Ford. While it is now fashionable to lament that there were few fine cooks until the postwar European migrants arrived, the women who could cook homely meals from basic ingredients formed then a higher proportion of the population than they do today. All in all, the experience on the farm was intensely satisfying. I feel lucky to have taken part in the simple task of harvesting which had gone on, little altered, for thousands of years, but was being transformed everywhere by the exit of the huge friendly Clydesdale horses and the arrival of the heavy tractor.

The Ford family, eventually selling the farm, acquired – unknown to me – a huge property of arid land in Western Australia. There, it so happened, I was invited in 1990 to declare open a new goldmine in the mulga country north of Meekatharra. Just before the ceremony, I found myself standing next to the shire president, easily recognised because he wore the mayoral insignia over his shirt and braces. Introducing himself with a handshake he said his name was John, adding that he held a sheep property over Wiluna way. Somehow his face seemed familiar. Half an hour later I said, 'Didn't you once have a farm in the Mallee?' 'I did,' he replied, looking at me intently. 'Well, I once worked for you,' I added. He scratched his head; he couldn't remember me. I gave him cheek, telling him with mock indignation that I worked like a slave alongside him day after day, and now he couldn't even recall me. At last he remembered, making amends in his own style by reciting the names of each of the draught horses working with us at that time. He phoned his wife who said, 'Of course you remember him.'

I had to admire the way he carried out his official duties at the opening of that remote Labouchere goldmine. In a marquee erected by caterers flown all the way from Perth, the guests and the mine's employees sat down together at a banquet; and during the meal John Ford stood, his thumbs entwined in his braces, and expressed the hope that the heavy traffic to the mine would not break up the municipality's roads, such as they were. Imploring God's blessing, he prayed for the safety of all who would work in and around the mine. He spoke so genuinely.

Not long afterwards, he died. He had received official permission to make a cemetery on a corner of his isolated sheep station, but on the day of his own burial the rain poured on the parched land, the newly dug grave filled with water, and many mourners on their way were soon marooned, the dirt roads being impassable. The Anglican bishop was already en route to conduct the funeral but his small plane could not land on the waterlogged ground. So reluctantly the funeral was postponed, and when the road finally was dry, the body of John Ford was carried on the long journey to the town of Meekatharra and temporarily placed in a hotel's freezer. Eventually his funeral took place, many mourners coming from far away, for he was widely trusted.

He was only one of my employers at vacation time. In Melbourne a day's work could easily be found at the long goods shed of the Spencer Street railway station. Bags of flour and sugar, knobbly bags of potatoes, heavy bags of cement and large boxes of machine parts had to be lifted onto the shoulder and carried onto a railway wagon and neatly stacked. Some of the men who worked there had the appearance of being homeless.

I was still eager, as a student, to visit places that highlighted Australia's history. Towards the end of one summer vacation, Sek Hulme and I hitchhiked around the coastal road to Sydney. Such exotic places as Eden and Batemans Bay and the Bulli Pass were new to us. It was an incredibly slow journey, for cars and trucks were few, and much of the coastal highway still consisted of gravel that was easily washed away in rainstorms. While Sek stayed in Sydney at his uncle's house, I hitchhiked across the Blue Mountains, spending the first night sleeping in the open air near the railway town of Blayney. Further west some roads, littered with the carcasses of rabbits run over by vehicles, were smelling high. The rabbit plague was at its peak, and the deadly myxomatosis virus had not yet been released.

I recall, one Friday afternoon, sitting on my small rucksack at a forsaken township out on the plains. I too felt forsaken. I ate an evening meal at a Greek cafe where the proprietor, a long-time resident, told me my chances of hitching a ride further west were small. He was kind: he arranged for me to ride on the back of a truck to Cootamundra where, at the railway station, I consulted the printed timetable and learnt that, sometime before sunrise, I could board a cross-country train that would take me to South Gundagai which was on the Hume Highway. Like all hitchhikers I resented the buying of a train ticket; it was a confession of defeat. Whenever I drive from Melbourne to Canberra I see, at the township of Coolac, the remains of the now-abandoned track along which my train moved towards Gundagai. There, on the Hume Highway, it was easy to hitch a ride in a semitrailer. About midnight, lying on top of the tarpaulin enclosing a load, I rode into Melbourne.

A few months later came an opportunity to visit Tasmania with a university friend, Peter Thompson. It was the term vacation, and we bought two of the cheapest berths in the tiny passenger ship *Taroona* and boarded her at Port Melbourne on a cold May afternoon. To make a voyage was such a rare event for our family that my mother and Donald, then aged six, arrived at the wharf to see us off.

As the ship steamed along the bay, I longed to be on the open ocean. Passing Queenscliff with its Norfolk Island pines standing like tall sentries we stood on the deck and felt elated. We were less elated when, passing through the narrow heads, we saw and heard the booming waves straight ahead. The ship began to climb wave after wave, sinking back each time into the deep trough. I felt that it was almost possible, while standing on the stern, to slide down the steep deck and straight into the seething sea. A bell rang, and we were summoned to the second-class dining room where a hot, heavy meal was served by uniformed waiters who skidded, darted and swayed in order to keep their balance. Half an hour passed, and most of us, back on deck to take in the fresh air and avoid the squeamishness, were wondering whether we would last the distance.

We could afford just four days and three nights in Tasmania. From the wharf in Devonport we walked to the outskirts of the town and were picked up by a Cadbury-chocolate man in his newly washed car. Like all sensible drivers he summed up his eager passengers – did he like them or fear them? – before deciding how far he would take them. When he discovered that we were going all the way to Hobart, which was Cadbury's home and his, he announced, 'I'll take you there'; he was generous and knowledgeable. Approaching the Midlands, and seeing the finger-signpost pointing to the small town of Ross, he announced that we must see its convict-built bridge. It proved to be the most stirring historical sight I had ever seen. Its yellowish blocks of heavy freestone shone in the faint midday sunlight. The three arches were rain-washed and clean, and the hundred or more stone carvings of faces and symbols, though sometimes eroded, seemed fresh. Erected in 1836, and now the third-oldest bridge in Australia, its presence had slowly altered the course of the river which was now a chain of ponds flanked by green rushes.

Tasmania was viewed by most people of my generation as a pale replica of the British Isles, and the area around Ross with its roadside hedges, oaks, elms and other English trees was seen as its heartland. Since most Australians – including me – doubted whether they would ever visit Europe, Tasmania was the closest substitute

The knowledge that convicts had built the bridge at Ross pleased me. The convict past, however, was still viewed with silent disdain or uneasiness by most people, especially those living in Victoria and South Australia, who did not foresee that eventually the convicts

I spent my first three years in Terang in Victoria's Western District. Above: our father (in clerical collar) with me, Joan and John. Below: our mother is nursing baby Joan, and next to her are John and me, wriggling. *Blainey collection*

The youngest students at Leongatha school, September 1936. I'm sitting in the third row from the front, seventh from the left, wearing the light pullover. Joan is in the back row, second girl from the right. *Blainey collection*

A family picnic near Anglesea in 1940: John, Ellis, Joan and me. Donald was not yet born. For some forgotten reason we were neatly dressed and well behaved. *Blainey collection*

Football hero, Ted Rankin, when young: he made us all barrack for Geelong. *Geelong Football Club*

Ballarat High School's youngest cricket team, 1941. In the back row, on the far right, stands my friend Rex Hollioake; I'm two places to his left. *Blainey collection*

I attended Wesley College from 1944 until 1947. I was later commissioned to write its history, and the jacket featured a watercolour of the old school. *Wesley College collection*

Mr Neil MacNeil, MC, was Wesley's headmaster. In August 1946 he suddenly died, just after taking us for Latin. *Wesley College collection*

We met every morning in Adamson Hall for what was called 'assembly'. A hymn was sung vigorously, a passage of the Bible was read aloud by a prefect, and on Friday the names of the war-dead were recited. *Blainey collection*

Outside Carlton's football ground in the winter sunshine: Jim Morrissey, Val Keast and S.E.K. Hulme in the back row, with me and Reverend Laurie Turner in front. *Blainey collection*

The Queen's students who had won first class honours in 1949 combed their hair and gathered in the large garden for a photo. I'm standing in the back row, on the left, and Ken Inglis is sitting in the centre of the front row. Four of these students became professors. *Blainey collection*

In the early postwar years Queen's College held about a hundred students and staff. Dr Raynor C. Johnson, the Yorkshire-born master, sits in his ornate chair, his gaudy doctoral gown touching his toes, while I can just be seen placing my fingers on the top of the chair. *Queen's College*

Pretending to read a book in an upstairs study at Queen's College. For much of 1950 I spent more time as editor of the *Farrago* newspaper than as a history student. *Blainey collection*

Looking out the train window, as I travelled through the rainforest in western Tasmania. Aged twenty, I was hopefully embarking on my first book. *Geoffrey Blainey*

I was lucky to meet Jimmy Elliott, who spent the cold days sitting beside the fire in the commercial travellers' room at Bowers' Hotel. In his eighties he felt fortunate to be alive, for in 1912 he survived an underground disaster in which forty-two miners were killed. He taught me about the prospector's life, which he had followed on Tasmania's west coast since he was a boy. *Geoffrey Blainey*

My first book, published in 1954 by Melbourne University Press, featured the eerie landscape of Mount Lyell.

The Tyranny of Distance began life as a cheap paperback with its ingenious Sadgrove cover that depicted a ship sailing upside down. The back cover rather boastfully proclaimed that this was my eighth book, 'and in his own opinion easily his best'.

Ann Heriot and Geoffrey Blainey were married at St George's Anglican Church, Malvern, on the late afternoon of 15 February 1957. The head of Ann's father, Commander F.W. Heriot, can be glimpsed just behind her bridal veil. Reverend Cliff Blainey assisted in conducting the ceremony. *Blainey collection*

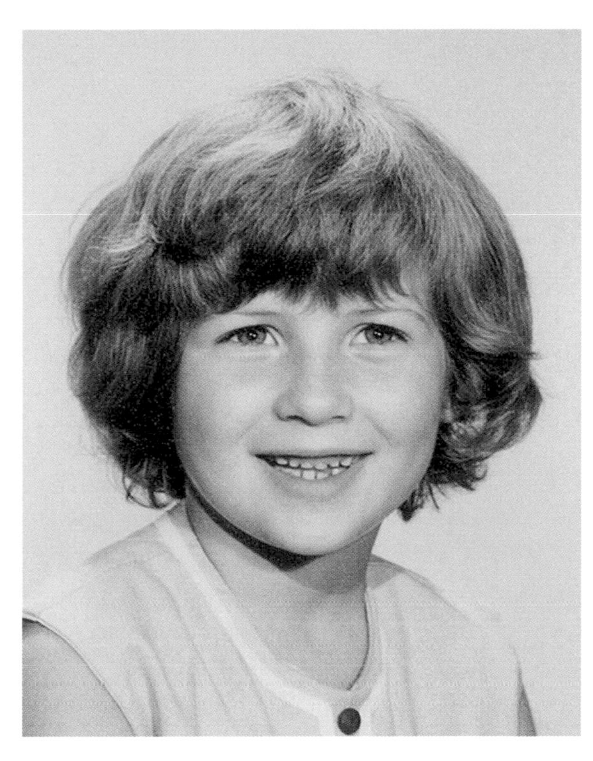

Anna, our daughter. She was born in the Mercy Hospital in East Melbourne on 3 September 1959.
Blainey collection

Anna and Ann, holidaying with the kind Oatman family in Illinois in 1970.
Blainey collection

John Campbell Miles, who discovered the rich minerals at Mount Isa while travelling west with his horses in 1923. His find was probably the most important made in Australia in the first half of the twentieth century. Living frugally and contentedly into the 1960s, his favourite menu was toasted raisin bread and a pipe of tobacco. *Mount Isa Mines*

This photograph was taken in the summer of 1958–59, and I had just written, to a tight deadline, the history book *Gold and Paper*. It was probably the last book I wrote with a fountain pen. *Blainey collection*

Two men with hats: Essington Lewis ('The Steel Master') and Ben Chifley (the former locomotive driver). Chifley worked for Lewis as an executive in the huge wartime munitions industry before winning back his seat in parliament in 1940. He was to serve as prime minister from 1945 to 1949. *Lewis collection*

The lightweight portable typewriter is now an antique, but for writers it was a technical wonder. In 1966 I carried one in a succession of trains all the way from Hong Kong to Holland; in Siberia its clattering noise sometimes caused a mild sensation. *Shane Stanley*

I regularly took the economic-history students to picnics at the abandoned Victorian goldfields, and sometimes tried to teach them how to pan for gold. Here at Blackwood in April 1967, Jack Potter and I are cooking the lunchtime chops. *Robin Mitchell*

In 1973 I was an Australian delegate (in my tropical white suit) at the first UNESCO conference held in Asia. At many of the sessions in Jogjakarta I sat next to the senior Afghan delegate, for the seating was alphabetical. Often I was greeted by his humorous cry, 'It's cold at Bondi Beach today.' *Blainey collection*

In conversation with Russian-born Judah Waten, who was almost the best known of this nation's Communist writers, before a Literature Board meeting in 1973. *Australian Council for the Arts*

A meeting of Mr Whitlam's new Literature Board in 1973. I'm in the chair and – going clockwise – joined by Joan O'Donnell (secretary), Dick Hall, Manning Clark, Richard Walsh, Tom Shapcott, Geoff Dutton, David Malouf, Alec Hope, Nancy Keesing, Judah Waten and Michael Costigan (CEO). Absent is Elizabeth Riddell. *Australian Council for the Arts*

Wandjuk Marika, Aboriginal leader from Yirrkala in Arnhem Land, yarning with me on the banks of the Yarra River. We met in 1972 and remained friends. Earlier he had been a sponsor of the celebrated bark petition-painting that called for a stronger say by Aborigines in their own lives. Sprinkling Methodism with the religion of his ancestors, he often announced in a deep soft voice: 'The Brolga is my great teacher.' *Blainey collection*

would be welcomed like long-lost relatives. Another reason for our lack of interest in convicts was that not much was known yet about them as individuals. I learnt that the ornate carving on the Ross bridge was the work of Dan Herbert, a convict who had once worked as 'a sign-board writer at Leeds'. Soon after reaching Ross, he married young Mary who had been shipped to Tasmania after stealing blankets from the house in Covent Garden where she was a servant. A likeness of his wife, carved with his stonemason's tools, can be seen on the bridge.

Hobart, where we met my schoolfriend Ted Sikk, was startling with its mountain hovering over the estuary and the steep streets of stone houses. Staying for only two days – we were in a rush – we learnt that we could return to the north coast and the Bass Strait steamer by a highlands route. At the Great Lake and its deserted countryside the motorist who had given us a lift from Hobart put us down and drove away in a westerly direction. All the motor traffic had long since ceased, and we began to walk. The arrows on a white signpost informed us we should walk in a northerly direction. It was a blue afternoon, with no wind and slightly chill, and the road was gravel. A smooth long lake soon appeared, only a stone's throw away, and strange white gum trees stood out, just across the water. We walked on and on, passing every now and then a fisherman's hut, deserted and boarded up, but seeing no cattle or sheep – not even a fence. Occasionally we heard the roar of a truck in the distance, but it did not come our way. The sun dropped just below the ranges and the cold air began to bite. At least, if no vehicle came our way, we knew that we could settle down, gather dry wood for a fire and keep warm all night.

At last we heard the faint coughing of a truck. Barely audible at first, the sound came closer, and to our relief the driver stopped and gave us a ride. Going down the winding road from the high country, we reached the warmth of Deloraine that night. Next day we hitched to Launceston, and downstream towards the mouth of the Tamar where we boarded the overnight steamship to Melbourne. Sailing into the open sea, I could see the low foreshores from which the first white settlers of southern Victoria had set out in small schooners or ketches in which sheep were crammed. That swift visit to Tasmania heightened my wish to be a historian.

In spare hours as a student in Melbourne I often visited the Public Library and took a seat in the newspaper room. It was the resort in winter of the overcoat brigade – oldish men who had fallen out of the race, and now spent the night in lodging houses or charity homes and the daylight hours in the warm Reading Room of the library. There, if you went to the counter and asked for a specific newspaper and waited patiently, a heavy bound volume of old *Age* and *Argus* newspapers for the requested period would be carried from the vaults below.

One cold day in the Reading Room I saw an unshaven old man wearing a shabby overcoat and my reddish woollen scarf which one week ago I had temporarily placed on the back of my chair and forgotten. I did not tell him that he was wearing my scarf. The loss of my only scarf was a tiny price to pay for the privilege of sitting in the stately Reading Room and communing with the past.

During a few years spent at the long reading tables I harvested a wide amount of Victorian, Australian and overseas political, sporting and economic news, especially from the 1870s and 1880s. I read about those decades partly because little was being written about them in Australian history books, and maybe because the gruff attendants, at whose mercy I was, did not have to walk so far to collect the newspapers published in those particular decades. The elation that I gained from burying myself in the everyday events reported in the tiny print of these papers was intense. In the second-hand bookshops I also gained much by speed-reading chosen books. Sometimes I read like a magpie, pecking here and there and chewing those morsels I fancied. It is no way to treat an author but I do not apologise to them.

As South Australia was the first foreign land I had visited, I had a sentimental feel for it, rather like many English people felt about Italy. Occasionally I paid more than I could afford for old Adelaide books, especially those that I imagined I might use as a writer one day. At a sale in a Bourke Street shop I bought for five shillings Ebenezer Ward's rare book of 1869, *The South-Eastern District of South Australia: Its Resources and Requirements*. The opening page was inscribed with the author's untidy hand – I had not previously owned a book that had actually been signed by its author. On page 33 he made the wild prophecy that Border Town was destined to become a 'metropolis'.

It was a wonderful feeling, on opening a second-hand book, to see the autograph of the author or the signature of a well-known citizen who once was the owner. In my early years I bought books carrying the signatures of Sir John Monash the soldier. Once I bought a pair of books originally owned by John Pascoe Fawkner, the jack-of-all-trades who in those days was recognised, more than he now is, as the founder of Melbourne. I still have those two volumes, describing Burma and published in 1834. To declare his ownership he had inked his signature in his large handwriting on at least six different pages. A few of these books, bought cheaply when I was a teenager, became valuable sources of knowledge when eventually I became a historian. The book that proved to be the best for a working historian was *Victoria and Its Metropolis* – two illustrated volumes, handsomely bound in leather, with the tips of the pages tinted in gold. Published in 1888, they were about as heavy as a large Christmas turkey. I carried them in triumph from Mrs Bird's narrow-fronted second-hand shop at the top of Bourke Street in 1949. They cost two guineas, but their details of Australian lives must have repaid the purchase price twenty times over.

As my second year commenced, I looked forward to the lectures by Mr Manning Clark who taught Australian history, which he began just after 5.15 p.m. so that part-time students, having finished work, could arrive by tram from the heart of the city. As we had heard much about Clark – not in the press, for he was then barely known outside the university – I expected to see a giant stride into the crowded theatre. He was commanding in his own way, above middle height, a large belt (it was still the era of braces) holding up his dark trousers, black gown clinging to him, and a folder of lecture notes which he placed on the lectern almost as if they were a Bible: in a sense they were, for he had a deep knowledge of Australian history at a time when the best lecturers, more than the latest books, were the main repositories of knowledge. The torrent of books on Australian history came later.

The son of an Anglican clergyman, and reared on Phillip Island and in the Dandenong Ranges, Clark studied at Melbourne and then at Oxford just before the war. He visited Nazi Germany, where his future wife Dymphna was studying, and saw the troops of armed men marching in heavy boots. After teaching under James Darling at Geelong Grammar School, which was slightly leftist in some classrooms, he came to our university where he initially taught political science and then Australian history – a topic not yet taught at most universities. Clark would become famous for his *History of Australia*, consisting of six volumes clad in a cover of fire-brigade red cloth, but he had published little at the time when he taught us. Even so, stylish writing being important to him, he drew our attention in his lectures to clear and powerful prose whenever he encountered it.

Clark's manner and his tone of voice were slightly gloomy. On the Beaufort scale of geniality his face normally registered no more than 30 per cent, but he had a sense of fun and a spontaneous wit. Cleverly he would mimic the voices or the demeanour of certain grand figures of Australia's colonial past, especially governors, divines and rich squatters. He also had the unusual gift of mocking himself.

In my pocket diary I called him 'Manno', though not to his face. He called me Blainey. He still had the disciplinarian manner of the more severe kind of schoolmaster, a manner that eventually faded. About seven or eight of us – all honours students – went to his weekly morning tutorial where for an hour he spoke more than we did. The only written works he expected from us were two long essays, and he encouraged us, when doing research for them, to read old newspapers and other documents. We had to let the dust of the past cover our hands.

When in his last years Manning Clark wrote an autobiography called *The Quest for Grace*, he graciously recalled me. One young man, he added, sat in the tutorial throughout first term and 'never said a word'. Amid the hubbub of discussion this young student seemed lost and rarely smiled. Though this swift portrait was a witty exaggeration, it held a kernel of truth. In his own words: 'At the end of the term one of the students whose name I had never heard before submitted a brilliant essay. I asked the class, "Is Mr Geoffrey Blainey here?" The silent one smiled and reached out for the essay.'

After he moved to Canberra as a professor, he looked back on his four years as a lecturer in history at Melbourne with deep pleasure. In the preface to volume one of his *History of Australia*, he wrote: 'There is a very special debt to those students in Melbourne whom it was my great good fortune to teach in the years after the war.' We also felt a special debt.

As he began to emerge as a national figure, his views on both earthly and ethereal questions were sought by news gatherers. The first volume of his long history certainly excited historians – indeed, more than it aroused the public at the time. In 1968 I received a letter from Kathleen Fitzpatrick who was busily reading Manning's second volume. She felt as if she 'were being swept along in a whirlwind, going dizzily around one of the lower circles of the Inferno. I don't know what to make of it, only what it makes of me. I wonder if you can keep your head better and form an opinion?' I do not recollect the opinion I gave her. At that time, like most of his readers, I was stirred and enlightened more by his small, fast-moving paperback history of Australia, though I was puzzled by his tendency to dismiss some of the country's achievements.

In due course I read most pages of his six volumes and marvelled that his prose was not only distinctive but that every sentence was polished. In his books many inaccuracies were pointed out by critics, but he was unusually methodical in facets of research. He visited scores of historic places to catch their atmosphere and geography, and his footnotes usually recorded the date of such visits: thus for the later volumes Clark visited the Melbourne Club on 21 December 1974 to see its painting of explorer Burke, and he walked in the ocean-view Waverley Cemetery in Sydney on 5 July 1976 to see the grave of the 'bellbird poet' Henry Kendall. About that time, at his request, I went with him to Ballarat to gaze at the site of the Eureka Stockade and then visited the graves of the miners and soldiers. That afternoon at the Ballarat old cemetery by chance I found the headstone of my great-grandmother whom I knew personally. Deep below her lay her husband, a Cornish migrant, who died almost half a century ahead of her.

Manning showed me kindnesses. Privately he invited me, when young, to put in my name for a newly advertised chair in history at the Australian National University, though in the end it was awarded to Mick Williams who was the professor in New England. Later I suggested that Manning be invited to join the Whitlam Government's new Literature Board, of which I was to be chairman, and we saw each other more than before. Our personal friendship blossomed, and he invited me to launch one of his books. I continued to admire him as a distinguished exponent of the craft of history writing. By the mid-1980s, I guess our views on certain current-day topics were moving far apart; while we rode comfortably in the same train we got off at different stations.

The History Department at Melbourne is said to have been the most influential of all the nation's departments in the humanities and social sciences in the early postwar years. Its leading place and much of its intellectual drive stemmed from R. M. (Max) Crawford. The son of the stationmaster at Grenfell in rural New South Wales, he came from a big and brilliant family. Moving from Sydney to Oxford, where he did a second undergraduate degree, Max Crawford taught in the Bluecoat School before coming home. At the early age of thirty-one he became professor of history at Melbourne. Into what was already a successful department, he injected his faith that history was the most important topic under the sun. Inheriting a few impressive lecturers, he recruited more. Nearly all were born in Australia.

Professor Crawford was thin and even ascetic, and as neat as his dark double-breasted suit. His speech was precise and slightly mannered, and he had a charming smile. He was almost too sophisticated to teach the weaker undergraduate effectively, for the structure of his sentences was ornate, and he liked to add an Italian phrase – the city of Florence during the Renaissance was his love. He flattered, indeed he encouraged, students by assuming that they knew nearly as much as he did. Talented scholars did not realise how often he sacrificed his own potential books by devoting so much time to writing references in their favour. At the peak of his writing powers, he and his new professorial colleague John La Nauze gave up their own research in order to complete the valuable book *Men of Yesterday* which was written but far from completed by a tutor in their department, Miss Margaret Kiddle, who died unexpectedly. Crawford lived through his students who, he believed, would have the chance to reshape the world.

As he was overseas in the year I studied the subject that he normally taught, I then knew him only slightly. I did not even read until last year his small history called *Australia* which he completed in 1951. Published in London, the first half was highly original, and he actually devoted one of his eleven chapters – a rare proportion – to the Aboriginal peoples. Two or more decades later he and his second wife Ruth became a loyal friend to our family: by then we were almost neighbours in a rural suburb on the Yarra River.

During my three years as a student I became indebted to many other teachers. They included John O'Brien who taught ancient history, and Norman Harper who specialised in American history – probably he was the only such full-time specialist in Australia at that time. Kathleen Fitzpatrick, assisted by the young Presbyterian theologian George

Yule, taught British and Reformation history; Yule later held a chair in Aberdeen while his son Peter was to become a most prolific Australian historian. European history was taught by Alan McBriar, who was just back from Oxford where he had earned a PhD – then a rarity in the History Department – and by Franz Philipp who was really a learned art historian. Nobody taught medieval history or Asian history – unless it was a smattering of the history of British India. Prehistory and economic history were not on the syllabus but a thick seam of economic history was hidden in the political history. The French and Russian revolutions we quickly walked past, at least in my years.

When, at the age of seventy, I completed the writing of a history of the world, I thereby acquired knowledge that I now wish I had acquired at the age of twenty. In gently reminding myself what was not taught in the university in my era, I hasten to add that in the space of three years we studied a wide range of subjects when judged by the standards of that time and even our time.

The History Department was said to be left wing. Perhaps it was – a few of its staff had been communists – but not aggressively so. In marking our essays, most of the staff were careful to praise students for their ability to build an argument rather than for their political allegiances. The department's public reputation for leftism stemmed partly from Crawford. In the middle of the war he had taken two years' leave to become the First Secretary in the first Australian legation ever opened in the Soviet Union which was now our wartime ally; and on returning from Moscow he felt a duty to support the Australia-Soviet Friendship League which then flourished. But his politics by 1950 were tending towards the mainstream and they continued so to tend.

As Crawford knew how to woo the university's major committees, a surprising quota of his bright students won overseas scholarships, of which few then existed. In the decade after the Second World War at least half of the Rhodes scholars from Victoria came under his influence. These scholars, all highly talented, included Geoffrey Serle, Creighton Burns, Hugh Stretton, John Poynter and Jim Gobbo. In many weeks, with the aid of his persuasive fountain pen, he must have spent hours in writing confidential references in favour of his students. He worked so hard for the sake of his staff and students that he had inadequate time for his own research. He sacrificed what he liked best.

The inner sanctuary of Crawford's course for the honours students was a subject called 'Theory and Method of History'. In my final year it was conducted by the Reverend Arthur Burns, an unorthodox Presbyterian. A curly-haired, fast-talking scholar in his late twenties, he was more the brilliant philosopher and theologian than the working historian, as he would have been the first to admit. Towards the abstract ideas and colourless principles that he rejoiced in, I felt little attraction. And yet I felt intensely interested in the practical questions of 'theory and method', such as the dangers of bias, and the frailties of memory.

Arthur Burns went on his dashing way, confidently tossing ideas in the air like a juggler and usually catching them as they tumbled down. If some ideas he did not catch, he smiled with boyish charm. Of the dozen or more honours students who attended his lectures, most were mesmerised though some were puzzled too. After weeks of struggling to follow him, I explained as tactfully as I could that my interests in the method of writing history were keener than in the theory. By then he must have known that I had just completed what was rare for an undergraduate: an article published in a scholarly journal. So he permitted me to skip most of his lectures and rather spend my time reading books written by notable narrative historians and to weigh the criticisms and praise made of their books. Relishing his promise to place on the exam paper a few special questions on these historians, I began to read them keenly, finally devoting as much time to his subject as did the students who sat gladly at his feet. Much later, in Canberra, he became an expert on the dangers of nuclear war, and strongly backed me in a controversy I initiated. Curiously we were blood relatives, though I did not know it when he taught me.

At his suggestion, I spent evenings reading the works of George G. Coulton who had aroused a mixture of friends and enemies between the two world wars by producing four volumes of a fascinating work, *Five Centuries of Religion* – the religion being the Catholic Church when it dominated Europe all the way from the Irish Sea to the Adriatic. I soon became absorbed in the history of a church about which I knew little: it was a sign of the tolerance of the History Department that a Presbyterian pastor should insist that I immerse myself in such Catholic stars as Francis of Assisi and Waldo of the French city of Lyon, along with side glances at a platoon of monks, nuns and friars. Coulton was skilled in depicting the working life of a monastery, and I still have the sheets of pink, yellow and light-green paper on which I recorded in blue ink his arguments. By luck I bought for a shilling or so a second-hand copy of his autobiography, *Fourscore Years*, which I devoured. I began to firm my own conclusions – more confident than they should have been – about the qualities a young historian should if possible try to acquire.

Thomas Macaulay was another whom I was encouraged to read. I already knew him, having bought for my nineteenth birthday Trevelyan's fascinating *Life and Letters of Lord Macaulay*. Two tiny black-bound volumes in the series known as World Classics, they could fit in the side pocket of a sports coat and be read on a suburban train. I still admire them, having read most pages at least twice. Already I had it in mind to become a writer – whether historian or journalist I was not certain. One advantage of reading the ever-confident, ever-eloquent Macaulay was to learn how he composed a chapter of history. He would gather evidence about an episode or event and walk over the site of the event, if necessary, and then ruminate about it. Then he would sit and ever so rapidly write his chapter, 'sketching in the outlines under the genial and audacious impulse of a first conception; and securing in black and white each idea, and epithet, and turn of phrase, as it flowed straight from his busy brain to his rapid fingers'. After he had completed this skimming draft he would elaborate on it and refine and polish it.

In years to come I was never able to follow some of his advice – everyone's working method is different – but I could see how he was able to use his pen almost as a lightning conductor. I read the story of his life before I actually read his unfinished *History of England* – several volumes that spanned just a few years.

Macaulay hoped to reach readers who normally bought the latest novel. Deep was his satisfaction when he heard that, far from London, working people had been assembling regularly to hear the reading aloud of volume one of his *History of England*. After the last page was read one listener stood up and moved a vote of thanks to Macaulay for writing a history that 'working men can understand'. The time spent reading these long-dead authors was part of my long apprenticeship as a historian.

Looking at old notebooks, in which I jotted half-thoughts for my own eyes, I now see that I was resolving, if one day I wrote a history book, to try to reach a wider audience as well as specialists. In ink I wrote my own impudent observation: 'rarely does a popular history come from a historian who holds an academic post at a University etc.' At the age of nineteen I warned myself: what if 'the common reader is smoked out & finally driven away in disgust?' I had more confidence in my own opinions than was appropriate!

10

THIS WEEK'S *FARRAGO*

Each week a free newspaper, usually of eight pages, was published by the students. Called *Farrago* it was one of the best-known casual newspapers in Victoria. When sensational news was reported by *Farrago* it would quickly be copied by at least one of the nation's daily newspapers. Just after the war, left-wing students who then controlled it devoted many articles to the class struggle in other lands. In the student elections late in 1948, however, the Labor Club lost control of the Students' Representative Council and its newspaper too.

The newspaper fell largely into the arms of an alliance of Catholic and Methodist students. Allan Griffith, a colleague from Queen's, became the coeditor of the new *Farrago*. An earthy Queenslander with a butcher's-shop background, he announced proudly, he had returned from the war with a determination to study political science.

He was the first person I met who sometimes bought, from newsboys, successive editions of *The Herald* in order to learn what had happened during the hour or two since the previous edition.

Griffith was a keen supporter of the small global organisation called Moral Re-Armament, founded by Frank Buchman in prewar England and quietly influential amongst a small circle of ex-servicemen living in Queen's College. 'Griffo' – his common name – had a strong physique, a visible jawbone and a loud laugh; much that he laughed at was unpredictable. Possessing what used to be called 'a heart of gold', he was perhaps nearer to orthodox Labor than to Liberal but his dislike of communism and its influence on trade unions was propelling him to the right. For much of his professional career he was to stand high in the prime minister's department, becoming personally close to Malcolm Fraser, and indeed influential at times in negotiating the peace agreement in Zimbabwe.

It was through Allan Griffith that I became one of the two sporting editors of *Farrago*. My colleague was Lindsay Thompson, who had served as a signalman in the army in New Guinea in the last half of the Pacific War and still suffered periodically from malaria. As sport in recent years had been largely replaced on the back page by students' political struggles in India, Hungary and elsewhere, we returned it to its previous place. It was easily achieved, for the university held numerous cricketers, footballers, hockey and tennis players, runners, oarsmen and mountaineers who hoped that their exploits or sporting scores would be printed. Their doings soon filled the back page, and crept onto page 7. Though Lindsay was many years my senior, we worked as equals; he was humble, intelligent and enthusiastic. His courage became known nationally when as Victoria's minister for education he heard that students and their teacher at a small school near Castlemaine had been kidnapped: he set out alone to negotiate with the armed man.

Towards the end of my second year at university I became the editor of *Farrago*. My coeditor was Tony Harold, a law student, genial and public spirited, and a warrior in Catholics' battles. A decade or so later he was to become the Victorian chairman of the Immigration Reform Group which worked to push aside the White Australia policy. While we did not argue or quarrel we eventually found that we didn't share the same ideas on how to run a newspaper, and so we edited on alternate weeks, though we often shared the same sporting and theatre editors, and reporters. The plan was effective, or at least we thought so, though from week to week the paper was different in style and tone. As we had to attend lectures and pursue our own university studies, the regular alternation of free and busy weeks was a bonus. We received no payment for editing the paper, and thought we were amply rewarded by the excitement and the adventure.

Set up in metal type in the old manner, our tabloid newspaper was printed at the city office of *The Argus*, the daily paper that was then in the last decade of its long life. I was ill equipped for the technical work, but soon after becoming editor I received a booklet setting out all the typefaces that were available. There was no attempt to teach me how to lay out a page and select a typeface for the tabloid: that was a measure of *The Argus*'s genuine tolerance towards the rowdy infant newspaper entrusted to it. Why that city newspaper, one of the oldest in Australia, accepted the potential threats of libel arising from amateur editors is a mystery.

When it was my turn to edit, I collected a variety of articles, news reports, and book and theatre reviews from contributors, edited them and provided a headline, and sent them downtown to the *Argus* office, high above Elizabeth Street, where they were set in type. When the night for printing arrived I would ride my bike to the printery, a big space where a multitude of busy men and apprentices raised their voices above the clatter of machines. There I would be shown long trays holding thin columns of metallic type – the pages ready to be printed.

The Argus's own experienced typesetter, who did our work, was warm-hearted, quick and helpful. Speaking in a barely intelligible accent from one of the British Isles, he was known as Jock. You had to hear him say a name two or three times before you understood it. He insisted that there were standards that a serious printing house should uphold. His instantaneous response to some of my layouts was 'But you can't do that'. If that warning had no effect he would send for Mr Cox, the head printer, whose crumpled dark suit made him stand out from the working printers with their dustcoats and inky hands. While almost genial at times, he stood no nonsense. On rare occasions an article we had written was deemed potentially libellous by Mr Cox and the lawyer who anxiously scanned the *Farrago* page proofs before all were ready for printing.

I felt proud, in the first weeks of my editorship, to walk into Union House and see the tall piles of freshly printed copies of *Farrago*, and the passing students taking them one by one. In the nearby cafeteria I could see a hundred copies held half aloft or sideways, so that they could be read at crowded tables. The paper was free: otherwise the circulation might have been small. On the other hand students, being human, liked to see their names in print.

During the university vacations, an occasional issue had to be prepared before the part-time staff returned. More than one issue I largely wrote myself. I had not yet learnt to use a typewriter. With pen I wrote the main news story, lesser stories for pages 1, 2 and 3, a book review or two, sporting news, and numerous letters to the editor which I then signed with suitable names. I found that, faced with a deadline, I could write with speed.

Normally a few articles were funny, but not as funny as we imagined. Fortunately we had faithful correspondents who could be relied on to write something arresting or arousing. 'Old Centre' was widely read not only for his descriptions of football matches but for his theological asides, especially those directed towards what he called 'the black Calvinists'. He once sketched, to clarify his account of a football match – as if there could be any doubt – a witch flying over the Ormond College spire. He had so much to say about his opponents that he barely had space for the final score. Who he actually was did arouse long speculation; his name was Jim Morrissey of Queen's College and later he became a fearless Crown prosecutor. The student reporters adopted names. Hugh Buggy, a graphic writer on crime and football for *The Argus*, must have noticed that crime reports in *Farrago* were written by a reporter called Buggy Hugh.

Of course there were serious and passionate articles. One to which I had given a front-page headline described the head of the adjacent teachers' college as 'Dictator' Law. It must have slipped past the lawyer holding the red pencil at the *Argus* printery. Our vice-chancellor, John Medley, who was so tolerant and benign towards student activities that I hardly knew who he was, invited me to call at his roomy office. He explained that he had received a complaint: he could not have been more friendly.

Farrago, though eccentric in its typography, had a standing among serious journalists. Sometimes intellectuals wrote letters to us – we accepted very long letters – rather than to city dailies. A visitor to Melbourne in the spring of 1949 was Pastor Martin Niemöller, who was perhaps the most famous German to have visited Australia during the preceding four decades, though in that category he had little competition. His visit was to provoke an indignant letter addressed to me as editor.

A commander of a German submarine in the First World War, and then a Lutheran pastor, Niemöller had courageously criticised Herr Hitler sometime after he seized power. Refusing to be silenced, the pastor was arrested. From 1937 to 1945 he was a prisoner in a German concentration camp, though at one time he did volunteer in vain to serve in Hitler's navy. After the war he confessed his nation's guilt, especially to the Jews, but some critics vowed that his apology came too late. But then how few of us, if a prisoner of Hitler, would have been so brave?

When I heard on the grapevine that the visiting German would be preaching on Sunday morning at the bluestone Lutheran church in the shadow of St Patrick's Cathedral, I and my friend Sek Hulme (*Farrago*'s new sporting editor) arrived early, found two seats among the expectant congregation, and heard him preach. Our knowledge of schoolboy German enabled us to understand about one-fifth of what he said when he spoke in his native language. Even if I had followed not one word, I would have been impressed by his dignity. Now in his fifties he was lean, slightly dark in complexion, his face alert but sometimes troubled. I am not certain, at this distance, whether I met him outside the church but I carried away an impression of his sincerity.

After his visit to Melbourne was over, a student wrote sympathetically about the pastor's struggles in Nazi Germany and sent the article to *Farrago*. I published it, thinking it defended Niemöller in what seemed a reasonable way. Promptly the talented historian Brian Fitzpatrick, the custodian of civil liberties in Melbourne, wrote a long and hostile reply, which I published in *Farrago*'s first issue for the year 1950. My sympathies – I did not make an editorial comment – were divided between the Jews and the German pastor.

Students I knew had actually fled, when boys, from Hitler's Germany but I cannot remember asking them about their endangered life there. One was Max Corden, now known by some as our nation's most famous living economist; and this year I heard him speak vividly in our old dining hall at Queen's College where the book of his own life story was launched in his presence. I had not realised that when stepping ashore in Melbourne with his parents on the eve of the war, a lad of about eleven, he was called Werner Max Cohn. Others of his extended Jewish family chose not to escape from Germany. His uncle Willy (a winner of the Iron Cross in the First World War) and his wife and two of their young daughters, residents of the north German city of Breslau, were exterminated by the Nazis. Max called his autobiography, which he signed for me with a few generous words, *Lucky Boy in the Lucky Country*.

As editors of *Farrago* we had the burden of sitting ex officio on the students' elected council. The days devoured by such duties eroded our academic time. Sometimes I missed two or three successive days of lectures and tutorials. In June 1950, with less than five months remaining until my final examinations in history, I realised that my essays and assignments had to be completed and a pile of history books and articles had to be devoured in readiness for the exams in November. I resigned as editor just in time.

Well behind in my formal studies, I resolved to harvest my remaining months sensibly. I pinned a sheet of foolscap on my study wall, and each morning with a red crayon I coloured in the number of hours I spent in studying. For the hours so spent in the afternoon I used blue crayon and for the evening I used black pencil. At a glance I could tell how I had performed on successive days. I did not include weekly time spent in university lectures and classes because they probably totalled no more than nine hours. I was scrupulous in consulting my wristwatch; and if I spent forty minutes in serious reading and the remainder of the hour in making tea and then in yarning with the person from whom I borrowed the sugar, I coloured in only the working minutes as true work. Soon I realised how much time I frittered away – I was in the presence of my work rather than working. In the first week, my most productive day totalled only eight-and-a-half hours.

Nearly all students then had the habit, when nervous about the approaching deadline for an essay or exam, of studying far into the night. The student way of life is not efficient. When later I taught at Harvard and lived in a residential college with a big communal study hall, I would see it, at exam time, packed with busy students long after midnight.

After four weeks of dutifully measuring the time, I realised how many hours I squandered daily, even when sitting at my small desk with a fountain pen in my right hand. The realisation, the lesson, was useful. Thereafter I tried to spend less time at work but to work hard in the hours set aside for work. Already a fast reader – so long as the subject matter was not difficult in concept – I discovered how to gut a book using the index and the list of chapters as a guide. Always I took brief notes of the main points and listed the page numbers that I might want to read later. If I had lived under an authoritarian regime and been told that I would be imprisoned if I did not read 100 books within a month, and write a clear summary of them, I would probably have passed the test.

Chance created my first public appearance as a historian. A conference of professional historians had been held in Tasmania, and Owen Parnaby, a history tutor, returned to our college with news of a tantalising address he had heard. The speaker was Professor R. S. Parker, a rising Australian political scientist who was about to take up the chair at Wellington in New Zealand. One of Parker's themes was that in 1898 and 1899 when the Australian people voted at referenda held to decide whether their own colony (now called a state) should join the proposed Commonwealth of Australia, they were partly influenced by their economic interests. Parnaby generously let me see a typed copy of Parker's argument, not yet printed. Why I was instantly dubious about this bright theory I cannot remember, but it is often instinct that arouses unease in a historian.

Walking the kilometre down to the Public Library, I waited impatiently for a few heavily bound volumes of the newspapers of 1898 to be fetched from the vaults. The more I read the voting results, the more I doubted the validity of some – not all – of Parker's arguments. It so happened that his case depended heavily on the actual voting results of each polling booth, whether in a Tasmanian mining town or a South Australian riverboat town. I felt now at home in old newspapers, though if I had had more experience I could have found much of the same information in the official papers issued by each colonial parliament. Before long it became clear that the people's votes for and against the federation often contradicted his theories. It says a lot for the overall atmosphere of encouragement among Melbourne historians that I, an undergraduate, was encouraged to do more research and to put down on paper my findings. Owen Parnaby later became the master of Queen's

College, while I became president of its governing council, and so we were to meet often; I spoke at his memorial service.

Travelling as a hitchhiker – and usually talking with the drivers – had taught me much about the geography and economic life of scores of small and big towns. It was as if they had partly prepared me for the task. My article was accepted by Norman Harper, editor of *Historical Studies*, which was then the Australian historical journal with prestige. He persuaded me, however, that my conclusions might be viewed as impertinent and unfair towards Parker, the professor whose article had just appeared in the same journal. Perhaps Harper feared that he himself would have to make his peace with Parker. I saw the light, and calmed down a few sentences here and there, even proposing that 'later historians will long lie indebted to him'.

Published in May 1950 it must be one of few controversial articles I have written that lavishes such praise on an opponent. Parker replied, calling my article 'exhilarating', and other historians joined in. Around the country it came to be known as the Parker-Blainey controversy. It was widely debated in universities and senior schools for several decades until, like most controversies, it began to fade. Contrary to my teenage prediction, later historians did not necessarily 'long lie indebted' to Parker nor, for that matter, to me. History rolls on, sometimes burying more historians than it resurrects.

Queen's College was unusual in that it had long-time links with China and India. Some of its former students had gone there as engineers, doctors and even missionaries before the Second World War. In turn, after that war, numerous Asian students came to the college. In my first year I came to know fairly well Dinka Khurdikach, an oldish and hardworking agricultural scientist who, before returning to India, sold me a newish black gown: it was compulsory to wear a gown at evening dinner. Dinka had a perfect set of white teeth which his dark face made even whiter. Later I became a friend of Majid Shaik, an engineering student from Singapore, who shared a study with Os Nelson, a Ballarat friend. Majid laughed inordinately, pointing out all kinds of oddities in the behaviour of those around him. When I christened him King O'Malley, after a controversial Labor politician of an earlier era, he laughed. He became widely known as O'Malley.

The postwar immigration program was just beginning. Spurred by the crisis of 1942 when strategic towns in northern Australia were bombed by the Japanese, Canberra's policy was to increase the population as rapidly as possible so that when a similar crisis occurred, the nation could fend off an enemy. While British migrants were still ascendant, other migrants were increasingly recruited from continental Europe.

Arthur Calwell was the minister for immigration and the architect of this dramatic change in the inflow of people. I invited him to Queen's College to explain his policy and his view of Australia's future. The invitation was easily made because I was the secretary of a public questions society called the William Quick, named after a founder of the college. Calwell promised to come, but cabinet meetings and interstate visitors made him defer. By the time he was free to speak to 'The Willie Quick', Menzies had swept into power and Calwell was only a shadow minister, though a powerful one. As one of his letters – his signature resembled a couple of cartwheels – reassured me early in 1950: 'Now that I am in temporary exile I shall be able to fulfil my promise.'

On the chosen evening I waited at the front of the college to welcome him. After his government car appeared out of the darkness, he greeted me with an unusual mixture of restrained warmth and innate dignity, saying to my surprise (I don't think I misheard him) that it was the first time he had accepted an invitation to speak at a university. Taking charge of his hat and overcoat, I escorted him to the common room which was packed with students, some sitting on the floor. He must have instantly noticed the Asian faces, then a rarity in Australia.

Everyone in the audience knew that Calwell had strenuously upheld the nation's so-called 'White Australia' policy in parliament and the press (though privately he permitted far more exceptions than was realised at the time). To the surprise of many, he gave a masterly speech. Even the Asian students were taken with his courtesy and clarity. He then called for questions, and Mr Wong jumped to his feet. Hong Kin Wong was an earnest student of electrical engineering but rowdy and humorous at a public gathering. Clutching the sides of his black gown he spoke with an eloquence not heard from him before or after. Mr Calwell responded with tact. When the meeting was over, many students vowed it was the best political meeting they had ever attended. That was high praise, for the university calendar was studded with public addresses by visitors of eloquence and, often, distinction.

Mr Calwell was then escorted upstairs to a simple supper and cup of tea. In the presence of half-a-dozen of us he spoke frankly about the new Menzies Government, and of his successor as immigration minister, Harold Holt, whom he respected. Of Menzies he offered the piercing words: 'Bob is a titan amongst minnows'. He spoke bitterly of the press and how they had hounded him when his spirits were low, especially when his only son, Arthur Andrew, was dying of leukaemia just two years previously. There was an immediacy about this family allusion because we sometimes walked in the Carlton cemetery, just across the road from the college, and knew the site of his young son's grave.

In the eyes of many of the public and many Liberals, Calwell was dismissed as a rough diamond with an abrasive cutting edge. To the joy of the cartoonists he had a curved nose and a strong rasping voice, but what was not publicly understood – because he did not boast – was that his mind was stocked with the fruits of wide reading, especially biographies. His formal education had finished at his Catholic school in North Melbourne nearly forty years previously but his mind was now more cultivated than the minds of all but the best university graduates of his own generation. Knowing him only through the press, or hearing his combative voice when parliament was broadcast from Canberra, we were astonished, that evening, to discover that another Calwell existed.

Another decade passed and I was in some trouble for expressing publicly what in fact were the mainstream views on immigration, and therefore it may seem that I am praising Calwell now because I had followed in his footsteps. As a student in 1950, however, I had no special interest in immigration and was not a Labor supporter. Calwell impressed me partly because of his deep affection for his country and his willingness to see the good in other countries, especially the United States, from which his grandfather had emigrated to the Victorian goldfields. The Aboriginal peoples, as Australians, also came within his affection, and he as much as any public figure of that time tried to help them.

Forty years on I came to think just as highly of B. A. Santamaria, the leading Catholic intellectual, as I did of Arthur Calwell, though they were bitter enemies. When you admire people you sometimes do so for the person they are, more than the viewpoint they represent.

I spent effort, as editor of *Farrago* and as secretary of the Willie Quick, in encouraging debate. 'Jo' Gullett, a winner of the Military Cross in New Guinea, was a rising member of the Liberals in the federal parliament, and I tried by a chain of letters to arrange a debate between him and a leading communist, either Ted Laurie or Ralph Gibson, whose brother incidentally was Melbourne University's professor of philosophy and a Christian. In June 1949 Gullett replied by hand, saying he would like to come as he knew the William Quick Society from his student days. Then came the crunch lines: 'Under no circumstances however would I engage in a friendly debate with Mr Laurie or any other Communist. To me these people appear quite simply as wreckers and traitors, accepting the benefits of life in a community to which they do not even grant fundamental loyalty.'

My final year at the university was rewarding. I did not share the global gloom that sometimes surrounded us. In our college a survey conducted by John McCarty, a bright economics student, revealed that one in every three students thought that another world war would be waged within five years. The war, if it came, would be fought between communism and the democracies, and already the two sides were fighting in Korea. Even if the third world war was averted, a global famine might arrive – or so it was feared.

Sir David Rivett, perhaps Australia's best-known scientist and the formal patron of our Willie Quick club, told us at one meeting that the soaring population of the world was fast outstripping the supply of food. When several students stood up and enthusiastically pointed to the new sciences as solvers of the world's problems, Sir David held high his thin fingers like a traffic policeman calling for unlicensed drivers to stop. Another warning came from a foreign professor who lived in the college. Wolfgang Friedmann, rather like a bald eagle in appearance, warned us that the police state might eventually displace democracy in much of the world. He spoke from experience, for he had fled from Berlin in the 1930s, served in political intelligence in the British Foreign Office and then, after the war, controlled the economic organisation supervising a zone in Germany. 'In vast parts of the earth,' he said in his strong German accent, 'the intelligentsia is today silenced.'

While some observers thought that the human race was at a crossroads, daily life in Australia gave a cheerful message. In 1950 the rationing of petrol was ended; new Holdens and Austins and Morrises were soon swarming on the roads, and the country towns were marvelling at the leaping price of wool. In cities the take-home wages were higher than ever before, and people who had never owned a refrigerator – my parents among them – were about to buy one. Unemployment was low, and everybody could find a job.

Hitchhiking to Brisbane during the August vacation of 1950, I passed through Newcastle for the first time. The smoke almost shielding the expanding steelworks, and the noisy shunting of the coal trains, were signs that the nation's pulse rate was rising. I hoped to be part of that pulse: three years at university were enough.

PART TWO

11

UNDER THE BARE MOUNTAIN

I went to the west coast of Tasmania on the back of a bouncing, empty truck. Most of the country was forest or grassland and totally uninhabited. Called the Lyell Highway it was a narrow, gravel road, usually winding but occasionally straight. When a car came from the opposite direction, which was not often, our large truck moved perilously close to the edge to permit it to pass. Several times, on this hot afternoon, we passed a lonely road mender whose only equipment was a shovel. The bushes within a few metres of the road were yellow-white, having been powdered with the fine dust rising from the sparse traffic. I was travelling with Dick Kent whose face, normally red, was now yellow-white.

A puzzling landscape came closer: a barrier of bare mountains. In some places this landscape was almost like the face of the moon. At last we reached the face of the moon. Here and there stood a few old or derelict hotels, scattered houses with roofs of rusted corrugated iron, and mysterious stretches of bare stony ground sprinkled with huge white-pink boulders. Now we entered a dangerous stretch of landscape. Down a twisting road – with a precipice on one side – the truck crawled in low gear. At last we glimpsed the straggling suburbs of Queenstown, with the smoke rising from the chimney of the famous smelters.

That night, after eating in the narrow main street, one of the most haunting in Australia, we slept in the grandstand beside a remarkable oval with thick gravel and not a blade of grass. By now I had the feeling – one of the rare times in my life I have so felt – that I had been in the town before. Where the feeling came from I don't know. One year later, in 1951, I arrived there to work.

It so happened that the mine and its railway, smelters, hydro-electric scheme and port had long been operated by a Melbourne firm with the proud name of the Mount Lyell Mining & Railway Company. Well known on the Australian stock exchanges, Mount Lyell had once been in the top five companies, measured by dividends paid. Sitting on its board was Walter Bassett, a Melbourne consulting engineer, whose wife Marnie was keen on history. She was just completing her excellent book on the Henty family, the white pioneers in south-western Victoria, and often she attended seminars in the History Department at the University of Melbourne. It was she who was about to pass on to Professor R. M. Crawford the news that the Mount Lyell Company would like a student to do research on its history. I was then completing my final year as an undergraduate and had little idea how I would spend my life.

The prize for the best of the undergraduates in the Arts Faculty was an offer to become a tutor in the university. About this time Crawford asked me whether I would like to be a tutor in history – if an offer were made. Cheekily I replied: 'Are you short of hands?' Several who overheard me were surprised that I made such a casual or even cavalier reply. I knew, however, that I wished to write and not to teach. It must have been about this time that Crawford, having heard from Marnie Bassett, suggested I might like to consider becoming the historian, or more correctly the researcher, for the famous old copper mine at Mount Lyell. Crawford had no idea that I had already been there and had fallen under the spell of those strange-coloured mountains and wild-west streets.

First I had to be inspected and certified as sound by Marnie and Walter Bassett. They invited me to lunch at their house in the Melbourne suburb of Armadale. It was a Sunday just before Christmas: they were agnostics or atheists and did not share my unease about transacting commercial business on that day. For the occasion I dressed in my white shirt and dark pinstriped suit, bought at a sale at the Leviathan department store in Swanston Street, and wore a discreet tie. Slightly apprehensive, I caught the train from Dandenong, which was then in the country, and walked from the Armadale railway station to the Bassetts' house in Kooyong Road. The tall man who opened the front door was dressed less formally than I was.

Sir Walter Bassett – he was knighted later – sometimes concealed the kindness that was part of his make-up. On first impressions, and not just to me, he could be intimidating with his air of authority and his slow and considered way of speaking. His long jaw jutted as he spoke. An airman in the First World War where he won the Military Cross, he had lost a leg in a flying accident; and almost as compensation he had acquired a stout walking stick that served many of the purposes of a long arm. When he spoke of astronomy he gestured with his stick towards the sky, and when he described the workings of an underground mine he pointed his stick at the ground. When he disagreed strongly he thumped the floor with it, and when he wished to impose his personal authority he even pointed it at the person who was challenging him.

We ate lunch, just the three of us, with maybe a helper bringing food from the kitchen. A French window, partly open, allowed us to see the front garden and to hear the street traffic. In my memory I seem to hear a mantelpiece clock ticking away, but perhaps it was the slight pounding of my heart. The rambling old single-storey house had an air of elegance, and when we moved from the dinner table to a drawing room my knee almost hit a low polished table on which lay new books. All books in the house were serious. As Walter and Marnie spoke, they hinted in passing – they did not dream of boasting – about learned friends and relatives. I found out later that one of Marnie's brothers was the vice-chancellor at Sheffield University and that her only sister had married the famous anthropologist Malinowski (of whom, to my shame, I had not heard), and that her scientist father had been a Fellow of the Royal Society. In Scotland her grandfather David Masson, whom she recalled vividly, was a friend of the writers Carlyle and Thackeray and had written a widely read life of the poet Milton. Walter Bassett in contrast was a Wesley College scholarship boy who became a notable engineer, but his background was bookish, his father having worked in the nation's largest bookshop, the Cole's Book Arcade in Melbourne.

Over the years I was to gain from the Bassetts' encouragement. Inch by inch I grew to admire them, even the stern Walter. After I married, my wife Ann came to admire them too. Slowly the Bassetts and Blaineys became close friends and dined together often, usually at their house. Indeed Ann was to give the address at Marnie's funeral though in age they were half a century apart.

Meanwhile the directors of the Mount Lyell Mining & Railway Company had to inspect me, to decide whether I was worthy of the task. I was invited to attend, one morning, a tallish office in Collins Street, in what was then the corporate heart of the nation. Wearing my dark suit, neatly pressed with a hot iron that morning, I was ushered into the presence of the directors. As I was only twenty, and about to be in receipt of the humblest of wages, the invitation to occupy twenty-five minutes of their meeting time was a generous misplacing of priorities on their part. In the boardroom, dark with varnished wood and dominated by a heavy table in the centre, I shook hands in turn with Ken Niall who was also chairman of the great wool house of Goldsbrough Mort, Sir Robert Knox who was an exceedingly tall and large man of much personal warmth, 'Don' York Syme who was the head of the Melbourne Steamship Company, Peter Johns whose family made structural steel and city elevators, and Noel Brodribb and Sir Harry Lawson. After Bassett genially pointed his stick towards the large leather chair where I was to sit at the polished boardroom table, I noticed an oblong piece of blotting paper sitting like a white tablemat in front of each director. The paper was to dry the wet ink when they signed official documents with the nib of a long pen.

I was attracted to old Sir Harry Lawson, who had won the goldmining seat of Castlemaine more than fifty years previously and had served as Victoria's premier for six years. Taking the lead in the conversation, he posed to his colleagues the question of when exactly the company was founded. I found it inconceivable that this question was met with silence, but most of them were successful businessmen for whom history was a matter of passing interest. Sir Harry then invited the secretary, who was simply known as Parsons, to provide the answer. In old blue-ribbon companies the titles such as general manager were apportioned frugally, and to be called the secretary was to be somebody of importance. Parsons had a slightly glum and ruddy face, and knew when to keep silent, but he was, as I came to realise, full of common sense, and capable of many kindnesses. He explained to the directors, just as cups of tea were being passed around, that their company had been founded in 1893.

In a sympathetic way I was questioned about what I would do at Mount Lyell. It was the company's intention, I think, that I should find out facts about its past which would then be written up as a large report and filed away in the hope that one day it would be deemed useful. I did not tell them that I was ambitious and had it vaguely in mind to write a history book.

It was agreed that I would investigate the history of Mount Lyell for one year. The university, on the advice of Professor Crawford, would pay me a research grant of £3 a week and the company would pay me £3 a week as well as all travelling and hotel expenses. The wage was less than that of a labourer but to me it was princely.

For a young scholar to study a mining field would now be deemed shameful by many academics, especially those with forthright views about the defects of capitalism and the virtues of the environment. For my part I felt proud. The prestige of mining then was high, for it was seen as an energetic creator of work and a mighty contributor to the nation's earlier development. It was also a force for decentralisation, in which most Australians believed. Furthermore virtually all my male ancestors had been seduced to Australia by gold, and all my great-grandfathers had dug for it. In each generation my father's family retained the gold connection, and my brother John had completed a mining course at the Ballarat School of Mines before transferring to civil engineering at Melbourne University. So, when I went in the small passenger steamer from Melbourne to the Tasmanian port of Burnie and travelled south by train and bus, I felt at ease. Indeed at times I was on top of the world.

The landscape at Lyell was more eerie than I remembered. Bare-topped mountains in the background might be capped with snow. In the foreground were round hills that in some regions would qualify as mountains. When the sun was sinking, and its slanting rays lit up the hills around Queenstown, it illuminated a patchwork of yellow, ochre, deep brown, light brown and white.

The colours came from the bare clay and rock. At first sight nothing seemed to grow there: not even a spindly bush or a tussock of grass. When later I walked over the hills there came into sight a little moss, a few cramped patches of grass, and some pathetic plants growing only as high as a candle. Here and there squatted the black stumps of trees that had ceased to live more than half a century ago and now were disintegrating.

Hardly anybody on the mining field knew what had happened to create what is now called the moonscape. They simply assumed that it was the sulphur – a strong constituent of the sulphide ore – that poured from the smelters, day and night. At times I beavered away at this historical puzzle: why had the landscape changed? There were no environmental specialists in those days, or if they existed they were not easily found. I began to realise that the cause of the denudation was complicated. At first the woodcutters had felled the tall trees, after which summer bushfires had removed the undergrowth. The massive rainfall was another destroyer. It scoured the topsoil and the soft clays until only the spine of the countryside remained. The ever-present fumes of sulphur and the denuding of the topsoil prevented new growth. Helped generously by Hugh Murray, the general manager, I finally pieced together this sequence of events that had created the astonishingly bare landscape.

Queenstown's main street was one of the narrowest in Australia, with a line of verandah posts on each side. Straight up the sloping street, and almost hovering over it, was bare Mount Owen which in the sunset occasionally glowed a breathtaking pastel-pink. The local sports ground had no grass – just white gravel, regularly spread by the truckload. Here I began to play football for the Smelters Club, kicking twenty-four goals in one season; but I was rather slow to learn how to fall without incurring gravel rash and bloodied knees and elbows. Around the oval, and part of the football arena, was a steep professional cycling track, and the fast wingmen such as my teammate Des Burton (winner of the famous Burnie Gift) would grab the football and run to the bitumen track and race along it, cleverly bouncing the ball on the smooth, sloping surface. Queenstown was one of the few large towns in Australia that owned no racecourse: flat ground was scarce.

The mine and smelters dominated the town. Regularly their whistles blew a series of warnings that a new shift was about to begin. The big open cut worked daily for sixteen hours, which were divided into two shifts, each of eight hours, while the mill and smelters worked twenty-four hours, divided into three shifts. The changing of the shifts were the main events of the day. On Good Friday it was always announced on the national news that this was the only town in Australia that worked flat out on that sacred day. And yet it was not entirely a godless town, for four churches financed their own ministers, the Presbyterians even welcoming a female pastor, unusual for that era.

The mining field followed its own social traditions and had its own way of expressing sorrow. A custom when a man died in the mines was to express sorrow to the male relatives and friends not with words but with a warm, strong handshake. I came to learn that simple custom, and sometimes I find myself practising it even today, though it occasionally puzzles the recipient. When a funeral procession came slowly down Queenstown's main street, the owners of shops honoured the custom of closing the shop and putting up the wooden shutters over the plate-glass windows until the mourners had passed. Often a brass band or a highland band played in the procession. Death was accompanied by a wake. For only 4000 people the mining field had eleven hotels.

Another custom was surprising. In Melbourne, the carrying of an umbrella, folded or in use, by a young man was looked on askance in some circles, being seen either as 'feminine' or as ultra-aristocratic. At Mount Lyell, however, miners on their way to work would often carry a wide black umbrella. As this was the second-wettest region in Australia – a coastal strip in north Queensland was wetter – the wide umbrella was a necessity.

Unmarried girls, unless they were under the age of twenty, were few – or at least they seemed to be few until square dancing became the vogue, when they came to the dance hall from everywhere, even from Gormanston – a slow zigzag journey by mountain road. Women still were far outnumbered by men. Of the young men, some were Italian, Baltic, Polish and North of England immigrants, but even more were nomadic workers who 'came down' from the Snowy scheme, from mining fields in Queensland and Kalgoorlie, or from Tasmanian farms. They worked at Lyell for a year or so before leaving with a large cheque, 'overtime' at high rates of pay being readily available at the weekends.

My time in Queenstown made me intensely sympathetic to mining fields, their traditions and way of life, and the way they coped with danger. My sympathy has not waned.

The twin towns – bustling Queenstown and vanishing Gormanston – were often the heartland of Labor politics in Tasmania. They had an influence out of all proportion to their size. Queenstown was among the few towns where visiting politicians continued the custom of addressing a crowd, without the aid of a microphone, from the balcony of a two-storey hotel; political meetings were balcony meetings. Eric Reece, a 'west coaster through and through', was on his ascent. He was to be premier of Tasmania for longer than anybody else, and you could see why. His political antennae were alert. At the same time in Queenstown, though not yet making his career in politics, lived a young teacher, Lance Barnard, who some twenty years later was to become deputy prime minister in the Whitlam Government.

It was exciting to unravel the history of the mining field. I spent months with the pages of old newspapers published in Queenstown, Hobart, Launceston and Melbourne. I found copies of obscure London financial weeklies which in the late 1890s were entranced by Mount Lyell, seeing it as a highway along which inexperienced investors were robbed. Everywhere I wrote notes of what I read in absurd quantities, gathering more material than I could ever use. The invention of the cheap photocopying machine has reduced that form of hard labour, the intellectual equivalent of rock breaking.

Determined to see the site of former townships and abandoned railways, old hotels of significance and overgrown prospecting camps, I set out on foot. Pockets of the country were wild. Several of the early towns were deserted and overgrown. Bush covered the streets of certain ghost towns; trees grew on the site of churches; and ferns rose from the vaults of the banks or the cellars of general stores. The route of former railways could more easily be picked up. True, the rails had gone, the stations and the hissing locomotives had vanished, but the embankments remained. I felt that I should see these places, not only to imagine how they once were but also, once or twice, to test the accuracy of people who spoke to me about earlier days. If their description of the geography of ghost towns, in which they claim to have lived, proved to be astray, I was entitled to be slightly wary of what else they told me. I soon discovered that most people were unfailingly accurate if they themselves had witnessed an event. Hearsay was a different matter.

For my story a vital place was Argenton or 'Silver Town', which stood on the plains towards the ocean. Here the first copper ore from Mount Lyell, carried along the steep slopes by mules, was smelted in furnaces and tested for its richness. If the test had failed, the rise of Mount Lyell might have been thwarted. One Saturday, determined to find Argenton, I went by bus to the sleepy mining town of Zeehan which once operated its own street trams and called itself (with a touch of exaggeration) the Silver City. There nobody whom I asked had even heard of Argenton. After walking rapidly for an hour or more, I found the site of the vanished township and railway junction and pottered around the slender ruins and then stood in the wind, trying to imagine how busy, noisy and smoke-filled the scene must once have been.

I could also see, by standing on a piece of rock, the embankment of the ghost railway curving in a wide sweep towards the ghost town of Dundas, at the foot of its blue mountain, and in my mind's eye I could hear the whistle of the locomotive and the rumble of the ore train.

The wonderful specimens of the chromate of lead, coloured red and orange – now on display in the Smithsonian Institution in Washington, perhaps came down that very railway from Dundas, which alas was now as dead and as coffined as Argenton.

'Forgotten Argenton. Dead these sixty years,' I wrote in my notes after returning that night to my shabby hotel in Zeehan. To be certain that I had identified the site of Argenton I had collected several chocolate-coloured pieces of slag – once molten – from the site of the smelter and put them for safekeeping in my coat pocket. Eventually they were tested in the assay office at Mount Lyell. Sure enough, they contained 0.8 per cent copper. I did not have the literary imagination to do justice to the silent town in my notepad.

Back at Mount Lyell I pieced together its history. In its heyday, about 1900, more than forty companies worked side by side, forming a chequerboard of leases. The main contest was between Crotty's North Mount Lyell company of London and Bowes Kelly's Mount Lyell of Melbourne. Each company built long railways from a port to its mine, and each built its own mining town and smelting town, with its own wharves and foundries. And yet the two mines were along the same mountain spine, the Philosophers Ridge, and within easy walking distance.

I was fortunate to have such a dramatic story landing in my lap. Moreover much of the detail was bizarre. James Crotty, a local prospector who had become a magnate, left a fortune but his will decreed that his wife could have a large annuity for herself only if she entered a convent. The town of Crotty, named after him, is drowned, at the bottom of a new lake, but when I first visited it the ruins of the town and the scatter of broken bricks – Crotty had its own brickworks – conveyed a lonely magic. Nobody lived there, but nearby stood an elegant, meccano-like railway bridge, the rails having been dismantled long ago.

At Mount Lyell itself a miner named Jimmy Beattie, learning that I was investigating the history, offered to take me underground in the evenings to explore old workings. We would walk along the North Lyell tunnel to the abandoned mines and, carrying a miner's lamp on our belt, venture into areas where stout vertical logs, like thighs of wood, held up the roof in weaker sections. Sometimes we would hear the ground 'talking', a sign that zones of rock were silently settling down after all the excavations made by thousands of men year after year. We climbed up ladder-ways through narrow openings, bursting into vast man-mined underground chambers with the rock gleaming wherever our lamps focused their thin shafts of light.

I had no idea that in the same mine there should be such narrow travelling ways in one area while nearby such huge stopes or chambers, unsupported by one single upright of timber. The silence too was uncanny, the most common sound being the slow dripping of water, but in the years when these underground areas were being actively worked the noise of the jackhammers would have been deafening. Here was a dark abandoned city with 40 or 50 kilometres of narrow main roads, the remains of iron tramways along which the ore had been hauled, at one time by horses, and a network of subsidiary walking ways. In the following dozen years I was to go down nearly all the big underground mines in Australia, and some of the smaller, without tiring of the experience.

Aborigines were not the only people to invest their spirituality in rocks and earth, though their religion was distinctive. In the Western world, mines had long been the home of supernatural beings, and many of the miners coming from Cornwall saw Australian rocks and earth in a similar way. Small men known as knackers – virtually cousins of the German dwarfs in the story of Snow White – reportedly inhabited the Cornish mines and were heard to sing carols at Christmas, and if rock was likely to cave in, were seen pointing to the danger. Belief in these strange beings, if it ever existed at Mount Lyell, had vanished by my time. But travelling in a silent mine with a working miner who was proud of his calling and saw the mine as partly peopled by the spirits of old friends enabled me for the first time to see how a hole in the ground – simply a source of profit to shareholders – was a special place to others – a mysterious habitation, a meeting point of life and death. In the early 1950s at Mount Lyell the huge quarry or open cut and its procession of roaring tip trucks was superseding the underground mine, quaintly known by the Spanish name Royal Tharsis.

People said, 'Have you met Jimmy Elliott?' Eventually I went into Bowers Hotel, where he slept on an enclosed upper verandah. Told that he might be in the parlour where the hotel's guests congregated, I half-opened its wooden door. The wide fireplace was bare and cold, and the room seemed empty. Then I noticed that a heavy armchair concealed a stooped man. With difficulty he stood up to shake hands. He confided – much of his conversation was in the form of loud whispers – that he was just on his eighty-fourth birthday. His cheeks and eyes were sunken, and his fingers were long and bony. His eyes glistened, however, when he spoke of the rip-roaring days.

He told me that he was only an infant when his father died in Victoria in the late 1860s; and his mother had advertised for a husband – whether in print or by word of mouth I do not know.

A candidate came forward, promptly they were married, and Jimmy was brought up at Steiglitz, Barry's Reef, and other small gold towns near Ballarat. Perhaps he had a quarrel with the stepfather but he was no more than twelve when he earned enough money, by felling a tall gum tree and selling its timber, to pay his fare to Tasmania. On his last night in Melbourne – he was never to see it again – he stayed in a boarding house filled with German-speaking artisans who had just arrived to help build the grand Exhibition Building.

Jimmy travelled in the hold of a ship that, having carried sheep and cattle in its previous crossing of the strait, reeked of manure and the smell of animal skins. After stepping ashore in Burnie, rather the worse for seasickness, he set out for the uplands. On the first day he walked more than 30 kilometres through the forest, reaching at nightfall a rough-and-ready boarding house where he paid one shilling for a bed and one shilling for a meal. Eventually reaching the booming tin-mining town of Mount Bischoff he personally sought a job from the general manager, Mr Kayser, who replied that he should be at school. At last some of the workmen, taking pity on the small boy, dressed him up like a man and tied bowyangs to his trousers, thus giving him the confidence to approach Mr Kayser again. 'Vell, vell, ha ha,' replied Kayser with good humour. 'If it isn't Jimmy!' He gave him a job. Soon Jimmy became a prospector, and one of the first to pitch his tent at Mount Lyell.

Thereafter he spent much of his life in mining camps where there was no curtain on the window, no tablecloth, and tin pannikins in place of cups. One evening, calling for a cigarette and a yarn at the boarding house where I lived, he was offered a drink of tea. When he observed the cup and saucer being handed to him his eyes lit up and he exclaimed: 'China! China! You're well set up here.' Before long,

I went in the bus to Hobart to read old documents and he was puzzled by my absence. When I returned I told him where I had been. 'Hobart!' he replied in astonishment. 'You certainly get around.' His own last visit to Hobart – indeed to anywhere – had been at least sixty-five years earlier. He had carried his swag most of the way on a rough bush track, crossing mountains and fast rivers.

For some reason, he called me Jimmy. As I naturally called him Jimmy, there was confusion when others were present. A few of my friends from Mount Lyell still call me Jimmy.

Becoming more trusting, he divulged snippets about his personal life. His wife was a sister of a popular pugilist but eventually the marriage sagged. He told me that when last he heard of her she was a stewardess in a passenger ship, from which she had written him a letter. Soon after reading her letter, he placed it in his pocket and set out on a prospecting expedition to the south side of Macquarie Harbour. I tactfully enquired whether he replied to the letter. 'No' – it had become sodden after he waded across a flooded creek. He also had a brother who followed the gold rush to the Klondike in north-western Canada. What happened to him? Jimmy was not sure.

I felt elation in hearing this old man talk frankly of his experiences of long ago. Here, sitting in an armchair and fumbling for his box of matches, was someone who had seen the mining discoveries unfold. I eventually discovered that as a boy he had had a hand in the first gold find in the district, even before Mount Lyell itself was found. Later he ran a poky bush hotel where the mainland financiers and promoters stayed on their first visit of inspection. Two decades later, working as a miner, he was trapped underground for five days in the worst metal-mining disaster in Australia's history.

Half a century ago the appreciation of eyewitness history, of events as seen by ordinary folk, was little valued by practising historians. When I studied history I was not informed that ordinary people could be precious sources. Within a few years I was to reach the contrary conclusion – that someone with little education was more likely than a professor to retain an accurate memory of events they had actually experienced.

Jimmy enjoyed talking but did not like me writing notes in his presence. Each time I had to record his main reminiscences as soon as he had departed, though occasionally – if I had a copy of the day's newspaper in my hand – I scribbled notes on the white margins of the paper. I own a copy of the Burnie *Advocate* for Monday 27 August 1951, and all over the front page – written in ink that instantly soaked itself into the paper – are my hurried notes. Virtually everything he told me was accurate, or so I came to realise, because in the end I was able to check his recollections against other sources.

Jimmy, or half of him, lived in the future. Glorious deposits of copper and gold were just waiting to be discovered, he confided, and he knew where they were. Osmiridium, used in making the nibs of fountain pens, came into his optimistic talk. The west coast was a map in his head – every creek and every ridge engraved. He would give me directions, drawing a map on the arm of the chair or pointing aloft with his bony forefinger. 'You know that big boulder in the Comstock valley – that's your indicator. Climb high, and follow the spur' to the point where the conglomerate meets the schist rock. 'Here's where you sink your shaft,' he would proclaim.

One night in about 1954 Jimmy caught a virus and became delirious. Mrs Lang who worked in Bowers Hotel and felt motherly towards him told me how, that morning, though he was almost too frail to stand up, he managed to dress himself in his old work clothes.

He announced that he had to inspect a discovery in the hills. 'I've no time to lose,' he said. His time had almost come.

Only a few people holding vital information about the past were reluctant to reveal it. Understandably they saw me as young and untested. The dynamic man in the early history of the mining field was an American, Robert Carl Sticht, a metallurgist and also an art collector whose smelters had transformed the landscape at Queenstown. I respected him and still do. He died in 1922 but thirty years later one of his sons was living in Melbourne where he was an executive in a chemical works. The son was persuaded, reluctantly, by Walter Bassett to meet me. He finally agreed to be interviewed one afternoon while travelling in his car from the chemical works to his home. I went to Yarraville by train, and duly appeared at the gate of the works at knock-off time. Inviting me to sit in his car, he answered questions with few words and dropped me off at the Flinders Street railway station. My request for a photograph of his father was a matter to which he said he would give thought. What his thoughts were I did not learn. He did not reveal that his family held a box of valuable letters and papers that would have eased and aided the writing of parts of the history. Ultimately his brother who lived in California heard of my project and showed every sign of genuinely wishing to help, but by then the book was printed.

The people I interviewed on the mining field did not worry in the least that I seemed young for the task. They were only too pleased when I sat by their fireplace and listened, especially if I was willing to go outside and fetch more firewood. When I went to Hobart to consult old files, the archivists Robert Sharman and Peter Eldershaw were kindness itself.

On the other hand Hugh Murray, the general manager of the Mount Lyell Company, was not quite sure how to handle me. I had been selected and sent by the head office in Melbourne, and those living at a distant mine are sometimes a little suspicious of head office and its ways of interfering.

Murray let me see the scrapbooks that had been kept since the turn of the century but for many months did not show me the wonderful files of letters flowing year after year between Queenstown and head office – the most important of all sources. Slowly his trust grew. Eventually he showed me volume after volume of bound letters dating from about 1895, some written by hand and many emanating from an old typewriter with a purple ribbon. Finally he showed me volumes of very confidential letters, a few of which were potentially explosive. To the best of my knowledge no public company in Australia had previously released its innermost files to an outsider, and here I was reading them week after week. Much that was exciting in my story was plucked from these files.

After one year of investigating, my research grant ran out. I was, in effect, unemployed though busily at work. To have no income did not pain me. Born in the Depression, seeing many young men calling at our back door for sandwiches and hot tea, I had expected that my own life would have phases of unemployment. Indeed, at this time my mother's brother Harold Lanyon suggested that I should think of a more secure career. He had worked in Chicago in the early 1930s before returning to Melbourne where he set up a small factory producing the suture or catgut that was then used by surgeons when operating and by makers of tennis racquets. Finally he studied medicine – he was not far ahead of me at university – and became a doctor, but the recollection of his own struggles made him sensibly warn me that a career as a writer was a financial risk, for hard times would come again.

I had collected a pile of evidence about the past but had barely begun to write. Maybe one year and a half of full-time work lay ahead. Meanwhile I needed an income. Recently I had come to the conclusion that on the west coast of Tasmania might exist lodes that could again be payable because the price of copper had risen or the cost of mining had been cut by new methods. If one such mine was capable of resuscitation, what a discovery – or rediscovery – that would be. I put this idea to Geoff Hudspeth, the mine manager. Wearing a hat with a brim wider than almost anybody's, he was fascinated by the ups and downs of mines. He liked my idea. Where would I find the mines? I told him I would go into the old newspapers with their drilling records and company archives.

Mount Lyell agreed to pay me £4 a day, and gave me a small office alongside that of Mervyn Wade who was the company's new geologist. At Hudspeth's request I went to Hobart and stayed in the old Customs House Hotel by the waterfront and ransacked mining reports in the government archives and old newspapers. He was especially interested in the early workings of the North Lyell mine. I compiled a short history of those workings, complete with my own roughly drawn charts of where shafts and tunnels were placed and which grades of copper ore and which patches of barren rock they passed through. I finally pointed to the existence of a big area of low-grade copper ore that might now be payable. He was excited. After a week he came to me and said that he had looked at the old mine drawings in his possession. Alas, the ore I pointed to had been mined long ago! Finally I rediscovered a large area of copper-bearing clays in a forgotten mine called the King Lyell. The clay had been unpayable using the treatment methods of 1900 but it was now payable, and the company eventually mined it at a handsome profit.

The life of the isolated town absorbed me. One Saturday, I won third place in the long-distance wheelbarrow race which followed the 40 kilometres of hills and valleys from Zeehan to Queenstown; it was said to be the longest barrow race ever run. Occasionally on the radio station, on the eve of local happenings, I would pretend to be an old prospector and under the name of Titus Mehaffey give my reminiscences in a quavering voice, thus provoking much discussion about who on earth that old-timer could be. When square dancing briefly became the rage I was the secretary of the club.

I wished not only to record history but to make it. I had the idea that I might discover useful minerals in the wild country, and Russ Hibbert, a diamond driller from Mount Lyell, was eager to join me. We had little equipment, no tent and not even a truck, but then there were few roads in the entire region. Early in 1954 we set out, our equipment on our backs. On Mount Sedgwick we passed tiger snakes sunning themselves on the exposed peaks. We then went to the deserted Chester mine, following a track from the Emu Bay railway. We explored – or perhaps we imagined that we were exploring – in damp, thick bush near the Magnet silver-lead mine, which was utterly deserted but in its day had its own hydro-electric scheme, railway station and football team. I saw white daisies growing in the manager's deserted garden.

The food we carried was the simplest. We had potatoes and onions, bacon which supplied the fat for cooking in the frying pan, and a large quantity of flour which, mixed with water and spiced with raisins, provided johnnycakes, either fried or baked over glowing coals. As a luxury we carried a few tins of preserved peaches or apricots, and we had tea, sugar and a tin or two of condensed milk. We lit a fire for breakfast and another in the evening for warmth, and if rain seemed likely we erected a shelter. In a few places we came across a wooden hut with a crooked chimney made of iron, a fireplace with a crossbar on which could be hung the billy full of water, and a bunk or two made of used potato bags. Water was easily found; there were few places in Australia where clean running water was more plentiful.

Even when following the narrow bush walking tracks, we met no other human being. Birds were so rare that the sound of one was arresting. Journalists and even geologists wrote that large areas of the west coast had never known a human footprint, but my reading of history, my talks with old prospectors, assured me that nearly every hectare of the west coast had been seen by someone. In unlikely places could be seen the evidence – the neck of a half-buried bottle or the point of a pick – and yet I had more faith than most of the professional mining engineers that major mines would still be discovered. While they thought, and the evidence of the previous forty years supported their view, that the great era of discovery in western Tasmania had passed, I saw a future for mining. Indeed in 1956 I gave a short lecture tour of Tasmania on behalf of the adult-education program and argued that major discoveries would still be made, though I had no idea which minerals would be found, or where.

We were attracted to uranium, the glamorous metal being discovered in tropical Australia. To the best of my knowledge, nobody had seriously sought it in western Tasmania, and yet this was one of the most mineralised regions in the nation. Why should uranium not be found here? At that time the latest and most portable instrument for identifying radioactive ores was the Geiger counter. Probably the only such instrument in the whole of Tasmania was with an energetic syndicate of prospectors at the once-famous tin mine of Mount Bischoff, and for a deposit of £45 – a lot of money for us – we took possession of it. Though it fitted into a brown shoulder bag, it was heavy to carry. When turned on, it gave a continuous series of signals which we had to count. If there was radioactive rock just under the ground, the count would be very high; we never found ourselves in the presence of it.

After examining rocks around the fading town of Waratah, we decided to visit the Pieman River. A truck driver promised us a ride, and we paid a launch owner to take us down the river. The mouth of the Pieman was impressive, with the windblown froth from the surf, and hundreds of logs, littering the beach. Floated down by the floods, most of the logs had lain there so long that they were smoothed and bleached.

Here, early in the century, had lived a Scandinavian named Ahberg, and in a five-room house of Huon pine he dispensed hospitality to miners who, walking along the coast, requested that they be ferried across the wide river. He owned a collection of the cylinders through which the early Edison gramophone played music, and sometimes travellers could hear the sound of Wagner and Bach before they saw his house. We could not find its remains but the wild seas were roaring, just as Ahberg had so often heard them. All the way to South America lay no intervening land to block the swell of the ocean.

To the north of the river we walked over the buttongrass plains, on and on, with a view of the Southern Ocean to the west. Here and there, in high hopes, we turned on the Geiger counter. Normally it emitted about fifty signals to the minute; at the Black Cat, an abandoned wolfram 'mine', the count reached sixty in a minute; and on a rocky hill near the foaming mouth of Pieman Heads it was to reach seventy-four. It was not high enough. There were two consolations: we were handed back our £45 in crisp notes, and even today nobody has found payable uranium in Tasmania.

12

'CALL IT *THE PEAKS OF LYELL*'

To write a book was more difficult than I had imagined. It called for stamina, for literary stamina. You don't know whether you have stamina until you have shown yourself that you do.

To write the early chapters I used long strips of shiny yellow paper recently obtained in Hobart. The guillotined leftovers from a printing office, they were like a yellow scarf. I wrote on them with a fountain pen and very black ink, and for some reason I used black crayon to delete. Scores and scores of the corrected paragraphs I wrote in this way appear in the book, almost unchanged, but most paragraphs on the long yellow sheets were deleted. I had written about ten chapters when suddenly I felt at home; by groping and experimenting I had found a rapport with an imaginary audience and at last felt confident that the audience was listening to me.

Chapter 11 which I called 'A Land of Fire and Brimstone' was one potential hurdle. A gnawing chapter, it consisted of a mosaic of tiny facts culled or scrounged from everywhere, and yet with my new confidence it was speedily composed in maybe three or four days. It had a vitality that impressed me, though part of the energy came from bursts of short sentences that perhaps continued too long. The chapter concluded with my attempt to explain the most remarkable change in the terrain:

> Sulphur, rain and fire swiftly painted a new landscape. Fogs heavily charged with sulphur made green grass and plants yellow in a day. Bushfires raced through the scrub in successive summers and left blackened hillsides. No fresh vegetation grew, for the sulphur fumes killed almost all the plant life within miles of the smelters. Heavy rain began to erode the top soil. Early in this century the landscape was black and desolate, a cemetery of black stumps. Two beautiful valleys had become as ugly as battlefields.

By the end of 1953 my manuscript was almost completed. I knew that the book was too long. I counted 129 000 words before crossing out, with many strokes of the fountain pen, hundreds of sentences that did not pull their weight. I was guided by the skilled American writer Carl Sandburg, the biographer of Abraham Lincoln, whose advice I copied into my notebook: 'Write till you are ashamed of yourself and then cut it down to next to nothing so the reader may hope beforehand he is not wasting his time.' His advice, I thought later, was too extreme.

The heads of the Mount Lyell Mining & Railway Company were eager to read my typescript. As I had used many of the company's own confidential records, I required its permission before I could publish it.

Sir Walter Bassett, now the chairman, smoothed the road. He liked the book though several of his colleagues were worried about the chapter describing recent years, because conceivably it could affect the shares in their company, then an important one on the stock exchanges. For my part I wasn't very interested in the last couple of years, and wrote about them with a visible lack of enthusiasm. It was a legitimate criticism of the book that it fell away in the last chapter or two. The more remote past was my domain, because there I had freedom essentially to write what I wished.

Walter Bassett, now enthusiastic for the book, as was his wife, insisted that I must publish it. His company offered no money as a subsidy, but I hoped the book would stand on its own. Late in 1953 I took the typescript to the Melbourne University Press and handed it personally to Gwyn James, the manager. Keen on Australian history, he had compiled one of the few significant books to come out in the wartime years, *A Homestead History*. Kindly, almost fatherly, he questioned me about the typescript in his English Midlands accent. While I answered him, he swiftly thumbed a page or two. He suddenly remembered that on maybe his first day on Australian soil he had left his cargo-passenger ship at the port of Burnie and made a short rail trip towards the west coast. At once we seemed to be on the same wavelength.

I was astonished to observe that a skilled publisher could assess a potential book in a few minutes. Enthusiastically he confided to me, without exactly committing himself, that my book was very promising. After a few weeks he sent me a phone message to say that he would be pleased to publish it. I was in seventh heaven, as they used to say in that era when one heaven was more than enough.

He offered me a royalty of 3 per cent on the retail sales. Ultimately each copy of the book went on sale in the bookshops for thirty shillings, and so I would receive just under one shilling for each copy sold. It was a small royalty – the normal was 10 per cent – but I would have accepted an offer even if I had been obliged to pay him a royalty. A decade later Peter Ryan, who succeeded James as general manager, raised the royalty – without being asked – to 10 per cent, the book then being in its third edition.

Meanwhile it was a bundle of typed pages, not a book. James intimated that he had half-a-dozen books in the slow publishing pipeline and said that mine would be printed late in 1954. He himself edited the book, displaying all his literary skills. He made a few suggestions on every second page, chopping out half a sentence or adding a semicolon or occasionally a phrase that added clarity. With few exceptions I agreed with him. Sometimes, if precise accuracy was at stake, I insisted that my wording was the best, and he would give in. The whole editing process was amicable and decisive. Walter Bassett, Hugh Murray and the other heads of Mount Lyell had spent a long time discussing minor matters that came up in the typescript, but James usually overruled them all. If the book was to be published his word was law. I doubt whether they even knew of some changes he made to the manuscript.

James announced, being a traditionalist, that on the cover of the book I must not call myself Geoff Blainey, the name by which I had always been known, but should formally call myself Geoffrey. I was dismayed. To change one's name is a bold step. After protesting, I made the step. I felt like an impostor taking on a new name, even though I had been so christened as an infant.

For the book I suggested a variety of titles. He wanted colour but not dazzle. I have subsequently had no trouble in devising titles for books, but he it was who suggested the title for my first one. He based it on a passage in Chapter 7 that described how in the cold winter of 1891 two mining promoters, fresh from making a fortune at Broken Hill, led their horses along the narrow track and suddenly 'saw the peaks of Lyell, veiled by mist and rain'. Triumphantly he said to me, 'Call the book *The Peaks of Lyell*!' When some of the high officials at the mine heard of the proposed title, they protested that Mount Lyell itself was round rather than peaked. They did reluctantly concede, however, that if it were seen from certain angles or viewed through clinging mist, a few of its rocky outcrops did seem peaked. After the book appeared in print, the title increasingly won favour. Occasionally a book gains by adopting a title that is slightly askew.

After completing the book, I had time to spare – I had no job – and resolved on the spur of the moment to see Henry Lawson's country. Of all Australian writers he appealed to me the most. I do not know when I first read him; I am pretty sure that it was not in school, even though my English teacher, A. A. Phillips, was later a national expert on Lawson. Probably I discovered him in the second-hand bookshops where two of his paperbacks were available in the Australian Pocket Library. How primitive they were! If you ran your hand down the spine you could feel the iron staples that held the pages together. The cover was so thin that it could be torn by a kitten's teeth. One book of his short stories, entitled *On the Track and Over the Sliprails*, I liked best, for they were heartwarming sketches of life on the goldfields and small farms.

I wished now to see Lawson's country. Buying a second-class ticket I went by train to Albury, changed to the uniform gauge and went on to Sydney where late that night I caught the mail train to Bourke. As it began to rush through the night I thought of Lawson's poem 'On the Night Train' and its opening words: 'Have you seen the Bush by moonlight, from the train, go running by?' At daybreak we were out on the western plains, where sheep were lightly scattered in all directions. When we halted at the little station of Nevertire I knew I was in Lawson country, for one of his ballads, recited at bush concerts, was entitled 'Jack Dunn of Nevertire'.

In the afternoon the train reached Bourke, the base for Lawson's only visit to the arid outback. Next day I saw the old red-gum wharves and the brown Darling River and walked through the town before travelling by train to Mount Boppy and to Cobar where the abandoned copper smelters were a nostalgic sight. Only after my journey of nearly 4000 kilometres was complete did I realise, with my new knowledge of the countryside, that more of Lawson's finest short stories were centred around accessible Gulgong, an old gold town near the Great Dividing Range, than the pastoral country I had just traversed.

I longed for my own book to appear. I had no idea that the typesetting, proofreading and printing could be slow. Now entering its final stage at a printing works in Melbourne, the book's future was suddenly threatened by a few sentences I had written in a chapter appropriately entitled 'The Disaster'.

It so happened that in October 1912, after weeks of industrial tension, a fire began in the North Lyell underground mine. Really an underground city it consisted of miles of 'corridors' or narrow roads, the roofs of which were supported by props or columns of heavy timber. Fortunately the fire which began at the 700 level, or about 200 metres underground, did not spread so far as was feared, but unfortunately the smoke and carbon monoxide fumes spread with speed. In the space of an hour they penetrated to every place where miners were at work. Many men managed to escape, travelling in the fast cages up the shaft to the surface. When evening fell, ninety-five men were still missing, their rescue impossible because of dense and dangerous fumes. Jimmy Elliott, my friend, was among the missing.

While the nation waited for news, an intricate rescue plan was adopted. A ship carrying firefighting equipment, smoke helmets and diving suits steamed across Bass Strait in record time. At the wharf in Burnie fast steam trains waited to carry the rescue equipment to the distant mine. Meanwhile, attempts were made to reach those men below. In the end more decorations were awarded for bravery at Mount Lyell than for any previous event in Australian history – until the assault on Gallipoli three years later. After five days the living were rescued but forty-two lay below, dead. The mine remained dangerous. The vast workings had to be flooded, and the fire extinguished, and the mine pumped dry before, in the new year, the bodies could be retrieved. Curiously they were well preserved by the mineralised waters in the mine.

What had caused the fatal fire? A royal commission, after questioning numerous witnesses, expressed its uncertainty with this memorable sentence: 'Forty-two men are said to have lost their lives in various parts of the mine; and, with so many voices lost to us in the silence of death, the evidence is necessarily incomplete, and we can only deplore the fate of those whose testimony concerning the happenings in the mine on the fatal 12th of October will never be given before an earthly tribunal.'

In my book I came to a different conclusion. On the basis of fairly strong circumstantial evidence, I argued that the fire could well have been lit deliberately. The likely culprit was a militant miner whose brother, not long before the disaster itself, had been killed in a mining accident. On his brother's grave in the Queenstown cemetery had duly appeared the indictment: 'A human life sacrificed on the altar of dividends'. It was true that on the morning of the fire, the militant miner had been seen acting suspiciously. Moreover he possibly had another incentive to light a fire, and thereby expose what he saw were hazards, because on that very day a senior delegation was on its way to Mount Lyell to investigate the safety of the mines. If indeed he lit the fire, he had no intention of causing the loss of life. As I wrote in the book, 'He did not suspect that the fire would give off deadly fumes.' In essence, 'the guilt of the suspect should not be magnified'.

About three months before the book was published, I became worried about the libel implications of this chapter. Presumably a friend raised the risk with me – I was ignorant of the law. Indeed I had written the book with a fearlessness that might now be called naive or innocent.

As the day of publication came nearer, my fear persisted: what if the miner were still alive? If so, might he take legal action? If he were thirty years of age at the time of the disaster he would now be in his early seventies. Belatedly I made enquiries as to whether he was alive, and discovered nothing. Meanwhile I wrote from Melbourne to the registry of births and deaths in Hobart, enclosing my search fee of £1, and enquiring whether the miner had died in Tasmania in the years between 1920 and 1950.

From the registry office in Hobart came a receipt for my payment dated 3 October but no information was inside the envelope. The search among the records was slow, and eleven days passed before Hobart wrote to say that the miner had not died in Tasmania between the years 1920 and 1930. Eight days later it wrote to report that his death had not occurred, at least in Tasmania, in the following twenty years. I replied, enclosing more money for a final search of the remaining years.

As miners were migratory, it was possible that he could have died at Broken Hill, Bendigo or another mainland field during the past forty years, but a search in the interstate records would have been long and slow. I made further enquiries, without success. An urgent letter to Fred Jakins, who had been a young mining engineer at Mount Lyell during the disaster, yielded a more reassuring response. In his recollection, the miner had gone to Victoria and probably had died there. He gave no date or place: it was just his feeling, his vague memory. At that time I was writing a very short history of the old engineers Johns & Waygood; and the two brothers Peter and Owen Johns, hearing of my futile searches, generously engaged a detective agency to join in the search. So far as I know, it found nothing.

Perhaps I was worrying too much. Then, as distinct from now, Australian authors and publishers of books were rarely sued for libel. But for my first book the glow and anticipation were dimmed by the fear.

Just before Christmas 1954, I went the office of Melbourne University Press. Gwyn James, chatting in his genial way, suddenly picked up a book from the side of his desk, and handed it to me. It was the first copy of *The Peaks of Lyell*, straight from the printer. It was wrapped around with a dust jacket that, by the standards of the day, was spectacular. The book's front and back and spine displayed a sepia panorama of the Lyell field, with the steep, strangely denuded landscape staring at the reader. In the sky above the landscape was printed in green letters the title of the book. In a cloud-shadow on the slopes below was printed my unfamiliar name, Geoffrey, in such small letters that I could not possibly take offence. I instantly wondered how many pages were in the book, and turning quickly to the back I saw there were 310. That evening I took it in the train to Dandenong and showed it with scarcely disguised pride to everyone who happened to be at my parents' home.

Publishing was then more like a cottage industry, and James was vague about the date when the book would be first seen in the bookshops. I looked in vain at the windows of city shops to see if copies were on display. After two months I saw them.

So few books of Australian history appeared at that time that mine received a volume of attention that would be inconceivable today when a monthly flood of new Australian books pours into the shops. The largest book window in Melbourne, Robertson & Mullens in busy Elizabeth Street, gave most of its space to displays of copies of my book, along with handsome specimens of North Lyell peacock ore, rich in copper, and photographs of old Mount Lyell. On several days I dawdled on the busy footpath in front of the shop window, pretending that I was a neutral observer. A week or two later *The Age* devoted most of the front page of its Saturday cultural supplement to the book. It was a generous review but I, like every new author, did not think it was generous enough.

For a few months I was almost a talked-about author. I heard by word of mouth that among its readers were Douglas Mawson the Antarctic explorer, and Captain Davis who was celebrated for his navigation of Antarctic waters. Other readers wrote to me: bent bushmen who rarely took up a pen, women who had once lived at Mount Lyell, and the descendants of people named in the book. A retired New Zealand goldminer working in the packing department at the printery told me that he often sneaked a read of the book while wrapping copies in brown paper for delivery to the shops. He was now almost up to page 100. He never told me whether he reached 200.

Owen Paice, a leading trade unionist at Lyell, wrote the most engaging of letters, telling how his wife, a strong personality, wept when she read about her father's rescue role during the mining disaster. In the district most adults either read parts of the book, or heard it being read aloud. The housekeeper at Bowers Hotel in Queenstown visited Jimmy Elliott, who was now fading away in an old folks' home in Hobart, and heard that he had read the copy I posted to him; 'he was lovely to talk to', she wrote.

One day I opened a handwritten letter signed by Nevil Shute. He was at the height of his fame as a novelist, for his *A Town Like Alice* was reaching many lands and his *On the Beach*, and the filmed version, were soon to attract millions of fans. Presented with my book by a friend, he glanced at it and thought he would read just a few words – in case the friend asked for his opinion. 'Instead,' wrote Shute, 'the thing held my attention to the end, so that I looked forward each day to reading a bit more of it in bed.' He added his view that skilled writing 'can make anything interesting'. When I showed the letter to Gwyn James, he clapped his publisher's hands and proclaimed that an endorsement from Nevil Shute would boost sales. But it was a private letter not to be made public.

With some diffidence I posted the book to my old English teacher, Arthur A. Phillips, who eventually replied, addressing me to my surprise as 'Dear Geoff'. Approving what he described as my 'colourful succinctness', he also waved a stick at me: 'Whither has fled the Blainey I knew with the pure and wholesome milk of Marxism still wet upon his lips? Whence came this Running Dog of Capitalism?' He did concede that I bit the legs of the capitalists.

Manning Clark must have read or seen the book. After passing through Queenstown in the autumn of 1958 he generously sent me a postcard depicting the almost-deserted main street. On the back, with a sense of fun, he scrawled: 'Greetings to the historian of Lyell from Abel Tasman.' It pleased him to sign postcards with names other than his own; and when Alex Jesaulenko became a celebrated Carlton footballer he sometimes appeared as the signer of Manning's postcards.

There was then no bestseller list of Australian books. I assume that my book, though popular, would not have ranked as a real bestseller except in Tasmania where it was widely read. But Professor Grahame Johnston in his *Annals of Australian Literature* listed the more influential books published each year; and for 1954 my name was the youngest of the authors on his list, while at the senior end stood such long-reigning names as Miles Franklin and Mary Gilmore. My book recently was observed to be the only one of Johnston's thirty-six books of that year to have been in print almost continuously since it first appeared. I would like to imagine that it was a worthwhile book, but when I set out to read a page or two now I am not always sure. Part of the reason for its longevity was simply that I kept on living and so was able to keep it alive by periodically updating it.

The book was the kind one might now submit for a doctorate, but I had a perverse attitude to degrees. At the end of my undergraduate course I had been awarded a first-class honours degree but refused to take part in the ceremony in the fine old Wilson Hall. Whether out of penury or principle or sheer contrariness, I had decided that the fee for the graduation ceremony was a tax on knowledge. In British history a tax on knowledge was eschewed in certain intellectual circles, and perhaps I was tacking my colours to this old mast, just because a mast was needed. I also held even then a suspicion towards degrees. Too many people holding no degrees seemed mentally superior to those who held degrees. I had met numerous people who had had no formal education but by dint of constant reading had eventually surpassed the typical university graduate.

Upon leaving university I had resolved not to graduate in the formal sense, and so, strictly speaking, I held no degree. Later at the registrar's office the presiding official, the colourful Mr Glasson Williams, looked through the graduate rolls, making, I assume, his annual inspection, and could not find my name. He sent for me and, after hearing my reasons, chided me and gave me a knowing wink. He knew nobody else who had refused on principle to 'take out' a degree.

After I was awarded an MA for the first half of my book on Mount Lyell, the whole book being far too long for a master's thesis, I decided again not to take out the degree. In any case, before I could graduate as a master, I first had to take out my bachelor's degree and then wait for another full year. I sat tight, taking no action. Meanwhile I made no claim to possessing a university degree.

When eventually I taught at the university, first as a senior lecturer and later as a professor, officials at the University of Melbourne, slightly embarrassed, placed an MA after my name in official publications. I preferred not to budge from my position, though it had long ceased to be a matter of importance. The academic officials wisely bided their time. In 1982 I went to Harvard as a professor, and while I was there my friend Sir David Derham the vice-chancellor in Melbourne busied himself, arranging for the chancellor to confer officially on me the degree of BA (Hons), and then a little later conferring on me an MA, again in my absence. Through Derham's patience and shrewdness I was made legitimate. Officially, the seal of wisdom was conferred on me but I felt none the wiser.

13

'IT IS DYNAMITE'

Unemployed, I was not sure what to do. I wished to write books but could not afford to write them. In Australia the royalties from the annual sales even of the bestselling history books were relatively small. Few works on our history had much chance of reaching a large overseas audience.

One Australian freelance historian living in the British Isles tapped an enthusiastic audience in many lands and must have earned an impressive income in his bumper years. His name was Alan Moorehead and he charmed readers with his observant and engaging books *The Villa Diana, Gallipoli, No Room in the Ark* and *The White Nile*. A gifted journalist on the Melbourne *Herald* and the London *Daily Express* in the 1930s, and a dashing correspondent in the war years, he already had a name as a prose writer but did not write most of his books on Australian themes. Moreover the penalty for living his final years in England and Italy was that here he no longer possesses the reputation he deserves. Like many of his readers I admired the charm and clarity of his understated prose. I met him once, when he spoke unassumingly about his books to a small lunchtime audience at the Celtic Club in Melbourne, and my liking for his work increased.

As I knew that a full-time author in Australia earned little money I thought of other careers. With a friend I planned to launch a weekly newspaper in Devonport which was then perhaps the largest Tasmanian town without a paper. I would write most of the stories while my friend would run the business and sell advertisements. In the end the venture seemed too risky. I also mulled over an offer from the Mount Lyell Company which, realising that I knew much about their mines, hoped I would take up a new well-paid post called the cost comptroller, and cut the costs of mining. Tempted, I was not persuaded.

Frank Eyre, a cultivated Englishman who managed Oxford University Press in Australia, invited me to call at his city office to discuss his idea for a book. Since 1916 his firm had issued Sir Ernest Scott's ever-prescribed *Short History of Australia* which had been reprinted at least twenty times. Last revised in 1936, a few years before Scott's death, the blue-covered book was out of date but still selling. Scott observed his adopted land with the sharp eyes of the first-class journalist which once he was, but his writing was rarely exciting for my generation.

When Eyre confidentially showed me the sales of the book, and the royalties paid year after year to the estate of this long-dead author, I could only gasp. The conclusion of Eyre's charming speech was obvious: would I write a book to replace Scott? I should have instantly said yes. In retrospect I was unwise to be deterred. I could have borrowed enough money to keep me in food and tobacco during the eighteen months when, totally devoid of income, I would be writing the new Scott. Eyre could have eased my financial dilemma by paying me an advance payment, as is now the fashion, but most publishers did not then offer advances. And so forty years were to pass before I attempted my own *Shorter History of Australia*.

Soon after saying no to Eyre's invitation I realised how captivating it would have been to write the book he envisaged, for I began to write a miniature version, a little essay on Victoria. It so happened that the big travelling circus of learning known as the Australian and New Zealand Association for the Advancement of Science was to assemble in Melbourne in the winter of 1955. To inform those who were to take part in this huge and exciting conference, a book was to be produced; and I was invited to write, as the opening chapter, a history of Victoria. Hurrying to meet the deadline I opened my chapter, indeed the whole book, with a dash of paint: 'Seen from passing schooners, the southern coastline of Australia was barren and spray-soaked in the winter of 1834.' Wondering how to end the chapter, I pointed out that in 1834 London was the largest city in the world but today Melbourne, ever so young, now held as many people as that earlier London.

At that time it was easier for Australians to win a grant to study at Oxford than to win one enabling them to write a book about their own country. I made one attempt, early in 1955, to win a research grant to enable me to do so but my old teacher, Max Crawford, hatched another plan. The university was to reach its century in the following year. Would I write a history to mark the occasion? Offered an attractive salary I set to work at once, occupying a desk in an underground room in the sandstone quadrangle where the servants of the first professors and their families had lived and worked. There they had ironed and starched the clothes, and cooked too. In the dampness of the cellar, while experiencing a series of colds and fevers, I worked hard. Few tasks are as arresting as full-time research in a field about which one initially knows little.

The second-oldest university in the nation, Melbourne had begun humbly with only fifteen students, some of whom soon vanished. It was exhilarating to find their neatly penned letters, calling for a stable for their horses or a later starting time for their lectures, for they had to ride along roads that were 'sorely scorched in summer and sadly drenched in winter'. The few professors too were engaging, and I tried, without full success, to make them come alive: Halford who set up the country's first medical school and made a brave search for a remedy for snakebite, McCoy the wrestler-chested scientist who had no time for the fast-ascending theories of Charles Darwin, Irving the classical scholar who was the son of Thomas Carlyle's best friend, and the bewigged Hearn who was the professor of almost everything and extended his portfolio by sitting in parliament.

I found it rewarding to exhume controversies that were once time bombs but were now firecrackers: the decision to admit women to lectures for the first time, the financial fraud in the 1890s that disabled the university for years, and the absorbing question of whether the professor of music should be punished for writing suggestive poems in a book provocatively called *Hymns Ancient and Modern*. I did not realise that a university is a difficult institution to analyse because in some senses it is a large monastery, with dozens of cells, each absorbed in a different world. Moreover, which historian had wide enough interests and sympathies to do justice to fields as far apart as Latin, anatomy, philosophy and civil engineering? I certainly was not such a historian.

I had been at work for only a few months when the university decided that I should also write a short illustrated history that could be handed to overseas guests when the centenary was formally celebrated one year hence. I wrote the book, and more than 100 photographs, all in black and white, were skilfully taken by Norman Olver, a science lecturer. Nobody could have been more pleasant to work with than Norman. When a crisis arose he did not throw his powerful spectacles on the ground or tear at his hair, he just laughed. The book of 176 pages, miraculously, appeared on time.

My decision to agree readily to the university's request was a mistake. If you have to write a book, it is best to write it only once. The emotional excitement of telling the story is largely used up in the first and shorter version, thus making the retelling of the story in a longer book as much a task as a pleasure. The short book I had written with ease. The longer book, towards the end, became almost a burden.

Max Crawford, having entrusted this task to one so young, was slightly nervous lest I, through carelessness or lack of diplomacy, might jeopardise his department's proud reputation. On the longer book he sought the views of John La Nauze who had just arrived as a second professor. La Nauze, a West Australian who had been an infant when his father was killed in the First World War, pursued standards of accuracy that were so high that his own polished sentences and their content had difficulty in passing his own inspection: for years he produced little in printed form. He rightly raised his eyebrows at some of my interpretations. He puzzled me, however, by suggesting that I was open to an action for defamation by reporting with a splash of detail that Professor D. B. Copland, who was now one of the nation's five best-known economists, had once been highly ambitious to become the vice-chancellor of the university. La Nauze said of my comment: 'It is dynamite, and in any case cannot be based on evidence (however much we believe it, in fact, to be true).' I could not see why it was dynamite but, being inexperienced, accepted his advice.

When it was Crawford's turn to read my typescript, he showed his modesty by suggesting that I delete my praise of his department as the best of its kind in Australia. He also proposed in the kindliest way that I tone down my criticisms of his predecessor in the chair of history, the late Sir Ernest Scott. 'I believe that, with all his faults, Scott was a great man,' Crawford told me. At the time I did not fully appreciate how generous it was for these two hardworking historians to read my manuscript, nearly every page of it.

During the eighteen months I was working on the two university books, I made long-lasting friends. One was John Mulvaney, a young history lecturer who was determined to bring serious archaeology to Aboriginal Australia. The son of an Irish-born teacher in Gippsland, Mulvaney was about to take part in the Lancaster bomber raids over Germany in May 1945 when the European war ended. Taking up history at Melbourne University he told me later that he felt stimulated by what he learnt every day; 'I regret,' he wrote decades later, 'that modern undergraduates seldom seem to derive the same sense of excitement and purpose.' After several years of tutoring in Melbourne he studied anthropology and archaeology at Cambridge and was taught how to excavate in lands as different as Denmark and

Libya before he returned to lecture in ancient history at Melbourne University. A country boy he was practical as well as theoretical, a useful pedigree for an archaeologist who, in the bush, would have to be a jack-of-all-trades.

His plans for 'digging' in South Australia in 1956 were well advanced when he casually mentioned that he needed transport and unskilled labour. I could offer both, having put nearly all my savings into a second-hand Jowett Javelin, an English car with an engine so unorthodox that, when some garage men lifted up the bonnet to check the oil, they let out a whistle of astonishment. Mulvaney so far had enlisted only one car to convey his small team of excavators. I doubled his transport and also volunteered to be cook and woodchopper for a fortnight at camp, tasks for which my time on the west coast of Tasmania had prepared me – but 'not quite', as his endearing wife Jean in her droll way was to observe of my cooking.

So we drove from Melbourne to Fromm's Landing, near the South Australian town of Mannum, where Mulvaney was proposing to dig on a cliff near the meanderings of the Murray River. There the mouth of a limestone cave or shelter overlooked the river; and inside the cave Mulvaney began the patient, meticulous process of examining and removing the successive layers of soil and ash.

Over the centuries, Aboriginal families had intermittently sheltered in the cave and cooked their meals and even slept there. Indeed it had a high ceiling when they first inhabited it, but they were to light on the floor so many cooking fires that the thin layers of discarded ash, supplemented by sand and rock falling from the roof, slowly raised the level of the floor. In the end it was edging uncomfortably close to the ceiling, so that a gap of barely a metre separated parts of it from the rock above. Sometimes those Aborigines using the cave in later centuries must have had to crouch or rest on their elbows.

I was surprised to see how painstaking was Mulvaney's process of excavation. It was done on hands and knees with the help of small steel trowels and even fingers and hands. Whatever was dug or prised up was placed on a sieve, so that the dust and fine soil fell to the bottom. Anything solid stayed on the sieve where it could be examined and then stored in labelled bags. A slow routine, it was like digging with a teaspoon. The prolonged tedium helped to enhance the excitement when something was found, whether a bone from an animal eaten long ago, or the chips of a shaped stone once used as an implement.

Outside the small cluster of tents at night, under the sparkling stars, there was high discussion. Mulvaney said that we were camped on the banks of Australia's Nile, and here, with luck, a leap in knowledge could take place. In the morning the patient excavating was resumed. Sometimes kindly old Mr Fromm would walk from his farmhouse to inspect activity in the cave. His idea of classifying was simple. When I described to him a local snake and asked what species it was, he exclaimed: 'That's an ordinary snake!'

On a long-awaited day a newcomer with strong muscles arrived at our camp. Felix Raab was a brilliant history student who had recently made a public stir in the Myer Emporium in Bourke Street when, in front of a curious crowd, he allowed his beard to be tackled by a new brand of electric razor. His beard gone, he said, 'I feel like a peeled orange.' He was soon to do research on Machiavelli at Oxford. On a summer holiday in the Italian Alps, he fell to his death.

Archaeology in our land was to gain enormously from an innovation known as radiocarbon dating which, then in its infancy, was being practised in a few laboratories in the United States. There, two samples of carbon dug from the lower part of our cave eventually arrived for examination. At last – long after we had all gone home – the first analysis reached Mulvaney. His cave contained the oldest evidence, so far found, of the Aborigines' presence in Australia. They had begun to live beneath the cave's high ceiling, about 5000 years ago. Into that cave they had first carried their river fish, newly killed kangaroos and fresh yams at a time when Rome and Athens were not even paddocks. Carbon remaining from their cooking fires enabled accurate dating of when they had first inhabited the cave.

Mulvaney's successful excavation promoted searches elsewhere. He himself in Queensland pushed the date back to 15 000 years. His friend Jim Bowler, another South Gippsland boy, doubled that span of time after his discoveries at Lake Mungo. By the early 1970s some experts were confidently speculating that Aborigines had lived in this continent for at least 40 000 years. Few finds did as much to underwrite the rising respect for Aboriginal people as this evidence of their antiquity. Mulvaney himself had done so much to prove that they had a long chronological history.

Meanwhile, around the university the gregarious low-cost social life bubbled along. On evenings at the weekend, lecturers put on parties in the inner suburbs with chairs for their guests, whereas at the student parties, most guests sat on the floor and heard music from a gramophone and drank cheap flagons of claret and port in scavenged glasses. It was a Saturday night when I was invited to one of these informal parties by Judy and Evan Jones, a rising poet; and in the course of pouring beer I spilt a dash over the dress of a very attractive girl.

Her name was Ann Heriot; she was five years younger than me, and was most of the way through a combined honours course in English and history. I first asked her if she would 'go out with me', as the saying was, on Anzac Day in 1956. That national day still conveyed the air of a Sunday, and few eating houses were open: not that many restaurants were open even on a roaring Saturday night. After calling at her parents' house in East Malvern, where I was no doubt inspected, I drove to a fashionable but not expensive Italian restaurant standing above the Young & Jackson Hotel, and run by Dante Triaca, late of Italy. Parking was still free and easy, and we left the car at the kerbside opposite the Flinders Street railway station. We quickly found that we had a lot in common: she had an excellent memory and her knowledge of English history and literature was superior to mine, but I soon guessed that she was not as interested in Australian history.

A Saturday or two later, I invited Ann to see a match in which Geelong was playing Hawthorn at the skinny Glenferrie Oval: she had not often been to the football. On 22 June I was sufficiently in favour to be invited to her twenty-first birthday, with her father presiding. Working first as an officer in the merchant navy in the era of deep-sea sail, he had entered the Australian navy in the First World War, and been the naval officer in charge of the port of Melbourne and nearby coastline in the Second. Frank Heriot, not innately an extrovert, was the heart and soul of a party, once it gathered speed – a time that he ensured was quick in arriving. The Commander, as he was called, spoke in a quarterdeck voice. When he lifted up a phone and spoke he gave the impression that he could manage without the help of the telephone wires.

Ann's mother had been brought up on a farm between Ballarat and Bendigo, and Ann and I sometimes visited it. We seemed to be driving everywhere. On one expedition, in rain and cold, we drove John and Jean Mulvaney to see the abandoned Aboriginal stone quarry at Mount William, the first time John inspected that ancient site which lay, forgotten, in the paddock of a Lancefield farmer. Stone axes from there, we later learnt, were traded far and wide in ancient Australia.

Eventually I asked Ann's father, as the custom was, whether I could marry her; she had already said yes to me. Ann was an Anglican – she had studied at Korowa Church of England Girls' School – and so we were married in the bluestone Anglican church of St George in Malvern one Friday evening in February 1957. My father was generously allowed to take part in the marriage ceremony, and Ann's father and mother put on a great wedding breakfast. A few weeks after our marriage we set out to make our first home at Mount Isa, close to the Gulf of Carpentaria.

14

SPINIFEX AND GUINEAS

Sometimes we misread our atlas. Thus Mount Isa in Queensland is not far from the north Australian coast but its nearest state capital is in fact Adelaide, on the southern coast. Mount Isa lies further from Brisbane, its own capital city, than from various Indonesian ports. Therefore Mount Isa suffered from its remoteness when it became the most dynamic mining field in the continent in the 1950s. Among startlingly red ranges, huge lead-zinc-silver deposits lay next to massive deposits of copper, one of which was discovered below a school built in the confidence that its playgrounds would never be disturbed. The school has long since been swallowed by the mine.

George Fisher, the head of Mount Isa Mines, invited me to write its history while pioneers were still alive to tell their stories. George actually lived in the town, the only chairman of a major mining company since the days of Bendigo and Ballarat to live at the mine rather than in a large coastal city. Having gained his underground experience at Broken Hill, he was skilled in industrial negotiations which at that stormy field was almost a martial art. He was not yet fifty when he arrived to lead Mount Isa into a new era.

I made my first visit to Mount Isa late in 1956, just before the Olympic Games were opened in Melbourne. Approaching in the plane from Sydney, I did not anticipate that the landscape would be fiery. After circling hills tinted red by the sunset, the aircraft touched down just before dusk. As soon as the door was opened, hot air poured in. Soon I was being driven along a narrow plain towards the town, while darkness set in with tropical swiftness. But not far ahead the mills and smelter and big buildings and high chimneys were so illuminated that they resembled a huge passenger ship at anchor.

Next day, meeting George Fisher for the first time, I was impressed. He struck a rapport with strangers without a hint of effort. While this was a formal era in clothing, he did not normally wear a suit coat at Mount Isa – just a white shirt which might be speckled with red dust at the end of the day. His own single-storey office, of wood and iron, was spartan, as was an adjacent shed which shaded his long car. His large Spanish-style house, on the rocky edge of the town, was called Casa Grande, and there his wife Eileen entertained all kinds of visitors. When directors came from New York or Sydney her open-air parties were spectacular, with ice-cold beer the favoured drink in the evening. Forthright but hospitable, Mrs Fisher was to die in an air crash in western Queensland in 1966. George, who was knighted in the following year, was to live well beyond his 100th birthday, and his second wife Marie remains a special friend.

George had the knack of striking a balance between present and past. A nationalist, he felt deep respect for what earlier Australians had achieved in mining but was determined that his generation should do even better. At that time a giant New York firm, originally founded by the Guggenheims, held the controlling interest in Mount Isa, but eventually he helped to achieve control for Australian shareholders. Today, alas, the mine is in Swiss hands.

Fascinated by history, George insisted I should look not only at his mines but also at a primitive outback camp so that I could imagine what infant Mount Isa must have been like. When the chance arose for me to visit a remote new mine in the Northern Territory, I jumped at it. His company was exploring a large zinc-lead deposit at the McArthur River, near the derelict town of Borroloola. The only port on a long stretch of the Gulf of Carpentaria, Borroloola once was known for possessing a fine public library, presented by the American millionaire Andrew Carnegie and housed in the iron courthouse. The town originally had a freakish ratio of books to residents – until the white ants ate the shelves, or borrowers left the district with books under their arm. Bill Harney, who won a name as a storyteller in the heyday of radio, once spent three months in the local jail, but as compensation he had access to the town's library, and it provided one of the turning points in his life: 'As night fell and we couldn't read any more, we would discuss far into the night the things we had read about that day', he recalled. His recollections made me eager to see Borroloola and thereabouts.

A small Proctor aircraft was to set out from Mount Isa at 7.30 in the morning. In the plane the pilot and a geologist sat in the two front seats and I shared the two back seats with a wooden case of oranges which had to be delivered to an outback camp. The plane, as it took off, reminded me of a Baby Austin car, tossed about by gusts of wind. Often looking out the small windows before consulting the map on his knee, the pilot shouted, above the roar of the engine, the name of a river or a hill that he recognised in the roadless country below. When we landed to deliver supplies at a prospecting camp near a lagoon on Corinda cattle station, a burly man came towards us: he had a dusty beard, shirt hanging out, pants at half-mast, and no boots or shoes. An Irishman, he had the billy on the boil, ready to give us tea.

Boarding the plane again we sat tight as it bounced along the dusty airstrip before soaring suddenly. Flying across a sweeping, dry expanse of country, we saw the rugged ranges called the 'China Wall' in one direction and the distant sea in another before we landed on a makeshift airstrip maybe 15 kilometres from the McArthur River mining camp. Several Aborigines, one of whom was smoking a large pipe, were ready to help when the plane landed near a row of petrol drums. In the afternoon we called at a nearby cattle station where the barefoot owner was tinkering with the engine of an old army truck. His homestead was almost roofless. While waiting for the roof to be repaired, he had pitched a tent in the front room.

Along a bumpy road we reached the prospecting camp where four or five tents sat alongside a bark-roofed storehouse containing enough food to last four months – in case the monsoonal floods isolated the camp. Five men were at work, sinking shallow shafts. The scene seemed almost a replica of early Mount Isa. When darkness descended, with the heat and humidity still overbearing, we gathered for dinner and talk in a shed clad with flywire. The big ore body they were exploring was rich but difficult and remote. More than thirty years would pass before barges carried the zinc to deep-sea ships anchored in the Gulf of Carpentaria.

After a few weeks at Mount Isa, I flew to Townsville, the nearest port, and then to Melbourne. There, to my intense satisfaction, I met John Campbell Miles, who had discovered the minerals at Mount Isa. Now in his early seventies and enjoying his rather solitary life, he had not before explained in detail how he came to find one of the world's great mining fields. Though he possessed a retentive memory, most of his recollections had to be gently squeezed out of him. Often his hesitant flow of words was halted while he relit his pipe, a task to which he gave total attention, for he did not like wasting a match. Frugal in an engaging way, he liked simple foods such as toasted raisin bread and had a connoisseur's eye for a large lump of boiled mutton.

Having worked at a variety of jobs in the mining fields and sheep country in the eastern half of the continent, he was truly the jack-of-all-trades. He had stamina, whether carrying a swag or making a long journey with horses. In 1908, in the hope of joining a new gold rush, he even rode a bike all the way to Far North Queensland from Broken Hill. He recalled how, along the dusty road, the tyres were punctured severely by thorns or sharp stones and he filled them with dry grass.

In 1923, the momentous year of his life, he was travelling with a riding horse and packhorses when he stopped to camp beside a lonely bush road between Cloncurry and the border of the Northern Territory. Close to his makeshift camp, on his very first day, he observed a heavy, dark-coloured rock which he broke up with his horseshoeing hammer. He rightly surmised it was rich in silver and lead. And so Mount Isa was born.

Miles had his own way of measuring time, and each particular year was engraved on his memory with the name of the horse that won the Melbourne Cup. After he had recalled an episode or incident, I would often ask, 'And what year was that?' After a pause, perhaps after peering down to chip charcoal from the inside of his pipe, he would look up and say, 'Now, that was the year Sister Olive won the Cup.'

Eventually I showed him a long typewritten draft I had written about his first months at Mount Isa. He read it word by word, and seemed more intent on how I described his horses and his equipment than himself. His deeply felt criticism was that I had assigned to one horse the wrong sex.

As some thirty years had passed since he lived at Mount Isa he was eager to see what had happened to his discovery. George Fisher asked me to arrange his air tickets but Miles had no intention of flying, and gave me a variety of ingenious reasons why he would not travel in an aircraft. He was sympathetic, however, to the idea of driving overland with his brother Steve, and I easily gained the consent of George to buy him a new station wagon in place of the ancient jalopy he drove: promptly George sent me a cheque for the wagon. So the discoverer set out to cross the continent. Arriving at last in the bustling town on the site of his discovery, he was greeted as a benefactor, and his hand was shaken and his photo taken a thousand times.

Meanwhile, it was March 1957, and Ann and I set out to live for some months at Mount Isa. In the mining boom the population was growing so rapidly that there was no house for us, save a small bachelor's hut sitting up a gully all alone. Ann was not overjoyed, and George promised he would quickly find us a house: 'Please could you come back in a week?' He provided us with a large Dodge utility – the company must have owned several hundred vehicles – and we set out to cross the red ranges to Cloncurry, the nearest town. The road was called the roughest in the continent, as the Redex around-Australia car rally had just discovered. We crossed creeks with no bridges, skidded down steep hills and bumped over large boulders, the rust-coloured dust trailing us. There was no other traffic except for a van carrying two men who, we learned later, were wanted by the police. The most memorable sight was a rocky ridge in the late afternoon light where a dingo stood still with a commanding dignity and stared at our truck.

Visiting the ghost copper-towns to the south of Cloncurry we drove along dismantled railway tracks and saw huge steam boilers sitting in the sun, the other machinery all gone. The towns' boom days were in the First World War, and much of their copper must have ended up in munitions factories or in the scarred earth of battlefields on the Western Front. At night we slept on the tray of the truck, under the stars: there was no prospect of rain, and it was too dry for mosquitoes. For breakfast we lit a fire and cooked in a frying pan and boiled the tea water in a billy. A brand-new house, simply furnished, and a truckful of red soil for a garden were waiting for us at Mount Isa when we returned.

People who had lived their life on the cattle stations or mining fields of the north-west of Queensland were proud of what they had achieved and eager to see it recorded. On some Sunday afternoons we would follow a dusty road to visit Arthur Campbell. An old widower, his cattle had been thinly scattered across the hills of Mount Isa long before there was a mine.

On the simple verandah he would be waiting for us, dressed in his Sunday best, with spotless white trousers, white shirt and white hat. As a mark of honour for special guests he would have the teapot ready on the kitchen table, the cups and saucers arranged, and a new tin of condensed milk. Ann was his favourite visitor. He would tell her of the life lived by him and his wife and children in the years before the First

World War when their house lay further away, amid lonely ranges: how their little daughter Chubby died far from medical help, how he himself dug the grave not far from the homestead, and how eventually a camel driver arrived with the headstone for their daughter's grave, a headstone carved and inscribed in a town hundreds of miles away.

About the future of this region an intense debate was being waged: what should be done with that vast tropical territory that extended more than a thousand miles west of the north Queensland sugar fields and the coastal spine of the Great Dividing Range? 'Here,' I wrote in my forthcoming book, 'the sun is merciless, the rains sparse, the distances vast, and most rivers are dry wrinkles on the earth.' This tropical expanse was almost as large as India but held few people. It was then the belief of all political parties that Australia had to develop and populate the more fertile parts of this vast region, but they were reluctant to accept that the cost of development would be high indeed. My view was that the history of Mount Isa, the success story of the region, showed how high was the price – 'a price which the nation did not want to pay'. In the following forty years the rise of the powerful green movement and the birth of Aboriginal land rights provided a new blueprint for tropical Australia, but the old dilemma remains: what is the future for this vast region, much of which sits opposite one of the most densely populated parts of the world?

Not long after my book was published, Campbell Miles was to make what was to be his last journey to Mount Isa, and at his request I went with him. Travelling for five days and nights, we changed trains at Sydney and Brisbane, Townsville and Charters Towers. He kept in his pyjama pocket a paper bag of boiled lollies, and during the night I would hear from below – he occupied the lower bunk – the rustling of paper as he fumbled for another sticky lolly.

Back home again, he settled down, with two of his sisters, on the plains near Melton, a rural village that is now a major suburb of Melbourne. The house, standing on its high wooden blocks, lacked front doorsteps, and when I called on him he explained that he had plans to build them: he was never one to rush events. Then one day the sad news came: he had cancer. When first I saw him in the Bacchus Marsh Hospital he was stoical, but after he was moved to a bed in Ringwood he quickly faded.

One afternoon in December 1965 I saw him for the last time. Propped up by pillows in an old-time iron bedstead, he resembled a pirate, for his glass eye had been removed and his bushy eyebrows were untrimmed. He grasped my hand and held it for minutes. Next day he died; he was aged eighty-two. I rang the ABC, and his death was announced on the national radio news at 10 p.m. He was the last of that breed of lone prospectors who, travelling with a horse or two, made discoveries that changed the nation.

Perhaps sixty friends and relatives attended the funeral. Some had come from the far inland, bringing memories of when he camped at this waterhole or shoed that packhorse in a shady spot beside a road. A forgotten generation assembled to pay tribute and swap yarns. George Fisher, chairman of the company, came all the way from Mount Isa – a return journey of two days – to take off his hat as the hearse departed.

Miles's partner during the first year at Mount Isa had been Bill Simpson. A returned soldier invalided home from France, the ginger-bearded Simpson was a joker and spender. Upon receiving his share of the proceeds from the sale of the original Mount Isa discovery he travelled across country from Duchess to Brisbane in one of the most expensive taxi journeys ever made in Australia. On the way, with the same impulsive generosity, he bought drinks for all and sundry until, crossing a street in Brisbane, he was accidentally killed. For four decades there was no connection or contact between Miles and any member of the Simpson family. Now, determined to attend the funeral, a younger brother of Bill Simpson made his way from the Riverina. After the funeral we met in Lygon Street in Carlton and had lunch together, Fisher and Simpson and me.

In the long era when so many jobs were created by rich mining fields – jobs in the mines and jobs in the cities – the discoverers of those fields were folk heroes, and deservedly so. Without aid from the public purse, they created what governments often tried to create at considerable expense: a host of new jobs. I am not sure what, in the public mind, is today's popular equivalent to the discoverer. Perhaps it is the pop star and the music group. But while they have fame, they exert less economic influence on the wellbeing of the average Australian than did Charles Rasp of Broken Hill, Paddy Hannan of Kalgoorlie and Campbell Miles of Mount Isa.

George Fisher, though a most persuasive individual, must have had trouble persuading the New York directors that they should allow my book to be published. I heard nothing for a long time. In 1960 it came out at last, in Sydney. It was called *Mines in the Spinifex*, that being the name of the tall prickly grass so common in that dry part of Queensland. Updated several times, and reprinted at least seven times, the book is still in print.

When the National Bank, then one of the big five banks, invited me to write its history, I knew almost nothing about banking. When I learnt that the book had to be published on the day of the bank's centenary – just fourteen months away – I remained more confident than was advisable. In that era, the editing and printing of a full-size book normally occupied eight to ten months. I was so eager to write it that I overlooked the fact that the deadline was impossible. Even in England where impressive histories had been written of the Bank of England and other banks, the task of research and writing usually took at least two years of full-time work. I can't understand why I slid into such a spider's web.

The National Bank offered me the handsome sum of £3000 for the task. As a gesture, they turned the pounds into guineas. The guinea, a sum of money then in its dotage and surviving mostly on accounts submitted by lawyers and surgeons, equalled one pound and one shilling. The bank, because time was precious, offered help with the research. Two talented young university graduates, Deirdre Hartnett and Margaret Rendell, were eventually engaged to investigate the bank's history since the First World War, while a regular officer of the bank, the faithful Colin Pollock, rounded up old records in remote branches. Rarely in my life have I had the help of research assistants, but probably I was too young and inexperienced to gain the most from their willingness and eagerness.

Wearing a dark or grey suit each day, I was set up in a managerial room in the head office with high windows looking down upon the classiest strip of Collins Street. At the same hour each morning a British butler wearing a white coat knocked at my door and came forward with a cheerful grin and placed on my desk a hot cup of tea and a small plate containing a few fingers of buttered white bread. I was working so hard that after a few days I hardly noticed his silent coming and going. Full of cheek and eager to chat, he rightly resented my absorption in my work. He looked at the piles of leather-bound ledgers and letter books piled on my desk and – so he told me later – regarded them as enemies. To me they were friends. I was enthralled by the stories they told of youthful managers arriving at remote gold rushes with a revolver, an iron safe and a pile of gold sovereigns, and promptly opening a bank.

'Rowley' Mountain, the chief economist of the bank, and his wife, Lyndsay, became friends to Ann and me. Sometimes they invited us to dinner in their rambling house in Spring Road, Malvern, where, in addition to their older daughters, their friends 'Ref' and Betty Kemp were usually present. Kemp was Australia's leading ideological exponent of private enterprise – so long as it behaved itself – and Betty was gracious and captivating. The Kemps' sons, David and Rod, then at school, were to become members of the Liberal ministry led by John Howard four decades later.

One morning I was invited, with only ten minutes' notice, to join the National Bank's annual general meeting: the attendance was small and needed boosting. Opposite the sprinkling of shareholders sat the directors, and Stanley Melbourne Bruce was with them. Long a resident of England – and indeed a member of the War Cabinet under Winston Churchill – he represented the National's London board, and this was probably his last visit to the land of which he had been for six years the prime minister. A trifle deaf, he leaned forward to hear more clearly. Informed, after the meeting was over, that I was writing the history of the bank, he recalled that when he was aged about ten his father, a wealthy Melbourne importer, had been almost ruined by the crashing of the banks. He hoped – a friendly gesture on his part – that I would 'get to the bottom' of that memorable event of 1893. I'm not sure whether I did quite reach the bottom, but I was fortunate to be the first historian to write, from a mass of confidential records, an inside picture of how that banking disaster occurred.

The banks bob up and down in public esteem, and when I wrote they were bobbing up. Their staff had successfully fought the attempt led by Labor's Ben Chifley to nationalise all the private banks, and most Australians rejoiced in or felt some sense of relief at the banks' victory. Moreover the banks were seen as rewarding their customers as much as their shareholders, and their branches were everywhere: they maintained too many branches. In the richer rural districts a road junction with only one hotel, one general store and a butcher might have its own bank. The average customer, without quite realising it, paid a high price in order to keep open this astonishing spread of rural branches. If today (late in 2018) I were writing a history of a bank, I might feel myself a social outcast, for the Hayne royal commission is exposing some of the misdeeds of the big four banks; but in that far-off time I felt some pride. The sense of loyalty inside the banks was impressive, and a typical young man worked in the same bank for his whole career.

I worked hard at my research, with few breaks. At lunchtime I took a stroll down Collins Street for maybe ten minutes, and bought a beetroot sandwich and a lamington which I ate in my room before resuming work. At night, for a month or two, I was still completing the last pages of my history of Mount Isa, the deadline for which was around the corner. When Easter came, and Ann went with her parents to Lorne for a holiday, I stayed behind, writing even on Good Friday. Desperate to make up lost time I was nonetheless writing with ease, indeed with deep pleasure.

I had not commenced full-time work at the bank until the last months of 1957. Before long, the book's publisher, Ted Harris of Georgian House, said he must be in possession of my completed typescript by the end of June. Already I was writing early chapters before I had done research on the middle chapters, and I had written only about forty pages of a book that was eventually to reach 430 pages. I consoled myself that the research on the bank's later years would not be so time-consuming, but eventually it became clear that the research on such later themes as the world depression of the early 1930s and the Chifley Government's attempt to nationalise the trading banks in the late 1940s would also be demanding.

The early chapters were set in metallic type, and the galleys and the page proofs corrected, while I was writing the later chapters. This was like writing with handcuffs on. In the era before the word processor and other techniques replaced the traditional setting of every page in metal type inside the printery, a book in the making was alterable only at high expense once it entered the production stages. About eighteen chapters were already set in type, and mostly in numbered pages, when I was still writing the last half-dozen chapters.

Years afterwards my memory became fixed on the belief that I had almost met the bank's deadline. One's memory, however, like a sentry on duty, sometimes falls asleep. The book, called *Gold and Paper*, was not ready in time for the day of the centenary, 4 October 1958, though it was printed and bound before the season of Christmas parties began.

The bank crashes of 1893 and the accompanying depression were such a landmark in people's lives that my book, when published, stirred older businessmen. It so happened that Australia's economy was again becoming overheated. The high priest of stockbrokers, Staniforth Ricketson of the well-known finance house J. B. Were, reading my account of the turbulent 1890s, issued a public warning and quoted my narrative to bolster his views. I was ill-equipped to comment on the health of the present economy, but he optimistically thought that

I might bring insights from the past and invited me to lunch in his office. It was all I could do to master the courtly etiquette of his table; and when a white-coated retainer placed a bowl of fresh fruit before us, and on the white cloth in front of me he set down a special fruit knife for peeling apples and bananas, I had to pretend that I didn't like fruit rather than admit that I could not handle this oddly shaped knife.

Ricketson could sniff the economic air; his premonition of economic trouble was correct. Late in 1960 a series of harsh measures labelled as the Credit Squeeze had to be imposed by the Menzies Government. They were so unpopular that Menzies was in danger at the next federal election, which he won only through the last-minute victory of that eloquent politician James Killen in his Queensland seat of Moreton. After the postal votes came in, Killen won by a mere 110 votes.

I tried to follow the rule that I would not approach a major company in order to enquire whether it might be interested in having its history written. It was preferable for me to be approached by the company. In such a situation my bargaining position would be stronger, and I could explain at the outset that I would write only a history of the company that was, as far as possible, fair and true. The risk of waiting to be invited was that I might spend a lot of time waiting. In the second half of the 1950s I did not have to wait long. Even before I had finished *Gold and Paper*, I was invited to write the history of Imperial Chemical Industries of Australia and New Zealand, a mouthful of a name best known by its initials.

Peter Ryan, who was head of its public relations, then a new profession, believed that the history of the big company should be investigated and perhaps publicised. In later careers he was to be the head of Melbourne University Press and then a political commentator who in the words of Les Carlyon displayed 'the toughness and clarity of Orwell', and a literary critic remembered for the campaign he conducted in the 1990s against Manning Clark's books. But when I first met Ryan he was unknown in literary circles. Busily in his spare time he was completing the extraordinary story of how as a teenage soldier in wartime New Guinea he risked his life operating behind the lines of the invading Japanese army. His book was called *Fear Drive My Feet*, for it was on foot – sometimes bare feet – that he crossed the tropical mountains on a wartime patrol, only to be trapped by the enemy. His companion Les Howlett was shot dead by hidden Japanese soldiers but Peter escaped, hiding in a muddy swamp while, within his hearing, the armed soldiers searched for him.

His wartime book was published while I was working for him. Now a classic, it was notable for the publicity heralding its birth. For that event Peter and his wife Davey had invited down from Port Moresby a brave wartime colleague, Sergeant-Major Kari, now of the Papuan Constabulary. In Melbourne, the handsome black face of the broad-shouldered Manus Islander was much photographed and his homely remarks were enjoyed. One of his requests was to inspect Pentridge prison to see where 'the white fellows' were locked up.

When I joined his company, it had just moved into a monumental glasshouse, the first real skyscraper built in Melbourne for more than sixty years. There I was allotted a room – or rather I was shown to a space within a vast room in which female employees wore stylish uniforms of Prussian blue. This was the era when the cult of open living was capturing modern architects, and nearly all internal partitions – and even personal privacy – were seen as individualistic intrusions. Only the most senior employees were allocated their own space, hidden by walls.

The company's glass tower was the head office for a range of factories, spread across Australia and New Zealand and making chemicals, explosives and ammunition, fertilisers, plastics, soda ash, phosphorus, synthetic ammonia, paints and even zip fasteners. Its activities had commenced in Victoria in the 1870s as a maker of explosives for the Bendigo goldminers, and had expanded into most corners of the economy. There was an air of competence in all its operations. Tariff protection, especially from the 1920s onwards, became an additional backstop. I was inclined to think, rightly or wrongly, that the firm – like most Australian manufacturers of the time – received too much protection; and my history must have sometimes emphasised that point. The company decided not to publish my typescript, at least 'in the near future'. They kept their promise.

If my finished work had bubbled with excitement and had also offered deep insights into the rise of Australian manufacturing and the links between politics and big business, I would have prayed that it would become a printed book and see the light of day. But the story, on which I spent one full year, appealed largely to those who worked in the company or bought its products. I could not seriously complain when the manuscript was placed in a locked filing cabinet, for I received my full fee; moreover there had been, from the outset, no firm commitment that the company would publish it. As the era of effective photocopying had not yet arrived I did not retain my own copy of the history, but by chance I did receive one more than half a century later. Reading it I was rather pleased; the story was more readable than I had imagined, though I am not always an impartial judge.

It was odd to spend a whole year on a book and yet reach only six or eight readers: but that happens to many authors. One reader did respond in writing. Miss Thelma Marks was a loyal and intelligent secretary or 'personal assistant' who, after spending her working life with the firm, retired about the time my typescript was handed in. A short time later it was lent to her in the hope that from her long experience she might offer confidential comments or corrections. Eventually she wrote to Peter Ryan a two-page reply, meticulous in its typing and capped with a slightly ornate signature. She was not sure, however, about the request that she offer an opinion and any corrections:

> I don't know if I can make you understand that I found this rather difficult: it was all so interesting and there was so much which was quite new to me as well as that which was of course familiar, that somehow I was so carried along in the narrative that I found my critical faculty as to accuracy or otherwise was more or less dormant.

Some professors and many company chairmen today are incapable of composing such a delicate, complicated sentence and guiding it to a safe landing.

Miss Marks, after hesitating, did make a suggestion: 'There is just one criticism (if such it may be termed) which I think I should make, though doubtless it is quite a minor one as far as the history itself is concerned.' She had noticed that in writing about Sir Lennon Raws, for years the chief executive, I had called him 'almost eccentric in his aloofness', adding that he once instructed his staff not to greet him or even outwardly recognise him when they passed him in Collins Street. Miss Marks, maybe quite correctly – I now have no means of knowing where I obtained my facts – thought that my description of Sir Lennon was out of keeping with the man whose letters she had typed and whose telephone she had answered during so many years: 'I would like to register a protest – I'm quite unable to reconcile such an action with my knowledge of Sir Lennon – it was entirely foreign to him: whatever his failings may have been, he was neither vain nor pompous.'

She wondered whether my source of information had walked along the street at a time when Sir Lennon was walking to or from a conference and was therefore 'abstracted and deep in thought'.

I respected the letter written by Miss Marks. If my history is ever published, the offending page will be so rewritten that Sir Lennon, when he walks along Collins Street, does nod to his employees. If the passer-by is Thelma Marks, he will even smile.

Just before this history of the chemical company was completed, a momentous event happened. On 3 September 1959 our daughter, Anna, was born, in the Mercy Hospital in East Melbourne. As I soon lacked a paid job, I was free in the early afternoon to wheel her pram proudly around the streets of East Ivanhoe in the hope that she would finally fall asleep.

I was optimistic that something would turn up, perhaps an invitation to write a book. Not for one moment did I believe that my writing future was uncertain. So when a travelling salesman knocked at the door and wished to sell the latest edition of the *Encyclopaedia Britannica*, we bought the twenty-four heavy leather-like volumes without hesitation, though we perhaps paid for it in instalments rather than in a lump sum. A minor bonus: the Chicago editors of the same encyclopedia later invited me to update several of their articles on Australia. Much later I joined their advisory board.

Realising the value of sound reference works, I bought in subsequent years various encyclopedias including the wonderful 1910–11 edition, printed on rice paper before the *Britannica*'s office was moved from Cambridge to Chicago. At home, encircled by books, I assumed that my writing career, so precarious, would flourish.

15

A RUSH THAT NEVER ENDED

The rushes of mineral seekers to dusty deserts and green valleys were close to the heart of our history. Rushes were so widespread that the surface of virtually every little corner of the nation had been explored by gold-seekers before the time of the First World War. Few nations had been so influenced by the discovery of minerals, but no book told that history. I myself hoped to write it. I did not yet realise that, covering so much territory and so many different minerals, it would be difficult to assemble and to write. That was why even in the mineral-rich United States, no worthwhile history of mining had been attempted.

Sir George Fisher, always a good friend, and a few of his colleagues who headed the Australian mining industry raised money enabling me to do my research and to meet the high cost of travel. Quickly I made my travel plans. To Broken Hill I went first, with hopes high. In 1961 it was still a 'silver city' with a population of 30 000 and professional talents such as no Australian mining field had so far assembled. I felt exhilarated to stand on the broken hill – or what remained of it – and look across the arid reddish plains. In the course of my stay I visited countless surface ruins and closely watched men at work in deep mines. I visited the shipshape cemetery with its obelisk engraved with the prayer 'Workers of the World Unite', and the city memorial honouring the musicians who played as the *Titanic* went down in the chilled Atlantic Ocean in 1912.

Maurie Mawby, whose company ran two of the four big underground mines, arranged for his fiery old friend 'Floss' Campbell to drive me in his runabout truck around the district; we saw the ghost town of Silverton, the fading opal town of White Cliffs, and ancient Aboriginal waterholes and rock carvings along dead-end tracks. Much of Floss's working life had been spent in humble jobs in the mines but like many other Broken Hill people he had enthusiastically gained knowledge, vast in total, about such diverse topics as mineralogy, native plants and the Aborigines' stone implements, one of which – a large, smooth axe – he presented to me. Radical politics had once absorbed him; and an hour before a local crowd assembled in a big local theatre he had secretly climbed into the ceiling, lowered himself down the long chain that held an ornamental lamp illuminating the crowd below, and hung there, interjecting loudly during each speech. 'That was one night when they failed,' he said, 'to throw me out of the hall.' He spoke as if he was normally thrown out.

Broken Hill, which for many years employed more people than any other mining field in Australia, paid high wages. Skilled miners in Britain had a much lower standard of living than their counterparts in the silver-lead mines at Broken Hill. On the other hand, facets of its way of life were spartan. In summer the corrugated-iron houses were so warm that a man working the night shift, on arriving home, often was unable to go to sleep. In earlier years when the shallow or oxidised ore was being mined, there was a danger of lead poisoning for those working in mines or smelters. Rarely did the mining field hold more than 35 000 inhabitants but it was, for about twenty years, one of the world's more ingenious small cities, being the main inventor and developer of a metallurgical process called 'flotation', which employed millions of bubbles to separate minerals from the ground-down barren rock and then to separate one mineral from another. Flotation plants, often on a huge scale, can today be seen around the world. I later wrote a book, *The Rise of Broken Hill*, about the town's history and way of life.

In 1961 I spent weeks in Western Australia. On the narrow-gauge train to the goldfields I shared a sleeping compartment with a policeman returning after escorting a prisoner to Perth. As he had assured me that the goldfields were a depressing sight, I was pleasingly surprised by the scatter of tall bushes and trees and the shining trunks of the salmon gums near Coolgardie – though, further on at Kalgoorlie, the huge dumps of discarded tailings resembled flat-topped burial mounds.

I spent days in the deep underground workings of the Golden Mile – walking in an eerie silence along mile after mile of abandoned workings, or being deafened by the chattering of the rock drills in the busier parts of the mine. The ore being low grade, gold was not to be seen with the naked eye; but at the Perseverance mine I was shown, after an iron safe was unlocked, a sugar bag containing specimens brought from Coolgardie. Most were lumps of gold set deep in the white quartz rock, like delicate jewels displayed on the white neck of a woman. It was the aesthetic as well as the monetary worth of certain gold specimens that once excited many Australians, and when these small nuggets or rocks in their native state were displayed in the windows of city jewellers they would attract crowds of spectators.

At Western Mining's guesthouse, a rambling weatherboard building in a suburb, I stayed for a week. There Sir Lindesay Clark, the chairman of that gold company, was also staying. Lanky, soft-speaking and slow-moving, he was a considerate host, and quietly convivial as a companion though he was twice my age. When I returned from my day at the mine or library he talked freely about the geology of the West Australian goldfields, a region in which he rejoiced. Most experts said that the fields were probably in permanent decline but he thought differently and he was correct. Nobody was to do more to revive the gold region. He enjoyed history, which of course is the young sister of geology: both topics are absorbed in the sequence of events though they lack all the evidence they need. When travelling, Clark carried a volume of Gibbon's *Decline and Fall*, and at the dinner table he argued eagerly about the historical theories advanced in many volumes by Arnold Toynbee. As I had recently met Toynbee, that enchanced my worth in Clark's eyes.

Guests came to dinner; and from the head of the table Clark would ring a handbell that summoned the housekeeper, Mrs Marie Eyles, to clear the plates and bring in the next course. One night, dining alone, I rang the bell and hid under the table. Mrs Eyles answered but could find nobody in the room. Twice I rang the bell and then hid. Clark – normally serious – laughed again and again when he heard about this prank.

On another night, in the warm twilight Clark held a garden party. I was put in charge of the drinks which flowed like water. His only complaint, when all the guests had gone, was a querulous aside: 'Who invited the bishop?'

Now in his mid-sixties he sometimes gave acquaintances the impression, quite false, that he was enamoured more with the past than present. His Western Mining Corporation, which did not earn large profits, was seen by some as a dying company, for it was tied to gold, but Clark was especially attracted to the intellectual riddles facing his geologists and believed in exploration more ardently than perhaps any other mining leader of his day. His senior geologist Don Campbell dined with us one night and spoke of the latest results from exploring the countless deposits of bauxite in the ranges near Perth. Clark was about to fly to Pittsburgh to discuss these discoveries with the heads of Alcoa, the world's biggest aluminium firm; and from that meeting sprang the huge Western Australian bauxite mines and alumina refineries as well as the smelters at Geelong and Portland. If, in any part of the globe, you flew in a jumbo jet or opened an aluminium food can, the chances at one time were one in seven that its aluminium was the product of the venture that Clark initiated.

In various remote corners of the continent other discoveries were in the air: Australia was at a turning point. Of these events about to unfold I had an inkling, and I visited many of the townships and sites that were soon to boom. I spent Easter of 1961 at Port Hedland, in the corrugated-iron Pier Hotel. What was soon to become a huge iron-ore port, the haven for the largest cargo ships ever to enter Australian waters, was then dilapidated and sleepy. A few Aborigines were fishing from the nondescript pier: no ship was to be seen. The manager of the hotel assured me that it was an exceptionally busy weekend because so many visitors had arrived from the struggling goldmine at Marble Bar to spend Easter near the sea. Some of the visitors slept on the verandah, under cotton eiderdowns, for there were not enough rooms to go around. A pregnant half-dingo slept under one bed; a huge cattle dog slept outside the room next to mine.

This tropical port was isolated. I enquired at the post office if I could ring Melbourne, only to be told that they could not even hear a phone call to Perth with clarity, let alone one to Melbourne. I then flew to Yampi Sound where I saw the monstrous tides sweep in and out.

In the Northern Territory I hoped to meet Jack White who twelve years previously had discovered uranium at Rum Jungle – the first such find in a region where was ultimately found several of the world's major deposits of high-grade uranium. White was elusive, until I learnt that he was confined to the leprosarium on an isolated arm of Darwin Harbour. The government had resolved that the image of the disease would be improved if official secrecy protected those who were receiving treatment. Therefore in order to gain permission to interview White, I had to call at the health office in Darwin and sign a document affirming that I would not publicly disclose his whereabouts.

At the leprosarium I found him sitting on the verandah of his own neat hut. Visitors must have been few, for he gave me such a welcome. It was not effusive: it was heartfelt. As we sat on the verandah, various Aborigines came up and shook me by the hand and, saying barely a word, went away. To touch another human being gave them pleasure. I was infected by the spirit of the occasion without knowing whether I was sensible in touching their hands. I was assured months later that there was little risk of a visitor being infected.

Now in his mid-fifties, White knew a lot about the history of Australian mining. He delivered with a poker face a hilarious account of how he squandered the money that he had earned from his discovery, including an impetuous ride in a taxi across a wide expanse of the Territory. He also explained, in answer to questions, exactly how he had discovered the green radioactive mineral sitting on the surface of the ground, and in my book I later published his version of his life story, to which the mineral bureaucracy in Canberra took exception, thinking its own staff deserved more praise for the discovery. Its head Sir Harold Raggatt announced that my version was mistaken. As I had actually visited White at the leprosarium and questioned him, I was not fully persuaded by a retort written from a desk in Canberra. I could not, however, publicly respond to Raggatt, because that would run the risk of disclosing where White presently lived. For more than thirty years I did not reveal that I had personally met White, let alone the place of our meeting.

I did not visit every living mining field or ghost town in Australia, but I saw most. None conveyed to me such a sense of magic as the site of the first large rush in 1851, the now-deserted bed and banks of the creek at Ophir, near Orange in New South Wales. Years later I returned there as the presenter for a documentary film; the atmosphere of the low hills was still compelling, and the same gold-bearing creek was trickling along.

A recession hit Australia at the start of the 1960s. The astonishing era of full employment, lasting almost twenty years, was temporarily halted. I felt unsure whether I could survive as a freelance writer. Contrary to what was often argued, Australians were eager readers when measured by world standards but there was one hitch: the population of readers was too small to provide a continuing income for all but a few authors.

My move away from full-time writing was spurred by chance. Out of the blue came an invitation to teach for one term at Adelaide

University. Ken Inglis, who taught Australian history there with skill and vast knowledge, wished to do research in the United States, and could find nobody to fill his shoes for a teaching term. Normally I would have said no, but in the gloomy economic climate I said yes. So in August 1961 my wife Ann and our two-year-old daughter Anna, after packing everything in our Holden station wagon, travelled with me to Adelaide where we rented a house in the hillside suburb of Wattle Park. It was a wonderful time, especially for Anna. Across the road lived the Bunney family and their three little children who proved to be wonderful neighbours.

In Adelaide I enjoyed the teaching and the students. Moreover on most days I could continue to write my history of mining or do research at the library.

Hugh Stretton, one of the most brilliant of Australian intellectuals – a description that he would have briskly disowned – ran the History Department; and only later did I realise that he ran in his benign way what was becoming probably the best of its kind in the nation. Near the end of my four months there he offered me a permanent job. While I was tempted I was also offered a job in Melbourne where we preferred to live. So early in the following year I became senior lecturer in economic history within the economics faculty at the University of Melbourne.

For me it was a long and slightly hazardous leap. Nearly all the students I taught were majoring in economics, and I knew little theoretical economics, having studied that subject only at school. Moreover I had no skill in the highbrow form of mathematics that was beginning to invade economics. Nonetheless I tried to fortify myself by reading in those branches of economic theory that I could understand. With a very bright undergraduate named Peter Jonson, who was to become head of research at the Reserve Bank early in the course of his influential career, I shared authorship of an article that seemed to undermine an important part of Keynes's economics. No overseas economics journal would publish it then, dismissing it as too radical. Now it would probably be seen as not even newsworthy.

Those economists partly understood by me included Keynes, Marshall, Jevons, Adam Smith and Roy Harrod, all of whom were masters of English prose. A decade or more later the declining mastery of clear English was to stem the influence of economists in national and international debate.

I began to teach the economic history of Australia, at first in a small half-filled lecture room. After a year, more students were attracted to the course, and also to the air of intellectual adventure gained from Allan Beever, a very serious young Oxford graduate who joined me in teaching the increasing numbers. Beever, whose father owned a bicycle shop in Huddersfield, explained in his Yorkshire accent some of those more complex themes I was almost incapable of teaching: and so we formed a useful team. The head of the department was Bill Woodruff, also from industrial England but by way of Illinois, and he was an eloquent first-year lecturer, many of his students moving on to our subject in their second year. For a time the teaching of economic history flourished, in a stimulating but unorthodox way, and the Melbourne department, by attracting many students in arts and law, must have become one of the larger teachers of economic history within the English-speaking world.

Many of the students worked in the city during the day and arrived by tram for the 5.15 p.m. lecture. One was a truck driver who parked his heavy vehicle in nearby Royal Parade or even inside the university's grounds; he became eventually the owner of one of the bigger transport firms in the nation. Weary after their day's work, some students had to be kept awake while others were eager to learn. Early on, I resolved that they should see the history that lay unrecognised; and on one or two Fridays in each year I would organise an excursion. All who owned cars would offer rides to the others, and we set out in a long convoy of forty or fifty cars to visit the deserted goldfields and waning towns around Ballarat, Creswick, Lal Lal, Mount Egerton, Newstead or Blackwood and other places near the Great Dividing Range. The eyes of the students lit up when, at the end of a lonely bush track, they found a small gold stamp-mill at work, or the remains of a blast furnace that had once glowed at night, or even an ancient arrangement of large Aboriginal stones in a circle. Sometimes we could crowd four or five historic sights into a day. At lunchtime, fires would be lit in a clearing, and the cheap chops and sausages provided by a friendly butcher would be cooked, and the bread and Boston buns and lamingtons eaten too. By the time the big billies were boiling and the hot tea was drunk, everybody knew almost everybody else.

A few days later, at the next lecture, I might hold aloft a copy of a newspaper from the locality and then read aloud, with a poker face, a vivid account of the picnic. The account had been scribbled by me and pasted on the unseen side of the paper. It was purported, however, to be the work of a local journalist who had eavesdropped on our visit. The reading aloud of the report caused merriment, and also wonderment that in such isolated places we should be unobtrusively observed! Some students, who became colonels of commerce, remember the excursions more than the lectures. A university can be a lonely place for many students, and excursions and other social events gave them heart and companionship.

In the second year I invited Brian Fitzpatrick to give half-a-dozen or so lectures and tutorials, for he had written the most influential left-wing books then available in Australian history. Being now out of touch with the current fashions, he wrote to enquire: 'Do you want me to wear a gown?' So that he could read aloud his lecture he requested a lectern, but the only one available was too low. At the last minute a suitable box was found by a student – a whisky box, of all things – and placed on top of the lectern. Fitzpatrick's hairstyle was of the 1920s – thick hair parted almost in the middle – and his dignity and courtesy and old-fashioned sentence structure conveyed echoes of the Deep South. In his political views he was the opposite of a Southern planter. On politics we did not agree, but I respected the way in which, as a very young historian, he had delved deeply into wide economic themes. Knowing that he earned little money I privately topped up the small lecture fee he received from the university accountant. At that time there was far more willingness than exists today to allow opposing views to be heard or even fostered.

Fitzpatrick was taboo in most history departments, though he had many private admirers and public supporters, one of whom was Harold Holt, soon to become prime minister. Several of the senior members of the university did not quite approve of my inviting Fitzpatrick to lecture. The disapproval came partly from his politics and partly from his drinking, but he was unfailingly sober when each morning dawned: most of my lecture times were then in the morning.

The teaching of my students I enjoyed. I did not write out my lectures but I made sure that I knew the points I wished to cover. One sheet of white paper carried a few headings – all I needed to know. If the lecture went well during the opening ten minutes, and the students were immersed, I consulted no further notes, as a rule. The discussions with students in tutorials or when they knocked at my door were also engaging.

I took on more book-writing than was sensible. During 1964, I was gathering material for the biography of a steelmaster – it did not appear for another seven years – and also beginning to ghost the memoirs of an international businessman. I was reading the proofs and making the index for a short history of the populous Melbourne municipality of Camberwell, preparing new editions of several of my earlier books, making headway on what I then called my 'distance book', and beginning research on the chapters I had promised to write for the centenary history of my old school, Wesley College. The shorter tasks included a long essay on Australia's economy for a coffee-table book produced by a Swiss publishing house, a wide-ranging essay on how technology had shaped Australian history, and an article on South African mining history entitled 'Lost Causes of the Jameson Raid' which was published in a major journal in England. Deemed controversial by some and eye-opening by others, it became one of the most discussed essays on the economic and political history of South Africa.

Looking back I can see now that I made a serious mistake. I responded too often to invitations from publishers and editors to write this book or that article. Instead I should have been blazing my own track in the direction that I wished to travel.

16

THREE PORTRAITS

Intense satisfaction came to me from a book I did not actually write. I was enticed to be its editor by Dudley Phillips, who ran the Australian end of the old British firm known as Sir Isaac Pitman & Son. An erudite bookman, a lover of fine music and expensive wine, his specialities were books on typing, shorthand and commerce. Therefore he was just about the last person to be given the option of publishing a worthwhile manuscript on Australian outback history.

One day in the mail he received a tattered manuscript that, at first glance, impressed him. It was an eyewitness story of the era when camels were the main carriers in much of the outback. As the manuscript was interleaved with brown stains from crushed shreds of tobacco, he guessed that it had been floating around to a succession of publishers and been read and rejected, read and rejected.

Phillips enquired if I would give a quick opinion. After a quarter of an hour I knew that the manuscript had a simple, earthy appeal but would need rearranging, culling and fine-tuning. He passed on my opinion to the author. A week later a dishevelled, one-armed man knocked at my door at the university, and stared at me after I opened the door. He did not say who he was but I guessed. The lower part of his face gave the impression that it had been chewed by an animal at a distant time. Whereas some people are embarrassed by a long silence during a conversation he seemed to feel relaxed when silence reigned. I came to know him well – he often called at lunchtime – but I did not think of calling him by his first name.

'Mr Barker' had taken up dry country in north-western Australia sometime before the First World War. His sheep run was far inland, close to places where many Aborigines had not yet seen a white person. Realising that camels were the most efficient method of transport in that dry country he became skilled in harnessing them, eventually training a team of fourteen or eighteen to pull his long four-wheeled wagon. As well as carting supplies to his sheep station, his camel team became a general carrier, hauling minerals, wool and settlers' supplies. When in the 1920s the new motor lorries superseded the camel teamsters, Barker moved on to mining and other activities. In his seventies, retired, he began to write down his experiences. It was the time of the Cuban missile crisis, when nuclear war seemed possible, and he was spurred to write in detail about camels and how to handle them, for he thought that soon the Western world might be in chaos. Deprived of petrol and motor vehicles, it would be forced to rely again on camels, bullocks and horses.

A charm of his frayed manuscript was the skilled way he captured a fleeting moment. He described his remarkable friend 'Dobson of Australia' who occasionally shaved off his beard by lighting it with a smouldering stick. Recounting incidents that had sent Aborigines into fits of laughter, he observed in passing that they 'laugh far more than white people'. He indelibly captured that day in 1922 when he halted his camel team on the road to Marble Bar so that he could witness an eclipse of the sun – a much-awaited eclipse which, when measured and analysed, was to validate one of Einstein's theories. The silence fascinated the watchful Barker: 'A solitary butcher bird in a solitary tree on the side of a rocky hill made the only noise during the eclipse, which lasted about twenty minutes. The bird began its usual evening song but soon realized something was wrong and stopped.'

The task of repairing Barker's manuscript was longer than expected. I spent at least two dozen evenings in clarifying and rearranging the story and retyping those parts that were barely legible. Sometimes Barker would phone me. I knew he was the caller because he usually rang from a public phone box and, as his only hand was needed to push the pennies down the slot, he had to let the phone dangle by the cord. I could hear it banging against the wall of the phone box before his voice suddenly emerged.

Barker's book displayed such powers of evoking an era that even I, as a helper, felt pride in its completion. Arthur Black, the main editor at Pitman, did the final polishing of the prose, and I wrote a brief foreword of two pages. Called *Camels and the Outback*, the book was printed in Edinburgh, and the ensuing delay vexed Barker. Periodically my phone would ring, and finally I would hear the slightly sad voice enquiring whether the ship bringing the books from Edinburgh had arrived. Then one morning in October 1964, I received an invitation to call at Pitman's office. The cargo of 4000 books had just arrived. Barker too had heard the news, and was sitting on the doorstep before the office opened. I found him rolling a cigarette with the aid of the wicker frame he had invented: thereby the tricky task of shaping and rolling the tobacco could be performed with his only hand.

When the first copy of the book was presented to him, his face conveyed a feeling of quiet pride. For at least a minute he gazed at the dust jacket with its line of pack-camels standing on a soft green background. He must have been delighted to see his own name, H. M. Barker, printed in large white capital letters. It was by then uncommon for a book to be published in the old-fashioned way, with the author's initials rather than Christian name on display.

After returning in old age to his native New Zealand he used to send me long letters observing that the winter, even when he had a warm fire to sit beside, felt harsh for a man who had lived so long in the hot outback. In August 1970 he wrote, 'My 2 oldest friends in W.A. died this year and none are left. Much the same here and the younger generation don't care a damn.'

Some years after his death, a letter arrived from a nun living in the West Australian pearling port of Broome. Having just read Barker's book, she explained that he, when living on his isolated sheep station, had fathered a part-Aboriginal son named Adam. The news was a surprise to me, for Barker had said nothing about a family and gave the impression that he was a lifelong bachelor. The nun noted that Adam had turned out to be a good man and now wished to know when his father died and where he was buried. Fortunately in red ink I had recorded, in my copy of Barker's book, the simple timeline:

Herbert McPherson Barker died at Christchurch, NZ,
on 28th March 1973.
In his 86th year.

*

W. S. Robinson was as immaculate as H. M. Barker was bedraggled. Robinson, usually known as W.S., was a kind of 'jetsetter' in the leisurely era when a passenger liner, plying between Liverpool and New York or between the Thames and Australia, was the fastest means of crossing the seas. At the captain's table or wherever he held court, a telegram – when a ship's telegram was blinkingly expensive – would occasionally be handed to him by a waiter bearing a silver tray. Robinson was rumoured to have been extremely influential not only in big business but also in international politics; probably he would now be called a 'fixer' as well as a middleman and unseen negotiator. I did not fully believe the folklore about the magnitude of his influence until, after his death, I was invited to meet several of his international colleagues and friends.

Few Australians were more influential on the world platform, and yet he was unknown to most newspaper readers in his native land. With his tall figure, his alert face, a full head of white hair which he combed carefully, tailored suits and a grey felt hat tilted at just the right angle, he looked persuasive. Increasingly deaf, he kept in touch partly through a stream of fluent letters sent to people in high places.

Robinson had worked away at his memoirs in spare moments but gave no priority to them. Suddenly it was too late: he died on the Sunshine Coast in Queensland in 1963, when he was aged eighty-six. He had already told a friend or two that he had almost completed his memoirs, and I was brought in primarily to enable him, after death, to keep his word. The trustees of his estate were Sir Maurice Mawby, who was the head of the mining house Conzinc Riotinto, and Sir Eugene Gorman, a legendary barrister. Their wish was for me to write a biography of Robinson, making full use of his unfinished memoirs and his files of letters. They thought that an outside writer would at last make him known to a wider audience.

By chance I had met Robinson at the company's head office in Collins Street not long before his death. Of course I was impressed – by his stature and intelligence, and the reverential way in which bystanders treated him. He said he had read some of my books; and much later, in one of his letters, I came across a sentence according me, as a historian, about 75 per cent of approval on his scale of values.

It might have been easier – or so I realised later – for me to write his biography than to edit and complete the story already written in his own words. And yet a story in the first person, told in his fluent prose, would be the more arresting. Moreover it was my view that, for Robinson's own sake, face had to be saved: to friends he had said so often that his memoirs were far advanced. I told Mawby that my preference was to fill gaps in Robinson's memoirs, and if at all possible to write nothing that he himself would not have written. His widow Gertrude, an Englishwoman of astuteness and charm, agreed.

I was shown folders in which were stacked maybe 300 sheets of paper, neatly typed by his secretary Kath Scanlan. In odd hours he had written down or dictated events and episodes as he recalled them: the story of a crucial business deal, the account of a Burmese mining venture, a pen portrait – ever so brief – of an English politician close to him, and a sentence or two about remarkable deals he had done in wartime America. The written episodes seemed random. On several phases of his life he was silent. Occasionally without realising it he had described the same adventure twice, though not in the same words. It was, when he died, a work in progress.

Born in Melbourne in 1876, the nephew of Edmund Barton who was Australia's first prime minister, W. S. Robinson was an orchardist in the Goulburn Valley, a financial journalist on *The Age* when it reached far more homes than any other Australian paper, and a stockbroker specialising in mining which was the bread and meat of the stock exchanges at that time. When still young he branched into mining itself. Becoming managing director of the world's biggest lead smelter, of the most promising mine at Broken Hill and of a famous mine in Burma – the same one in which his colleague Herbert Hoover made most of his fortune – Robinson was a somebody in the world's commodity markets.

Using his recollections and extracts from his letters, I wrote bridging paragraphs from a variety of sources. As I observed in the completed book, I tried 'as best I could, to conform to his distinctive literary style'. I knew that I was making some headway when I showed to Barton Maughan – one of Robinson's Broken Hill friends and also an official war historian – a draft chapter written by me and another written by Robinson. I did not tell Maughan which one was mine. He decided, though he was not entirely sure, that my chapter must have been written by Robinson.

I was halfway through the editing when Maurie Mawby suggested to me, out of the blue, that I should go overseas and meet Robinson's surviving friends. My reaction was cautious. Since the book had to focus on Robinson's view of the world rather than on the world's view of Robinson, it might not gain enough from the overseas trip to justify the expense. I explained my reluctance to Mawby but he thought that I should travel. 'Ask your wife,' Mawby said. 'See what she thinks.' If we decided to go, he assured me that the company would cover all our expenses for six or eight weeks. That night, I arrived home and put the suggestion to Ann. She said yes, instantly and enthusiastically. That first overseas trip, followed soon by others, was to widen my interests far more than I imagined.

We set out two days after Christmas 1964. Contrary to my expectations, even the first day of the journey in this period of slower travel was exciting. Boarding a plane at Essendon early in the morning and changing planes in Sydney, we flew by BOAC to Darwin where we landed after 4 p.m. The first foreign airport we approached was Singapore, and we peered down at a fleet of cargo ships at anchor in the open roadstead, their lights beginning to burn brightly and their reflections wavering in the dark and placid sea. We then crossed to Calcutta, where an aircraft engine was repaired in the darkness, and so to Karachi and Beirut and to Rome where the rain was driving down. With so many stops it was easy to see why it was called the kangaroo route. In the last stages of the journey we were lucky enough to view the snow on Mount Parnassus in Greece and the white cliffs of Dover.

London, though foggy and dank, still conveyed – without any swagger – the feeling that it was virtually the centre of the world. Perhaps half of the old empire was intact, though each year a few more colonies dropped like fruit from a tree. We walked the streets at every opportunity, revelling in the blue plaques fastened to the walls of the houses where Dickens and Thackeray, the Pitts and Churchill, and a host of the mighty had once lived. I carried a list of people to interview but the schedule was easy, leaving most of the day free for the discovering of more blue plaques, Wren churches and leafless parks – by now the winter was intensely cold but exhilarating.

W. S. Robinson had drawn his English friends from several networks, one of which centred on Brendan Bracken. A leading politician, he had risen far. Spending part of his childhood in Victoria where he studied at a country-town convent, Bracken travelled as a late teenager to England on his own, with enough money to pay his fees for a short period at the fine Yorkshire school Sedbergh. Skilled at the spoken and written word, he was adept at making both enemies and friends. In the 1930s he became such a close supporter and associate of Winston Churchill that it was rumoured, wrongly, that he was Churchill's illegitimate son. When Churchill became prime minister in the perilous days of the war, Bracken rose with him, becoming minister for information, and a very competent and at first gloomy one: he thought that the war would be the end of London as an influential city. Surrounding himself with mystery – at the end of his life he ordered that his correspondence be destroyed – he reaped rewards that mystery sometimes bestows.

Bracken had died about seven years earlier but a few of his friends were still in high places, and I met them. They adored him and his sense of fun, and they also felt admiration for Robinson, cloaking him also with an air of mystery. It was justified because Robinson did not take much part in public life, was not a Briton, and operated from a hidden power base in international base metals.

In London I discovered that Robinson's opinions had been prized by Churchill. Calling on Lord Chandos, I heard that he himself became a member of the British War Cabinet in 1943 after Robinson privately suggested his name to Churchill. I was shown, in case I might be sceptical, some of the handwritten correspondence that preceded this appointment. At that time Chandos, or Oliver Lyttelton as he then was, did not even hold a seat in the House of Commons. Among others with whom I shared long conversations were Lord Drogheda, the head of the *Financial Times*, which had been Bracken's fiefdom; Peter Quennell the charming biographer and poet who was married five times; and Lord Shackleton who was the son of the Antarctic explorer.

On our first Sunday in England we took the train to the seaside resort of Margate. Ann was advanced in the writing of a book on Richard Hengist Horne, the English poet and bohemian who discovered Elizabeth Barrett Browning and then migrated to gold-rush Melbourne – the most noted literary figure to come to Australia so far. Returning to England, Horne died in 1884 at Margate. On the morning we arrived it was hemmed in by dim daylight and a grey running sea: a sight unfamiliar to us for we associated the sea more with the shimmer of bright sunlight. Going by taxi to the cemetery we found Horne's grave. On the return journey to London we went in a double-decker bus through the farmlands to Canterbury, just in time to inspect the cathedral in the fading light. That day, England seemed very small.

One misty day we went by train to Oxford to meet the venerable financier 'Foxy' Falk, who had been a sparring partner and friend of Robinson. O. T. Falk, now in his mid-eighties, was a cousin of Professor Arnold Toynbee, then one of the most quoted of living historians. He confided to us that Toynbee was 'a dull dog' whose books should have been more attuned to economic factors.

Falk's life was linked with that of John Maynard Keynes who, though dead, was at the height of his fame, his economic theories having dominated the Western world since about 1950. Falk and Keynes had both been in the British delegation to the Paris peace talks in 1919, which inspired Keynes to write his celebrated *The Economic Consequences of the Peace*, a book of warnings. Falk, as a sharebroker and commentator and company director, had introduced Keynes, a Cambridge academic, to the intricacies of business, without which Keynes might not have been able to make his influential diagnoses of capitalism. Under Falk's tutelage Keynes learnt what it was like to speculate and finally lose what, for him, was a huge sum. Falk it was who personally introduced Keynes to the wonders of the Russian ballet, just when it had captivated London on the eve of the First World War.

Keynes knew nothing about ballet but on the first night he confidently said of the famous Lydia Lopokova, 'What a rotten dancer. Her bottom is too stiff.' Falk introduced Keynes to this elegant dancer with the stiff bottom, and eventually the economist married the dancer, and they lived more or less happily.

In Oxford in his old age, Falk often sat alone at the back of a small, closed antique shop at 36 the High Street, and there we talked. Confiding that he was sensitive to the atmosphere of people and places, he told us with a mystical softening of his voice that the poet Dante had lived for a time in that low-ceilinged room with the broad wooden beams. On this afternoon the room, though a coal fire was burning, seemed so icy that Dante, if he had really spent a winter there, must have longed for sunny Italy.

Soon 'Foxy' Falk took much more interest in Ann than in me, and his talk catered for her interests. He told her about his dinners or private conversations with H. G. Wells, T. E. Lawrence, Augustus John the painter, Winston Churchill and Arthur Balfour the philosopher who became prime minister, 'a great man'. Falk recalled how he first saw the Russian ballerina Pavlova, whose dancing in London excited him, night after night. The notebook I kept paraphrased Falk's memory of the exciting occasion:

> He went one night to the stage door – 10 or 11 men, her admirers, there. She appeared with her bouquets of peonies. 'I see you like my dancing,' she said. She gave him half the bouquet, highly scented. She told him to call on her at her hotel.

Falk reminisced about the politicians with whom he sat at the peace conference in Paris in 1919, observing the cleverness of Lloyd

George of England ('an unscrupulous rogue') and the brilliance of Clemenceau of France. He recalled how they began to dominate the learned United States' president Woodrow Wilson who had argued that Germany should be accorded a less humiliating peace treaty: 'They left him for dead.' A historian likes nothing better than listening to people who were actually there, even if they were minor actors and observers.

One evening we went to a two-storey fish and oyster restaurant near St James's Square, and in its cramped upstairs room we recognised one of two men dining together: he was the stylish actor George Sanders, near the height of his fame. In a loud but not ostentatious voice he was talking to his friend about Profumo the defence minister and Christine Keeler the glamorous one, who, sleeping together, had recently caused a political sensation. For an outsider to overhear such gossip was like standing unnoticed at the centre of the universe. At the airport later, we stood close to Malcolm Muggeridge, the writer and broadcaster, surrounded by cameramen. In the grand scheme of things such glimpses are trifles, but to a traveller they supply surprise and pleasure.

Other meetings with Robinson's old friends had been arranged in Frankfurt, Hamburg and Cannes. We travelled by train, stirred by the countryside, bleak as it was, and all its historical echoes. After a couple of days in Paris and Versailles we flew back to London from which we set out in a Pan Am aircraft to New York. There, staying in a hotel in 44th Street East, we marvelled at the views of the skyscrapers. On our only free Saturday we went in a fast Greyhound bus to Washington, stood by President Kennedy's new grave in the Arlington National Cemetery, were ushered into the tiny theatre where President Lincoln had been assassinated, and travelled in the bus back to New York, all in one dimly lit day. The human energy, whether the hustling pace of people on the pavements or the conversation of students sitting in the bus, seized us. It was not clear whether all those rushing young Americans knew where they were going but they would certainly arrive there first.

After Ann flew home – our daughter Anna was about to begin her first day at school – I interviewed other friends of Robinson. After brief trips to Montreal and to Corpus Christi in Texas, I flew west to Tucson and finally to San Francisco and Los Angeles. In South Carolina I spent a day and evening with Bernard M. Baruch. Perhaps I was the last outsider to have long conversations with him.

Of few Americans was the honoured phrase 'elder statesman' so often used, but a few critics less kindly remarked that Baruch sometimes was photographed sitting on a public bench outside the White House, waiting either to be photographed by the press or summoned by the president. An organising genius, he had been in charge of mobilising the United States' industrial effort during the First World War, prominent in Woodrow Wilson's delegation at the peace conference in 1919, and a shaper of the United Nations' policy on atomic energy after the Second World War.

A New Yorker, Baruch was spending the winter months on his estate in South Carolina, which could be reached by a train from Charleston. Sitting up in an iron bedstead, his back propped against a pile of white pillows, he greeted me with slight puzzlement at first, but soon he treated me almost as a friend, for he desired companionship. Tall for a man of his years – he was ninety-four – his feet nearly protruded from the bed. A rifle was standing upright at the head of the bed, and he intimated – or perhaps I misunderstood him – that it could be useful if there were intruders.

Baruch said that he would soon take a swim or do exercises in his indoor pool where his housekeeper Elizabeth Navarro kept an eye on him. I was about to leave his room when he pointed to several rather garish paintings on the walls. They had been painted, he said, by his friend Winston Churchill whose funeral in England had been only nine days previously. Baruch had watched it on television but, feeling too moved, asked for the set to be turned off. Later I learnt that President Roosevelt had stayed here with Baruch for a wartime month in 1944, trying to recuperate his strength, because negotiations with Stalin were at a difficult point.

That evening, refreshed by sleep, Baruch turned up for cocktails and dinner in a smart blue suit, and after dinner he put a red shawl over his shoulders and another over his legs – he feared cold draughts though the big house was warm. He no longer drank alcohol but was drinking a little that night: a big occasion, for Elizabeth confided that his visitors were few. He spoke generously of many people – W. S. Robinson 'had elements of real greatness' – but said with feeling in his voice that John Maynard Keynes was 'dishonest' and that General de Gaulle, France's leader, was 'not a man of his word'. Though he had not visited Australia he spoke highly of us as a wartime ally and questioned me about Ann and Anna and Canberra's foreign policy too. So relaxed was he, as the evening raced onwards, that I asked him about the long-term future. He quickly replied that Japan and China (he mentioned them in that order) would be troublemakers and perhaps allies. Russia, then the feared enemy, was less to be feared than a united and reinvigorated Germany.

When I used the fashionable term 'the Cold War' he intervened, not in a boastful way, to explain that he had been the first to speak in public that memorable phrase. Surprised, I looked to Harold Epstein for confirmation, and he nodded. An author, Epstein had written the first draft of Baruch's autobiography – much altered by the man himself – and had flown from New York to join us.

I left to catch the late-night train to Charleston with a sense of elation. Next morning I recorded in a small notebook much of what Baruch had said. He died that year and I was half tempted to write an obituary but decided that our meeting had been private, and memorable for that reason.

A week later the approaching era of space travel was displayed at the Douglas Aircraft Corporation in California. At lunch I sat between Donald Douglas senior and junior, father and son, at a table for eleven, a coloured globe of the world standing as a decoration in the centre. It was the day before the launching at Cape Kennedy of a major venture, and only a month or so before Alexey Leonov the Soviet cosmonaut emerged from his spacecraft and spent twenty minutes floating in space. After the Douglases spoke of space experiments – careful no doubt with their words – they asked me about old-time Australia. As they imagined that it resembled their own country in the frontier era, now vanished, I told them about my friend Campbell Miles, the discoverer of the minerals at Mount Isa, and his simple travels with packhorses and his love for boiled lollies. Laughing at my accent, Donald Douglas junior began to tease me. He had once been taken by Reg Ansett, the airline owner, to Hay in New South Wales for the duck shooting, and was amused that a town called Hay, so simple to pronounce, was called by most Australians as if it rhymed with 'high' rather than 'hay'. Donald Douglas Sr and his wife were not sure whether they could explain why W. S. Robinson had such influence but they singled out one quality: he had thought globally, at a time when a global viewpoint was rare.

Of the memoirs so far written by an Australian businessman, Robinson's probably reached the most readers. His life was laced with quiet excitement and achievement, and he had rubbed shoulders with or guided the great. In this digital era Bill Gates of Microsoft was to read the book with gain and give it to a friend.

Some readers felt peeved that they were not mentioned in Robinson's book or, worse, were mentioned too often. Sir Lindesay Clark was not pleased when he read a few pages describing his role in the creation in the early 1930s of Western Mining Corporation. Robinson had given to his unfinished book the title *If I Remember Rightly*. Lindesay's private reply was 'No, you don't.' I learnt later that he did not quite see eye to eye with Robinson. Nonetheless Robinson knew enough about the fallibility of human memory to give his book a title that hinted at that frailty.

To be a historian is hazardous. When editing the memoirs of Robinson, I included as part of Chapter 3 a fascinating little essay that he had received privately from his friend Dr Hedley Marston, an Australian scientist of high repute and indeed a Fellow of the Royal Society. In the essay Marston to his credit set out what no mining historian – me included – had previously known: that Charles Rasp in an earlier life had enjoyed a professional career in Hamburg that indirectly helped him to discover the silver-lead at Broken Hill. Marston knew much about the life of Rasp and his wife Agnes, but some parts of their life stories he seems to have made up.

Years later, R. Maja Sainisch, using the skills of a first-class detective and her knowledge of Germany and its language, began to piece together the real story. She found that Rasp had a strong desire to conceal his past. Serving as an officer in the Saxon army, at the height of the Franco-Prussian War in 1870 he fled to Australia where he adopted the name of Rasp and shrewdly concealed his past. It is hoped that the long-awaited book about the real Rasps will soon appear.

My involvement in Robinson's memoirs was a result of Maurie Mawby's interest in history. In fact he was interested in almost everything: he was a one-and-only. His mind was quick, his speech rapid, and he rained knowledge on his hearers. Coming from a humble, Cornish-flavoured background in Broken Hill, Mawby had studied mostly at night school until he became just about the most widely qualified man in the mining industry. He also knew much about native plants, not surprising because Broken Hill was the first stronghold of the 'green' movement in modern Australia; and the company for which he worked for most of his life, the Zinc Corporation, actually tackled the sand-besieged area around the mines in the late 1930s. The original vegetation – removed by axemen, droughts, wind erosion and a plague of rabbits – was restored in Robinson's era by the systematic planting of native trees and shrubs. One of the most effective environmental crusades, it was conducted when the green movement nationally was not yet born.

Promoted to the head office in Melbourne, Mawby from 1962 was chairman of Conzinc Riotinto of Australia. He was already well known as a developer of mineral deposits. The massive bauxite deposits on the shores near Weipa in north Queensland, the iron ore at Mount Tom Price in the Pilbara, and the copper of Papua New Guinea's Bougainville were being shaped by him. Not often in the history of world mining has one person been a driving force behind three such disparate and major discoveries.

When he died in August 1977, I was asked to deliver the address at his funeral in Melbourne. On the day before, his wife Lena showed me his coat of arms. I doubt whether he displayed it often – he was ambivalent whether he should accept a knighthood. There stood a wooden Cornish headframe or poppet head, such as supported the winding gear above a mine's shaft. As a field naturalist during his free weekends in old-time Broken Hill he wanted that pursuit recorded too, and so his coat of arms displayed the Sturt desert pea and that exceptional bird with its sprawling ungainly nest, the mallee fowl.

As I spoke, I saw the faces of people, row after row of them, who had come to honour Mawby from mining fields all across Australia. 'He loved this country,' my speech concluded. 'I need hardly say it in this gathering.'

Essington Lewis was rugged and masterly: few Australians have been more influential. A country boy from South Australia, he became head of the Broken Hill Proprietary Company and its rising steel industry; and during the Second World War he was also given extensive powers by Canberra and placed in charge of a workforce of hundreds of thousands of men and women busily making munitions and military aircraft.

He died in 1961, while riding a horse in rugged country, and a few months later his son Bob suggested that I write a biography. To do the research, I needed the help of BHP which in effect owned the Lewis papers, many of which were confidential and of national importance. The difficulty was that BHP, even after it became Australia's largest company, tended to be averse to publicity and especially to criticism. My argument was that a fair and readable biography of Lewis would actually help the public image of the company, 'irrespective of any skeletons it might rattle'. Eventually it was agreed that I could access the Lewis papers. In effect I had the right to write what I wished but BHP and the family had the right to refuse permission for the manuscript to be published.

I liked working on the book. To visit Newcastle and its steelworks, and its underground coalmines nearby and to visit distant Whyalla and its shipyards was exhilarating. To talk with Lewis's surviving circle of friends was to come closer to him. But a vital insight simply came from a piece of cardboard I found in his office desk. It said in capital letters I AM WORK. I ended the book on that note. Later it became the title of John O'Donoghue's splendid play.

My typescript on Lewis's life was completed – or almost – in April 1966, just before I went to China. BHP retyped it, handing copies to its higher officials and to a few members of the Lewis family. Helpful remarks and reminders came back. Bob Lewis said in his gentle but forthright way, 'There is too much talk about the man; and too little are he and his active life allowed to speak for themselves.' It was fair comment. Some readers said the story was too wordy, while others said the prose was too lean and tight. Inside the family circle one pointed out that it did not make enough of Lewis's sense of fun, though she did admit later that the sense of fun was 'rarely seen' by outsiders. Another relative complained that Lewis, contrary to my story, didn't smoke cigarettes, but the oldest son Jim explained that his father smoked them for years before he turned to cigars. Another reader sensibly pointed out that when he was at Whyalla and drove a buggy with two horses, named Iron and Steel, they were ponies, not horses. All authors owe a lot to a few people who, at the right time, take a microscope to the detail.

The story, however, remained unpublished and seemed likely to remain so. In January 1968 Sir Ian McLennan entered the fray. He liked the biography – maybe some of the points that offended earlier readers had now been resolved – but disagreed on a few major issues. One complaint was that I had described Lewis's disillusioned attitude to democracy during the world Depression. The other points were so minor that they were easily resolved on the basis of fact. On Lewis's reluctance to dress formally he reminded me that Lewis would, if need be, wear a dinner jacket but rarely if ever 'white tie and tails'. On Lewis's dislike of publicity he reminded me that in later years Lewis relented a little and allowed his own photograph, even a recent one, to be sent to the press. This did not mean that a press photographer could come and 'capture' Lewis as the photographer's eyes saw fit: Lewis himself controlled the capturing.

One complaint by McLennan was entirely valid. I had failed to point out that BHP had become a much larger firm after Lewis left. It had become a major producer of oil and gas in Bass Strait and of iron ore in the Pilbara, and those achievements had been largely carried through by McLennan and his generation. Sir Ian's complaint, holding some truth, was worded delicately: 'I think that perhaps the biography gives the impression that the building up of BHP was more of a single-handed effort by Mr Lewis than, in fact, it was.' It was a mirror of this old-fashioned company and its respect for privacy that Lewis was still formally called Mr Lewis.

One or two sentences still kept me and BHP apart, and another four years passed before the book finally appeared under the title of *The Steel Master*. It was still being read almost half a century later.

I must have written a dozen books before one of them was formally launched. To my surprise *The Steel Master* was launched at BHP's head office at 500 Bourke Street in Melbourne on a December afternoon in 1971. Sir Ian, as the chairman, made the main speech. Neither of us mentioned the long-running disagreement about sentences that now seem of little consequence. At the end of the launch we parted amicably. When he was very old we sometimes lunched together.

For the space of about a quarter of a century I wrote no more about the history of big institutions or those who led them. From early 1968, when I finished *The Rise of Broken Hill*, until the early 1990s when I began work on a short history of the Golden Mile, I was writing other kinds of history.

The prestige of mining was high when I worked in western Tasmania on my first book. A host of well-known Australians, including many prime ministers, had links with mining fields. Mineral discoverers were folk heroes; the major gold nuggets were prized as if they were works of art; and many of the older women in the countryside still wore tiny nuggets as jewels when they dressed in style. By the 1980s, however, the mines were chastised by critics as destroyers of nature. Many were denounced as foreign-owned – it was forgotten that nearly all the rich goldmines at Kalgoorlie during the 1890s boom were owned by Britons. Above all, several minerals – including lead and asbestos – were now singled out as enemies of health, and uranium was labelled the potential enemy of all humankind. Perhaps only a minority of Australians had turned against mining so far but they were soon multiplied by the articulate, surging green movement and its success in politics.

Belatedly, about 1990, I realised that 'green' as a political word carried contradictory meanings. In Perth, making a speech, I found myself coining two phrases to distinguish viewpoints that lay far apart. Most Australian people were Light Green; but many of the new political leaders were Dark Green and feared that environmental crises were endangering the world. I still see the distinction between light and dark as vital if there is to be constructive political debate.

17

TRAVELLING THE RED WORLD

In 1966 I was granted overseas study leave for eight months. It now seems preposterous that so many academics were allowed regular periods of overseas leave, on full pay, but that was the prevailing rule. Its aim was to promote research and to rejuvenate teaching. The favourable exchange rate of Australia's currency, and the money we ourselves had saved, enabled us to travel far.

After long discussion, Ann and I arranged that we would travel by different routes to London and meet there. I made last-minute plans to travel to Europe through China, Mongolia, Siberia, Moscow and the smaller communist nations of Poland and East Germany. My wish to visit Siberia was augmented by the book *Journey into Russia*, written by the South African, Laurens van der Post, who had recently travelled on the Trans-Siberian Railway across the vastness of the Soviet Union – though he did not visit China. I was spurred also to visit China by my friend Arthur Huck, a student of Chinese and much later the Dean of Arts at Melbourne. He found his brief visit to southern China, unusual at the time, stimulating and exotic.

From Melbourne we set out on the same day in May 1966 but travelling in opposite directions. With her mother and our daughter Anna, Ann flew to Fiji for a short holiday and then to the United States to do research on her first book, while I sailed in the Orient liner *Iberia* from Sydney to Hong Kong in the hope of travelling in a succession of trains across Asia. As Australia, like most Western nations, did not recognise the government of communist China, I could not collect a travel visa at home but instead had to apply for it in Hong Kong. As it allowed me to travel only in China, I knew I would have to apply, along the way, for further visas enabling me to continue the railway journey to Mongolia and the Soviet Union and so across Siberia to the Ural mountains, Moscow and Warsaw, East and West Berlin, and finally to Holland where I would take the channel ferry to England.

In Hong Kong the China visa was easily secured. I had to answer only one question: 'Have you ever travelled to Taiwan?' – Taiwan was the home of the exiled Chinese government. So on a bright Sunday morning I set out from the handsome old Kowloon railway station, since demolished. Crossing the border into China was slightly unnerving, because nearly all foreign travel to that country had ceased, and I felt at the mercy of an unfamiliar regime. The city of Canton (now called Guangzhou) was creepy. It felt strange after dark to be driven through dimly lit but crowded streets in a car with the headlights turned off. The hotel was full of guards and overseers, and in public parks an official loudspeaker boomed out instructions.

Hardly a foreigner was to be seen. The local interpreter assigned to me was nervous and apprehensive. When I asked questions he made it clear that there was only one view of what was happening in China, and that his duty was to express that view. The thought of speaking a few words privately to me was too dangerous for him to contemplate. Next day, after seeing many sights and visiting markets where almost nothing was for sale, it was a relief to prepare to travel to Beijing (then call Peking).

Reaching Canton's railway station, one of China's most strategic, I found that the main entrance was locked. My interpreter, about to farewell me, explained that train travel was a privilege, and that I was a privileged one. In our train, about to depart for the capital city, nearly all passengers were soldiers, but in one carriage several bunks were set aside for the four or five foreigners possessing visas and tickets. Finally the train chugged from the station, the loudspeakers playing martial music as if we were all 'marching as to war'. At wayside stations, where the train briefly halted, a crowd of simply dressed Chinese, each carrying a tiny amount of luggage, could be seen outside the entrance gates. For them the gates were locked.

The countryside through which the train made its long journey, the driver frequently and loudly tooting his whistle, was sometimes deserted, but elsewhere it was alive with simple activities. In villages the donkeys walked in circles pulling the big stone that ground the wheat into flour. Men marched up and down on a treadmill that raised irrigation water to the level of the fields. At new construction sites a line of men carried earth in baskets held aloft by bamboo poles, and on dusty roads men pushed handcarts stacked high with hay. They were like timeless scenes from an old illustrated Bible. I did not know, nor did almost anybody in the West, that in the past five years a total of 30 or 40 million Chinese had died of starvation. The erratic climate was partly to blame: so was the communist bureaucracy and the primitive farming methods.

I had no idea, before I reached Beijing, that the country was in political turmoil. The Great Proletarian Cultural Revolution had begun. Tens of thousands of intellectuals, politicians and bureaucrats, actors and musicians and authors, said to be in the grip of Western, bourgeois and even Soviet-like ideas, were soon hunted and caught. A host of downgraded or dismissed officials were condemned to house arrest, publicly humiliated or imprisoned and even beaten. Many committed suicide. The ultimate death toll was to be large.

Chairman Mao, in attempting to revive the communist spirit in China, enlisted young city people in their millions. Not long after I left the country, or perhaps even while I was there, the first of the infamous Red Guards appeared even if they were not yet identified by name. Teenagers or very young adults, they were soon acting as juvenile thought-police. All schools were to be closed – except the school of propaganda, which worked overtime. Workers and peasants attended compulsory political lessons, parades and re-education classes. In the inner circles, high leaders were overthrown or disappeared from public view. Even the whereabouts of Chairman Mao was not known with certainty, and for months he made no public speeches, finally appearing in public after swimming down the Yangtze River.

In Beijing I had glimpses of the coming persecution though I did not see its magnitude: nobody did. From the window of my room in a Soviet-style hotel, one of the few tall structures in Beijing, I looked down on a wide boulevard and saw at daybreak on Thursday 9 June truckloads of people travelling to protest at the behaviour of a high official. The flat trays of the trucks were crowded with standing people, some of whom waved large flags. In the purple dusk that evening, while returning from a Chinese restaurant, our car was halted by a procession – red flags waving, drums beating and cymbals clanging. Other processions, the young people predominating, marched here and there. All were assembling to applaud the deposing of the editor of the capital city's daily newspaper.

My youngish interpreter put on an earnest face and altered his voice when about to say something that was important politically. In a low voice he disclosed that 'some university graduates were working as farm labourers near Peking and would continue as labourers all their life'. I did not realise that they were being punished partly as a warning to others.

At the Great Wall, one of the noblest of the world's tourist sights, hardly a person was to be seen. From the nearby luncheon house with its gravel floor and its piping-hot cups of green tea, I could see in the distance a few people trudging towards us from the distant Green Dragon Bridge railway station. They turned out to be five Chinese – the first tourists I saw at the Great Wall – and my impression was that they were 'overseas Chinese'. Tourists had almost vanished from China, and foreign correspondents and businesspeople were not to be found. The voices of English-speakers I no longer heard. Even a car was uncommon – fortunately I had been compelled to hire in advance, at a reasonable fee, a Polish-made car and a chauffeur.

If by chance I ran into trouble I had no idea what I would do nor where I would seek help. The British operated a small embassy, but they were viewed locally as wild-dog imperialists who might be planning to join the USA in crushing communist China. I was also told that President Johnson might decide to conquer China if the present war in Vietnam provided him with the launching pad. Meanwhile nuclear tests were being conducted in China and long-distance ballistic missiles were being built.

In Beijing, a slogan-smitten city, no foreign-language newspaper could be bought. I had no radio – maybe foreign visitors at that time were not permitted to carry one – and phone calls to the outside world could not be made. I depended on my young interpreter for explanations of what was going on, but at first he was unable or unwilling to explain. Occasionally hearing the drumbeat of street processions, I enquired where they were marching. He told me that the mayor of Beijing – an ally of the official seen as a likely successor to Chairman Mao – had been deposed. Who, I asked, were these people filling the streets? I was told that many were peasants being trucked in to chant slogans condemning the mayor's behaviour, while others were teenagers conscripted to march behind red flags. We now know that the downfall of Peng Zhen, the mayor, was a momentous event in the Cultural Revolution. I enquired, what was the mayor's fate? 'We do not know where he has gone,' said the interpreter. In my subsequent book I was to note that there is 'something hauntingly tragic about a society which has to be content with such an answer'.

About a dozen years later, to my surprise, I was appointed by the prime minister, Malcolm Fraser, as chairman of the official Australian council that carried out many of the cultural, scientific and sporting negotiations with China. In Beijing I would be duly welcomed by Chinese cabinet ministers in the Great Hall of the People, and when I replied, in answer to their questions, that I had visited China in 1966 they expressed surprise. The official interpreter – as instructed – would courteously enquire whether perhaps I had misunderstood the question? No, I understood the question. When I added that it was in the month of June 1966 they expressed astonishment. What was a foreigner doing in the capital city when those tumultuous events were unfolding! Some, finding it difficult to believe, questioned me further: what date in June? They knew that the mayor had been dismissed on 3 June – in modern Chinese history a notable day – and yet here was this foreigner claiming to have been there just a few days later.

Back in 1966, I felt the tension and excitement in the capital city. Sometimes there were scenes or sounds of fanaticism in the streets and live theatres. They evoked the atmosphere visible in the films of Nazi street marches and mass rallies just before the Second World War.

I could have been tempted to try to find a way of returning home, but the calmness of my ever-present interpreter reassured me. For twenty-four hours he wondered whether I would even be allowed to leave Beijing and travel through Mongolia to Russia. When I visited the local Mongolian embassy to apply for a transit visa he hinted that the officials might refuse me: Mongolia was an obedient ally of the Soviet Union and therefore an enemy of China. Relations between China and the Soviet Union, close friends in the previous decade, had so deteriorated that a few months later, all Chinese students in the Soviet Union were expelled. Russian students living in China had already departed.

Eventually receiving my permit at the embassy I boarded the train that would travel to the Mongolian People's Republic and so to eastern Siberia. The country outside was soon arid. In the Gobi desert the sand blew lightly. By the time the train reached the Chinese–Mongolian border, only fourteen passengers remained. Maybe half were East European diplomats and bureaucrats returning from duty in China and in South-East Asia. The flow of people between China and the Soviet Union was now a trickle, so tense were the relations between the two communist governments.

The Siberian city of Irkutsk, in contrast to Beijing, seemed a haven of free speech and den of luxury. Women wore bright colours, the shops were passably supplied with goods, the bookshops and cinemas and beer stalls were busy, and young people promenaded the leafy streets. Not far away, however, were punishment camps where hundreds of thousands of people followed a spartan timetable. Much less was known about their plight then than now.

The true Trans-Siberian Railway passed through Irkutsk, on its way from the Pacific Ocean to Moscow; and in normal weeks a superior, comfortable train arrived to pick up a sprinkling of foreigners as well as upper-ranking Soviet citizens. Somehow an unforgivable mistake had been made by the remote bureaucrat who had authorised my ticket to Moscow. I was escorted to the railway station at Irkutsk, but on that morning the train with the special carriage for foreigners was absent. Instead, punctually at 7.34, the ordinary people's train arrived. As it was a strict rule that foreigners must not travel on that train, my tourist guides faced a dilemma. I could not stay longer in Irkutsk because I had to be in Moscow three days later: my official travel papers stood no nonsense. The only solution was to despatch me on the people's train. A small blonde conductress wearing a black uniform and a cheerful smile – revealing a black enamel tooth amid the white – stepped forward and escorted me to a special carriage. Settling me in a four-bunk compartment just before the train left the station, she kept watch in the corridor and forbade any other passenger to come near me.

When it was time to eat she led me along the corridors, carriage after carriage, until we reached the dining car. Suddenly it had become empty, enabling me to eat in isolation. I was segregated – until the overflow of hungry and impatient passengers could no longer be held back. As the train became full, even my sleeping compartment and its three spare berths were needed by incoming Russian travellers. For a time a military officer was allowed to sit with me. After I handed him my passport in order to explain who I was, he looked at it intently but without understanding it. After telling me that his name was Victor he said no more, though his silence was comfortable enough. At a small station I watched him leave the train. On the platform he hugged his waiting wife; his flaxen-haired young daughter looked so smart in her sailor suit.

Into my compartment now entered a burly man and his burlier wife. They were labourers, judging by their tough beefy hands. She wore a sleeveless dress – too small for her – with a pattern of red and white spots, while above was a floral scarf that made her head resemble a wrapped-up plum pudding. She carried a dillybag and two dilapidated suitcases tied with rope.

For a time the newcomers looked at me in puzzlement. Obviously they had been chosen for my compartment in the belief that there would be no effective communication between us. Soon he began to address me in Russian, sometimes leaning over in a confidential manner as if we were old acquaintances. She listened to him intently and proudly. When I took out a book and began to read he would look at me with some wonder, gesturing to his wife that I was reading, and finally tapping me on the shoulder so that he could resume his one-way conversation with me.

At every stopping place he rushed to the food stalls, ready to leap back on the train just before it moved away. With his bulky build and his black shirt it was easy to see him in the crowds jostling around private stall-keepers on the railway platform. In the course of three days he and his wife devoured cold chickens, frankfurts, a whole fish, loaves of bread, rolls resembling doughnuts, garlic sausages, and a blood sausage with a skin so tough that it had to be peeled with a pocketknife. When bottles of beer and vodka had to be opened, which was often, she used her teeth to tug the cap off the bottle. With their food and drink they were unfailingly generous.

Any hope of segregating me was abandoned. The train was packed with people and the conductresses could no longer keep me in isolation. Their remaining duty, if I walked on the platform during a brief stop, was to usher me to my carriage before the long train began to move.

The countryside sped by, a pleasing patchwork: the white bark of the birch forests, the orange and yellow and sherbet-pink wildflowers, sunny clearings in the forest, and rivers almost jammed with logs drifting towards a distant sawmill. In the villages, for an instant, a woman could be glimpsed drawing water from a well and carrying it away in buckets hanging from a yoke worn on her shoulders, while others were waddling in gumboots on muddy roads. We passed isolated villages where the timber cottages were unpainted but the wooden 'tombstones' in the cemeteries were bright with paint. At night a teasing incense came through the windows – maybe the smoke of forest fires.

Of the two bottom bunks in the cabin I already possessed one and the big Russian with the black shirt took the other. His wife did not want the top bunk but at bedtime we pushed her up. It had no side wall, and so – as the train lurched – she was in danger of falling all the way to the floor. She occasionally let out a pitiful miaow-like sound, like a cat stranded in a swaying tree. After a time I said that she could have my bunk, a minor gesture that was repaid generously. Again and again, until we reached Moscow, they tried to repay me. At wayside stations he bought a loaf of bread, clutched for safekeeping to his black shirt, and gave me first choice of the thick slices he cut. When I gave him two bottles of red wine he refused to treat them as a gift but paid me in Russian roubles. He swallowed wine in big gulps, wiping his mouth with the side of a hand.

Our little cabin and a stretch of corridor outside became a meeting place. People arriving to look at the foreigner stayed to drink and talk. One passenger, from the southerly Soviet republic of Moldova, wore a ribbon badge signifying the medals he had won as a soldier fighting the war against Hitler's invading army in the early 1940s. Towards the end of the journey he gave me the badge, pinning it on my left lapel. Other passengers rebuked him: perhaps it was against the law; perhaps he was being far too generous. When I unclasped it and handed it back he insisted that I keep it.

Eventually I was to write a book about my travel experiences but it had to disguise certain facets of what I saw or heard, partly to safeguard my interpreters from being questioned by the authorities. A book written by a foreigner after visiting China and Russia was likely to be examined by inspectors eager to detect any unauthorised thoughts or activities. I did not mention the kindness of the man from landlocked Moldova.

At night the twilight persisted. The long inlets of the Arctic Ocean – when I looked in my pocket atlas – were not far to the north. And yet in the opposite direction Central Asia also seemed within reach, for its snow-tipped mountains fed the wide rivers that passed beneath the railway bridges on which we travelled. Slowly one gained a sense of the vastness of the Soviet Union and the difficulties of effectively administering provinces so far from Moscow. It made me think – and later I expressed the thought in print – that the enormous

Soviet Union was not necessarily such a permanent empire. Just as the distant colonies of Britain were breaking away in the 1960s, so too might the ethnic outposts of the Soviet Union someday become independent. This dramatic event came to pass, far earlier than was anticipated.

Coming close to the Volga River, the onion-shaped domes of the churches could be seen through the gaps in the trees. As the train slowed down and entered the suburbs of Moscow, the big Russian changed the shirt he had worn throughout the journey. Well before the train halted his wife had the battered suitcases and various food bags in hand. We shook hands warmly before they clambered down the steps to the railway platform. I watched him pushing his way through the waiting crowd, like an icebreaker preparing a channel for the laden ship that was following him.

I spent time in Moscow and in Warsaw where I could find no hotel room until I was told that I must first bribe a tourist official. For four days I stayed in East Berlin but a tourist travelling alone was not easily handled by the communist authorities; I needed police permission to visit nearby Potsdam. Finally, one morning, I reached the Hook of Holland and the North Sea, grey and choppy. After such a vastness of land the sea seemed homely and small.

I left the communist lands with a few pocketbooks crammed with rough notes written in haste. There would have been more but for the fact that the Chinese guides had ordered me to put my notebook away. They were wary of anybody who might be a journalist. When I reached London, reunited with Ann and Anna, and began to read the press I realised that by chance I had the ingredients for an eyewitness book.

I should have promptly written the book, while my knowledge was red hot. Perhaps I was wearied by the nervous tension of the journey – a tension I did not feel so much when travelling as when the journey was over. Realising that I had seen much that was unusual, I began to write the first chapters. For the next three months we travelled by car in the Continent, and there was little time to write. Between Bergen and Sorrento we travelled more than 16 000 kilometres, mostly on the minor roads, before returning to London where I wrote the book on nearly every spare day without finishing it.

Ann was ahead of me. She had completed her first book, which I mentioned earlier. A life of the poet Richard H. Horne, it was eagerly accepted by the Longmans editor John Guest, who prepared it for publication in London. Her preface, dated May 1967, was written well before my book was finished. The dust cover of her book printed in psychedelic green, held a charming essay by her editor, twice her age, revealing that Horne had close links with Dickens and Carlyle and a mixture of British writers, and had exchanged letters with so many of them that he was seen as 'one of the more extraordinary figures' of the literary scene in the nineteenth century. The essay noted that 'in this splendid book, he is a man presented in such depth that, although one may laugh aloud at his absurdities, one leaves him with respect and more than a touch of affection'. The book was to be reviewed favourably and widely, especially in Britain.

Back in Melbourne, I showed my typescript to Robert Cross, an English publisher who had just arrived in Australia as the head of Macmillan. We signed a contract in Gina's Restaurant in Lygon Street, Carlton, which was not yet a street of restaurants. The final parts of the book, rewritten, were completed in October 1967. Publishing was still a slow business, and the printed book did not appear until

April 1968, which was two years after I had begun the journey. I had almost missed the boat. But *Across a Red World* was still highly newsworthy to readers in New York and London and not least in Australia where it was briefly high on the bestseller list.

Various readers of my book gained a strong desire to visit communist lands. In a perilous stage of the Second World War, at a very young age, one reader had been captain of a British destroyer that escorted the long convoys carrying aircraft and other military supples across the Arctic Circle to the north Russian port of Murmansk. Said to be the most hazardous convoy route of the war its ships were vulnerable to attacks from German aircraft and submarines. If in icy weather the attacks were successful, the British sailors and officers who fell into the sea froze to death; perhaps 3000 died in the space of a couple of years. It was a quarter-century later when, reading *Across a Red World*, he resolved to take his car and caravan to the Russia that he had helped to defend but could see only from the ship's decks. We discussed my book and his own journey only this year; he is now over 100, and still a traveller.

From scores of Australians, over many years, I learnt that my book persuaded them to make a similar journey. Some did not like the railway trip across Siberia; their view was bleak if they travelled in winter. Some wished they could meet Russian travellers but on the train, to their disappointment, they were segregated.

18

THE TYRANNY OF DISTANCE

I had written another book about travels, and I saw the first copy of it while in London, just after crossing the red world. Called *The Tyranny of Distance*, it was based on heavy research and only light travels. It led me into unexpected corners and down blind alleys and almost slipped out of control.

It began with Brian Stonier, the head of the branch of Penguin Books, newly established in Australia. Wishing to initiate local books rather than be mainly an importer of English books, he thought that a history of transport in Australia would fill a gap. He had in mind a shortish book of no more than 45 000 words, which I was happy to attempt; I signed the contract in January 1964. In the end, however, I was to produce a different book, two-and-a-half times as long with a wider theme.

Lacking adequate knowledge about early transport, I read and read, delving in out-of-the-way places. At first I collected material largely about the effects of the railways, steamships, cars, aircraft and other mechanical conveyances, thinking the book would largely cover the seventy years from, say, 1850 to the First World War. Then I began to see that earlier Australian industries such as wool and whaling had been profoundly affected by transport. I was surprised to discover that whaling provided Australia with its main export revenue as late as the year 1833. Some students tell me that they recall the lectures I gave in the 1960s on the whaling ships, how exactly the crews caught the whales and how they boiled down the flesh to extract the oil for lamps and for lubricating machines, in the era before petroleum flowed from the ground.

I looked at some themes and discarded them. Others became roads down which I travelled. Thus I asked myself why the British in the late 1780s sent a fleet loaded with convicts and marines to harbours so far away as Botany Bay and Sydney. Compared to nearer sites north of the equator, Sydney must have had some special attraction for English naval power. I began to wonder why Australia rather than New Zealand was chosen as the site for a large convict settlement. I first discussed publicly this question during Writers' Week at the new Adelaide Festival when I shared a section of the programme with Robert Hughes who was then a lively art critic in Sydney but unknown in New York.

At that time I had never been in a ship – except to Tasmania – and had never travelled to the Northern Hemisphere. For the first time in my life I was mentally travelling the seven seas. At night in the big domed reading room of the Public Library in Swanston Street, I read of long-forgotten voyages to and from Australia. I sat on the decks of the sailing ships, in my mind's eye, and saw the booming whitecapped waves approaching, and near Cape Horn I saw the icebergs on the sea lanes. In February 1964, Ann and Anna – now four years old – and I spent a fortnight by the ocean at Lorne, and at night I read bound volumes of back numbers of the fine historical magazine *The Mariner's Mirror* and seafaring books. It was the first time I had read much about the sea, and I was fascinated. I learnt what longitude meant and how it was made portable just before Captain Cook first sailed to the Southern Hemisphere. I learnt about fast clippers and the Great Circle route they followed on the long voyages from Liverpool to Melbourne in the 1850s when they were the greyhounds of the sea. I learnt about the distinctive role of the winds in Australian history – something so elementary but then little known – and how the sailing ships on their return voyage to England usually sailed by way of stormy Cape Horn, thus following a completely different route to that which they had followed on the voyage out. Coming to Australia from the west, they set out for home by first sailing in an easterly direction. So the prevailing winds, discovered by Cook and Hunter and other navigators, became the mainstay of Australia's overseas commerce for decades.

I investigated the coming of the first steamships and the opening, decades later, of the Suez and Panama canals which were shortcuts from Europe to Australia. The arrival of the overland and overseas telegraph from Asia in 1872 – a fast message might arrive in twenty-four hours – was perhaps more fascinating to Australians than the first wireless or radio. I examined early railways and the break of gauge. The first aircraft I studied but failed to do justice to their impact.

The book, expected to be small and completed in six months, grew beyond the expected size. I explained to Brian Stonier that it was grabbing me by the wrist and that I was its captive. He understood and accepted my changes of plan. The book became larger. The deadline – the date when I promised that the typescript would be complete – was left far behind.

So much material had come to hand about the early period that I intended to end the main narrative at the year 1914, on the eve of the First World War. Perhaps I would speed the story forward to the era of Kingsford Smith and Hinkler and worldwide flights mainly by using illustrations with long captions. Soon it made sense to take the story beyond the Second World War; and so I wrote two final chapters about the coming of the Model T Ford, the fast ocean liners, the defeat of Japan in the Second World War, and the postwar swing of our nation's trade from Europe to Asia. I ended the book with the mid-1960s when Australia was drawing close to Asia: distance had been realigned.

What had commenced as a short history of transport became something wider. In the book I tried to demonstrate how Australia's distance from Britain, and the long distances across Australia, shaped or influenced all kinds of events and attitudes, including the long-time male dominance of Australian society, the rise of the whaling and wool and gold industries, the power of the trade unions, the unusual role of spectator sport, and the inflow of Chinese gold-seekers. I was not bright enough to realise that distance had also deeply altered the old Aboriginal way of life which reigned for more than 50 000 years.

A mishap or two affected the emerging book. When I had completed one or two chapters, with many cross-outs and additions in ink, I would take them to Mrs Jean Edgar, the secretary of our department at the university, for neat typing. Inquisitive, intelligent and strong-willed, she was skilled in guessing what I intended to say if my handwritten corrections were illegible. One day, being about to fly to Mount Isa, I had no time to call at her office to give her the rough typescript of two long chapters now called 'Gold Clippers' and 'Black Cloud'. Instead, wrapping them up, I posted them to her office. The small parcel did not arrive. As it represented more than one-third of the writing I had completed so far, and about one-sixth of the final version of the book, I was stunned by the loss. In those days few writers kept a copy of their work in progress, finding it time-consuming and unsatisfactory to use carbon paper in order to make a second copy while typing. In any case I was busily correcting the typed copy as soon as it left the typewriter, and so a carbon copy ceased to be the up-to-date record.

For weeks I hoped that my missing parcel, after hibernating in what the postal officials of those days called their 'dead-letter office', would somehow turn up. When at last I was resigned to the loss, the prospect of trying to write afresh those two very long chapters that had vanished was so irksome that I postponed it, month after month. Most of the book was written, at least roughly written, before I set out to write again these lost chapters, which together occupy fifty-two pages of the final version. The new chapters were definitely superior to the lost originals – in short, I had gained – but the pain of losing the first versions and then having to rewrite them is still with me.

While actually writing the book, I was often living on a high. It's impossible, however, to be elated for more than a couple of days: that's why the elation, while it lasts, is so memorable. On a few occasions, when I was busy on the book, the thought fleetingly appeared: what if I die before it is finished? Some books acquire their final shape, the dovetailing of the separate arguments one into another, and indeed the power of their conclusion, only during the last three weeks of writing and correcting. Then everything falls into line – or seems to fall into line. If the author dies unexpectedly, however, the unfinished book can also be mortally wounded. Even if faithful friends bring the typescript to finality and arrange for it to be published, it will not be quite what the author intended: it might even be what the author would not have intended, if life had been prolonged. I was so immersed in my work, obsessed – unjustifiably so – with its importance, that I longed to complete it.

At last it was completed. The first paragraph in Chapter 1 was actually the very last that I wrote. My story began with the flights of birds – the long annual flights of the short-tailed shearwater or muttonbirds from Siberia to Bass Strait and the annual migrations of the swifts from Japan to Tasmania, at a time when no human navigators had ever made such long north–south voyages:

> In the eighteenth century the world was becoming one world but Australia was still a world of its own. It was untouched by Europe's customs and commerce. It was more isolated than the Himalayas or the heart of Siberia. The only European and Asian navigators who visited Australia came each season in flocks through the skies.

Looking back I am surprised that I gave prominence to birds; the modern nature movement had barely begun its meteoric rise, and moreover I was not a keen birdwatcher. The book, seen in retrospect, should have begun with the history of the Aborigines. Their long occupation of this continent was indelibly shaped by isolation and by untamed distance. The Tasmanian Aborigines especially lived in a kind of chronological quarantine; and few if any other people in recorded history had been isolated so long from other members of the human race. But at this stage Australia's long Black history had barely been touched upon by mainstream historians, of whom I was one. Aborigines appeared in the book only as ghosts.

Normally in my books I had not set out regular footnotes that indicated along the way my exact sources of information. Rather I had set out at the rear of the book an essay listing the main sources of information used for each chapter or each cluster of chapters. Kathleen Fitzpatrick, after reading *The Rush that Never Ended*, thought that I should draw readers' attention – at least the few readers who were interested in such matters – to the specific sources of information that lay behind each major assertion in a book. From her seaside escarpment at South Main near Lorne in January 1964 she sent me in her own hand a short note, accepting my view that footnotes at the foot of the page were a deterrent, an intrusion, for the average reader. In its place she offered a suggestion: 'There is a method I have seen used in some American books that overcomes this difficulty and I wonder if you would consider using it next time.' This was the unobtrusive method, used for instance in Barbara Tuchman's impressive book *The Guns of August*, whereby the notes were individually set out at the back of the book in the following style: *Page 40, 'icebergs in 1850s'*, followed by a brief statement of the source of that piece of information.

Fitzpatrick's letter finished with 'warmest congratulations'. I assume that she was congratulating me in advance for following her advice, rather than for writing a book worthy of her congratulations! She assumed that I was unlikely to disobey a former teacher who had taken the trouble to write to me, and write so graciously. Dutifully at the back of the book I set out my notes in the manner she suggested. Thanks to her, mine was one of the first Australian books to display a method that now is commonplace.

In July 1965 the typescript, virtually completed, was sent to Penguin

Books, as promised. Brian Stonier had recently left the firm to set up his new paperback publishing house called Sun Books, with its office in Little Collins Street; and so it was his successor at Penguin who read – or paid somebody to read – my typescript. He responded with an emphatic note of approval. Indeed he said he was 'tremendously impressed'. That was exciting news but it lasted only for ten seconds. He followed it up in the same letter by saying it did not fit the series he had in mind. This was another way of saying he was *not* 'tremendously impressed'. In effect Penguin, presumably with the support of its head office in England, refused to publish the book it had commissioned, and hitherto approved at every stage. To my surprise it offered no compensation. I then tentatively offered the book to Sun Books which hugged it with open arms. Stonier was even willing for Melbourne University Press – I was then a member of its board – to acquire the hardback rights and to share with Sun Books the cost of editing and typesetting and printing. It would be first a hardback with Peter Ryan and then a paperback with Brian Stonier, but this plan fell through, leaving Stonier in sole control.

The book when it was almost finished had no title. In my diary I used to call it the transport book or the transport history. Now it needed a title, and clearly transport was playing second fiddle. On 5 January 1966 I wrote a note: 'Almost decided to call the book *Distance and Destiny*.' Now at last, beginning for the first time to see the shape of it, I realised that it consisted of two equal halves. So I labelled the first half 'The Tyranny of Distance' and the second half 'The Taming of Distance'. But as a whole it still needed a title, and bit by bit I came to see, as did several others, that *The Tyranny of Distance* should perhaps be the title for the whole book.

Stonier, when presented with the proposed title, was more enthusiastic than I was. I held lingering doubts, because neither the word tyranny nor the word distance was very visual: I always want at least one visual word to be in a book's title. At the same time I sensed that the two key words sat in a kind of harmony, for each contained in a key place the letter 't' and the letter 'n'. The combined sounds proved to be arresting or attractive to many readers.

At the end of April 1966 the book was with the typesetter and printer in Adelaide, the Griffin Press, but the title was still slightly in doubt. Stonier's new firm could not afford to make a loss, and an enticing title for the book was vital. On Friday 29 April he drove me down to Geelong College to speak to senior students at an evening history gathering in the school library. They strongly supported the title; they cheered it, so Brian Stonier recalls. I had no conception that it would catch on, entering the everyday language.

I had set out to cross the red world some months before *The Tyranny of Distance* was ready for publication. Not until we returned to London in December 1966 did I find a waiting parcel containing three copies of the book. With pleasure I saw the dust jacket and then some of the printed pages and illustrations.

The book appeared in what was then a rare sequence, being published first as a cheapish paperback at a price of $1.95, and a couple of years later as a more expensive hardback and finally as a coffee-table book. The paperback editions carried a brilliant dust jacket, designed by Brian Sadgrove. I can say so impartially because I had no part in its creation. The cover showed the bottom half of the globe, in brilliant blue, with a white sailing ship mysteriously travelling upside down.

At first *The Tyranny of Distance* did not sell in large numbers. Most of the reviews were very favourable but reviews do not necessarily sell a book. Indeed it gained because some of the reaction to it was unfavourable. Several scholars were not convinced by my chapter, which argued that Britain settled Australia primarily for strategic reasons. Their argument did not convince me but like other authors I am not an impartial judge!

News of the book spread by word of mouth. It defied the bookshops' general rule by selling more in its second year – and also in its third year – than in its first year of publication. It was reprinted again and again. Eventually it appeared as a hardback with Macmillan in Australia, while in England it was offered by the History Book Club to its members. The Japanese translation came much later. Probably it was the first book in Australia to begin as a paperback and to blossom – in the space of half-a-dozen years – into a hardback and then an expensive coffee-table volume.

For a time the phrase *tyranny of distance* was anchored rather than airborne. There was only an occasional sign that it would acquire a life of its own, independent of the book. In March 1968 it was officially used to describe an event that in a dramatic way was to weaken that tyranny. A satellite, stationed far above the earth, could now transmit television news and programs between the Northern Hemisphere and the Southern. And on the day when the first images were transmitted between Japan and Australia, a speaker proclaimed that this was another blow against 'what an Australian historian has called the tyranny of distance' – or words to that effect. I felt secretly pleased.

Another sign that the phrase might soar was a headline in the London *Times*, written in 1970 when a reigning pope made his first visit to Australia. The paper announced that Pope Paul VI was conquering 'the tyranny of distance'. The origin of the phrase was not stated nor was there a reason why it should be. Year after year it was employed by more journalists and politicians, mostly in Australia but sometimes in North America and Europe. I could have no objection to the popularising of it. I did not own it; the language belongs to all.

The book aroused controversy among historians. One chapter was the pivot of their argument. Such influential and able historians as A. G. L. Shaw and Geoffrey Bolton argued that Sydney was settled simply as a convict town. They denied that it was originally envisaged in London as a seaport and a possible naval base on the route from England to China and that Norfolk Island far to the north-east of Sydney was seriously seen as a vital source of naval supplies – flax for making sails and rope, and tall straight trees that would serve as strong masts for sailing ships. The controversy was so enticing for Year 12 students, and relatively easy to understand, that it became the most contested debate in Australian history for the best part of twenty years. Meanwhile Professor Alan Frost of La Trobe University, in book after book, did the new research that buttressed my side of the argument and made it more persuasive. But I would say that my side was more persuasive, wouldn't I? The debate is not yet over.

In 1982 I heard that the phrase was capturing new territory. One day my secretary, Liz Carey, enquired whether I was the coiner of the phrase *tyranny of distance*. She added that somewhere near the top of the hit parade in England was a pop song performed by the New Zealand group Split Enz and called 'Six Months in a Leaky Boat'. After singing about the plight of a leaking boat near Cape Horn the group – she explained to me – vividly wailed or sang 'the tyranny of distance'. A week later, listening to the car radio, I turned by mistake to a pop station. There I heard the male musicians sing, in a haunting way, the phrase I had coined, and soon my daughter was playing the song on a vinyl gramophone record that was slightly scratched. I found out years later that the composer of the hit, Tim Finn, had been reading my book when he wrote his words.

My feeling by the 1990s was that the phrase had already passed its peak. As the World Wide Web arrived, my phrase was seen as outmoded. Rupert Murdoch borrowed it for a major speech that concluded that distance was dead. An English author, Frances Cairncross, wrote an influential book called *The Death of Distance* which, after explaining courteously that I originated the debate, argued that distance was being conquered by the new communications of the digital age. I accepted her argument that the world had shrunk, but after reading her book I was far from convinced that distance was defeated. Completing in 2001 a new version of my book, labelled the 21st-century edition, I concluded that distance, while tamed, was far from dead.

To the surprise of many historians the United States' generals and strategists began to emphasise the tyranny of distance, thus reviving my phrase. They knew the heavy additional expense of fighting wars in the Middle East and other regions far from home. To send fighter aircraft to Afghanistan, which lay far from the Americans' island bases and aircraft carriers in the Indian Ocean, called for aerial tankers that could refuel planes in midair. South Korea, Japan and Taiwan had to be defended, if necessary, by the United States. but they were far from the large American naval bases. In an international crisis there would be perilous delays if, at short notice, American aircraft carriers had to be sent from San Francisco and Pearl Harbor all the way to East Asia.

When a rejuvenated China began to confront the United States' forces during the first decade of this century, the 'tyranny of distance' was a key concern. Nowhere was the phrase used more often than in the island of Guam, the United States territory that lay closest to the South China Sea. Slightly smaller than Singapore it was being converted into a major fortress and naval and air base. During the North Korean missile crisis of 2018, President Trump expressed concern that even this island, if used by the heaviest US bombers, was almost too far away from continental United States. In flying time it was at least five hours distant from the Korean peninsula. The tyranny of distance still prevailed.

In the history of warfare, a succession of bold ideas and weapons had promised to curb the tyranny of distance. The horse and the cavalry had revolutionised warfare and tamed distance; but the Boer War, where more than 300 000 horses were killed in the fighting, foreshadowed the declining role of the horse. In the First World War the flimsy aircraft flourished high above the trenches without seeming likely to conquer distance; and yet in the Second World War the Japanese launched their devastating aerial attack on Pearl Harbor in 1941, and the huge American aircraft dropped the first atomic bombs on two distant Japanese cities in 1945. In various other phases of the war, however, distance was still a powerful obstacle. In the following decades the latest American and Soviet missiles covered vast distances, but many military leaders in the nuclear era believed that 'the tyranny of distance' was far from ended.

19

FOLDING LANDSCAPE

The English historian Thomas Macaulay believed that writers should not spend much time in the company of other writers. His advice could hardly be followed in Australia. Writers were few: if they lived in the same city most could not help knowing each other.

Melbourne in the late 1950s was the hub of the liveliest writers' organisation in the country, the Fellowship of Australian Writers. Most of the activist writers were left wing, and a few were communists, but they accepted the goal of a fellowship and were tolerant of nearly all opponents who treated writing as a serious craft. I was invited to join the committee which met intermittently at suburban houses. Prominent at meetings were Vance and Nettie Palmer (then the grand couple of Australian writing), Alan Marshall, David Martin, Stephen Murray-Smith, Frank Dalby Davison, A. A. Phillips and Clem

Christesen; and with nearly all of them I remained friends, no matter how much our political views differed.

One of our memorable meetings was in the university grounds, in an old two-storey house lent for the evening so that the famous prehistorian Gordon Childe could be welcomed during one of his rare returns to Australia. It was 1957, and his paperback book *What Happened in History* already had gained an enormous following, its Marxist interpretation fitting the postwar mood. In a speech to our little gathering he caused a mixture of merriment and indignation by praising Iceland above Australia. Childe, while mentally quick and impressively courteous, appeared frail and slightly lost. A week or two later, visiting the Blue Mountains, he fell to his death.

Through this committee I came to know closely the old-time man of letters Judah Waten, a loyal communist who had left Russia as a baby, and Stephen Murray-Smith, an old Geelong Grammarian and New Guinea veteran who had recently resigned in disgust from the Communist Party. Much later in the mid-1960s I was a referee of Stephen's successful application for a post in the Education Faculty. 'I hope you and the university will not have cause to regret it,' he replied. A Renaissance man, with more projects than he could ever finish, he was generous towards friends' projects. Every week or two arrived a short note, written usually in the railway train on which he commuted to the city, providing a morsel that he hoped would be useful in some forthcoming book. Universities as working places have a reputation for being catty but generosity is also present on a considerable scale. Stephen and his wife Nita were among the most generous.

Frank Dalby Davison, one of the oldest in this circle of friends, had a gift for writing about horses, dogs, heifers and other animals. He had made his name with *Man-Shy*, which for several decades was one of the most widely read of Australian novels. He was wary of the limelight, whereas his wife Marie wore very wide hats and gestured theatrically with her eyebrows, voice and hands. While each day he wrote a little – he was in his early seventies – Marie did the farming, viewing each calf as her infant. To their small farm called Folding Hills, just to the north of Melbourne, we went maybe twice a year, usually at weekends. As we drove slowly along the track between the main road and house, we sometimes saw Marie parting the curtains to see who was arriving. When the front door of the modest house was opened, the smell of the roast wafted out.

Frank had a mild strand of melancholy; and when he rejoiced he did not let the rejoicing last too long. His gift for understatement was rather endearing. When an oldish friend married again, Frank's confidential letter to us offered this whispered aside: 'I am glad that you met . . . and his brand new wife. She is quite a social experience, don't you think?' Reading a new book, Frank knew instinctively the chapters where the writer was succeeding or failing.

Absorbed in a long experimental novel set in a variety of Sydney bedrooms and workplaces, Frank believed that he was writing about sexual relations with a rare frankness, and at first he was. If his very long novel *The White Thorntree* had appeared in bookshops in 1950 it might have been publicly banned by the censor, but the social revolution of the following decade overtook him. When at last in 1968 his book was about to be published, it was no longer revolutionary. When we, eager as friends to support him, placed an advance order for two copies, we heard that so far he had received total orders for only half-a-dozen.

In the last twelve months of his life, when he appeared on television to reminisce about his life, the public response was warm. 'I am only now plugging my way through the fan mail,' he wrote exultantly.

After his death Marie cheerfully battled on, presiding over the cows. 'I am alone at Folding Hills,' she wrote.

Sometime in the early 1960s, Nan and Rohan Rivett became our good friends. Rohan, at least a dozen years my senior in age, was in Singapore when it fell to the Japanese, and he spent four years as a prisoner of war. His book *Behind Bamboo* was the first fluent account of that tragic episode to reach a wide Australian audience.

He was the editor of Rupert Murdoch's first newspaper, the Adelaide *News*. Later he and his proprietor parted. If ever an Australian had far more enthusiasm than could be harnessed to the normal day's tasks, it was Rohan. Even the family's dogs had enthusiasm. One day, when Helen Suzman the South African politician was his guest at dinner, Rohan's dog expressed pleasure by wagging its tail so forcefully that it hit a thin-stemmed wineglass standing on a side table. We saw the glass, almost full of wine and standing in a vertical position, flash by as if carried by a waiter on a tray.

Rohan wore his shining armour as if it were tailor-made. One Saturday morning in 1971 he phoned to say he would be calling around in half an hour. Hearing his footsteps, I opened the door, and he produced a letter all ready for signing. With his enthusiastic smile, he explained that he had only a minute to spare. All he needed was my signature: he already must have collected seven or eight. In vain did I explain that I rarely signed collective letters. His combined letter – soon to appear in newspapers in various countries – strongly opposed the idea that the South African cricket team should be allowed to tour Australia later that year. When Rohan died at a relatively young age we found that we missed him deeply.

*

I took more notice of the politics and economics of writing after an invitation came from Harold Holt who had succeeded R. G. Menzies as the prime minister. The unexpected letter, signed by Holt himself, invited me to become a member of the advisory board of the Commonwealth Literary Fund (CLF), which was the oldest of all the federal government's agencies for promoting the arts. It met twice a year in private, and twice a year in the presence of a political committee consisting of the leader or nominee of the three main political parties. Menzies, while prime minister, had personally chaired the committee, enjoying the chitchat about writers and the discussion about those books that merited a publishing subsidy; but thereafter a cabinet minister took the chair. The board itself consisted of two of the nation's influential poets, Kenneth Slessor and Douglas Stewart of Sydney, the novelist Kylie Tennant, and the Canberra literary critic Professor Tom Inglis Moore, with Sir Grenfell Price as chairman. I learnt years later that it was Price who had lobbied Holt – to the point of pestering him – that I should join the board.

Sir Grenfell presided with a puckish and occasionally an indignant face. Seventy-five years old, he was white-headed and slightly stooped, his reddish face was a little pixieish, and like nearly every member he smoked a lot, except that his cigarette burnt away on the edge of the ashtray. An Adelaide geographer and for long the master of a university college, he had written many books, the best known of which focused on tropical Australia and on the Antarctic. In the early 1940s he had sat briefly in the federal parliament, just when Menzies gave way to Curtin, and he remained a Menzies man. At meetings he referred to him affectionately as 'Bob', an affection not shared by Gough Whitlam who, attending our meetings as leader of the federal Labor Party, seemed to be on the verge of winning office. Whitlam, I should add, was an impressive member, and spoke eloquently on all kinds of topics with emphasis and fluency. Of all the hundreds of federal committees, boards and commissions, the Literary Fund was probably the only one where the leader of the Opposition was part of the decision-making process.

An aura surrounded the CLF. On the evening of the first meeting a black Commonwealth car called at our house in East Ivanhoe and took me to the airport, and in Sydney another black car was waiting to go to the Australia Hotel where the board met the next morning. The meetings were fascinating. There might be a confidential petition requesting that a literary pension be awarded to an old writer who had given much to the nation and was now in need; a literary magazine applying for a subsidy so that it could stay alive; a publishing house pleading on behalf of a volume of verse that was financially risky; and numerous requests by established writers for a fellowship that would enable them to write full time for the next year or so. Between the meetings, manuscripts arrived in the post with a request for a written comment. I was sent most of the non-fiction works by the hardworking staff consisting of Bill Cumming, Brendan Kelson and Valda Leehy.

I was much the youngest member and probably Douglas Stewart was closest to me in spirit. We exchanged notes about trivia. Many of his letters, on small sheets of Angus & Robertson notepaper, were written with blue ink in a spidery script. With tongue in cheek he would sometimes refer privately to other publishers as 'our reptile rivals'. He had a talent for spotting a rising writer, and I remember his delight at discovering Eric Rolls, who was farming near Boggabri in the interior of New South Wales when he became absorbed in Australian history. Rolls' long manuscript on the coming of the rabbits and other pests to this continent, aptly called *They All Ran Wild*, needed a Commonwealth subsidy if it was to reach the audience it deserved; and I was told to report quickly on a work that was now in the form of long galley proofs, and close to publication. With no academic training and only one small work – of poetry – to his credit, Rolls' new history, both in its research and its prose, was an eye-opener, and I wrote: 'It impresses me more than any Australian work of non-fiction I recall.'

Another work that could not be published without a very heavy subsidy was T. G. H. Strehlow's massive *Songs of Central Australia*. Not only a scholar and a linguist, Professor Strehlow was intimate with a vast dry region in Central Australia, having travelled far 'in the company of various old native men of authority' and the camels that carried his supplies in the early 1930s. As a guide to Aboriginal religion, poetry, love and war, his book was unsurpassed. For the first time, again with subsidies, a cluster of books by Aboriginal authors appeared in bookshops. It is easy to think of the excellent books that we helped, with government money, to see the light of day, but no doubt we subsidised others that did not deserve it.

Price eventually reached the end of his long term of office and put it to the other members of the advisory board that I should be chairman – if the prime minister, William McMahon, and the minister for the arts, Peter Howson, consented. I was in London late in 1970 when I received from Price a letter hoping that I would accept. 'You will be greatly wanted,' he wrote. So I became the last chairman of a board originally created by Alfred Deakin in 1908 as the first Commonwealth venture in the arts, and then in 1973 I became the chairman of its successor, the Literature Board of the new Australia Council.

The year or two on each side of 1970 was a special stretch of time. Inventiveness and new technology, especially in weapons and spacecraft, were a source of fear and also wonder. Few events in human history were as spellbinding as the first human landing on the moon in July 1969, and for hours on end we watched the ghostly astronauts 'live' on television. Events in outer space were matched by travel far below, and suddenly it was cheaper to travel from Australia to Europe by jumbo jet than by ship, and thirty times as fast. Those days were intellectually exciting and dislocating too. The counterculture, the rise of feminism, the surge in the green movement, the youth uprising in the United States and France, and briefly the ascent in China of the young and ruthless Red Guards – these movements marched in step. Those protesters who challenged the legitimacy of the war being fought by Americans, Australians and others in Vietnam increasingly disputed the legitimacy of the industrial and liberal civilisation that fought the war. Our own big cities experienced long street marches in protest at our involvement in the Vietnam War.

Many of my students wished to know why the causes of war were not on the syllabus, and so I began to lecture on the causes of war. Big numbers crowded the lecture theatre, many being students who belonged to other faculties. I began to develop the idea that any valid explanation of why nations stopped fighting – in short, an explanation of peace – must be logically linked to any explanation of why they had begun fighting. In order to test existing theories about the causes of war I tried to examine every international war fought since the year 1700. Soon I reached the conclusion that theories widely held by historians and political scientists were contradicted by the weight of evidence. One of my own conclusions was that most wars began with undue optimism on both sides. It was common for both sides to expect victory: unreal expectations were a vital cause of the decisions of leaders to go to war.

It is always exciting – and risky too – to enter new intellectual territory and be only a few steps ahead of the students. Boldly I began to turn my lectures into a book, called *The Causes of War* and eventually published in London.

In about 1970 tumultuous changes were experienced in politics, international relations and in social and intellectual life. A new nature movement was in the air. To my surprise I heard in tutorials a few young members of the green vanguard – and their enthusiasm was infectious – speaking affectionately of snakes, crocodiles and all living things. My generation even as toddlers had been taught always to be alert for poisonous snakes, but now they were welcome in the Garden of Eden. As I knew where nearly every one of my students came from, whether city or country town or farmlands, I realised that the passionate pleas on behalf of nature came mostly from city students. In the coming clash between nature and technology I was slow to appreciate that in the history profession, as it gained young and ardent recruits from the counterculture, several existing books might be seen as sometimes barracking for the wrong side.

Amid the rising interest in nature, whether tamed or in the wild, the climate was not prominent. In 1970 there was no deep fear of global warming. Actually, in some learned circles, global cooling was predicted. Climate change was not the topic of the decade in Australia. Few historians were then interested in climate as a major theme, and I am not sure why in May 1971 I chose to speak at a major science conference in Brisbane about the influence of climate on our nation's history.

One sidelight was curious. By chance I discovered that Captain Cook and his travelling scientist, Joseph Banks, during the single week they spent at Botany Bay in 1770, misjudged the climate, with profound consequences for all of us. While their ship *Endeavour* was anchored in Botany Bay they made busy excursions on foot into the sandy interior. Impressed by the 'vast quantities of grass', Cook thought one green meadow was as rich 'as ever was seen'. When in the following decade the British government resolved to send convicts to Botany Bay, it was confident that in such a lush environment they would soon grow all the food they needed. They saw that landscape at the wettest time of the year, but when the First Fleet arrived from England in January 1788, the long waving grass had vanished, the meadow was nowhere to be seen, and even the fast stream – so powerful that, day and night, it could surely turn the waterwheels of a flour mill – was no longer full of water. If the exploring ship *Endeavour* had chanced to visit the Sydney region in the dry months of 1770, would a convict settlement ever have been planned for such a dry region?

As Indigenous history came into prominence for the first time, climate was seen as more influential. It was realised that human beings had long been settled in Australia and New Guinea before the climate began to change dramatically. The increase in temperatures dwarfed any increase predicted in this modern era of global-warming fears. The sea levels rose massively, beginning about 18 000 years ago, and Australia was cut off from New Guinea at one end and from Tasmania at the other. Here was the most far-reaching event in the human history of Australia, more momentous than any event in the last three centuries. For the first time I began to write and lecture about climate history, and to try to piece together the fragments.

Here, more than in most other nations, history was becoming central to national debates. For historians, they were exciting years.

*

I must end this story, for the time being. I have given too much space in these pages to my work, when all kinds of other events also held my attention. Our house was almost surrounded by wastelands, and the gorse and young hawthorn bushes grew on the slopes leading down to the Yarra River. Sometimes pet animals were abandoned there. One morning in 1971 three female kittens appeared near our carport, in the shade of a lemon-scented gum. Tumbling over one another, they were energetic and healthy except for a dose of the 'cat flu'. When I said, 'We can't keep three cats', I was outvoted. Our daughter Anna, then aged eleven and beginning to read widely, chose names from Shakespeare, calling them Titania, Perdita and Cleopatra.

The smallest, named Cleopatra but soon to be called Baby, became the undisputed leader. After we found at the grocer's a large cardboard box for them to play in, she took charge, using her paws to prevent the others from jumping in. As they crowded into our bedroom at night, we decided to exile them downstairs, but eventually Baby, by pushing her head at an unusual angle against the bottom of the locked door, learnt to open it. The other cats just looked on.

One morning a few summers later, near a fence facing the wastelands, the placid black and white cat Perdita, known widely as Perdy, cornered a large tiger snake and rocked to and fro as if about to grasp it by the neck. It was a tense time: for Ann to interfere was futile. Perdy and also Titania, who was crouched nearby, could not be diverted. Eventually, after the snake was frightened away, the two cats were rushed to the local vet. He feared that they might have been bitten: certainly Perdy was frothing at the mouth. The vet, just to be sure, prepared to give them an antivenene injection. 'It will be very expensive,' he added. Ann quickly consented, explaining that the cat was one of the family. She did not recant from that statement of kinship when later she opened the bill-envelope and discovered how expensive were the injections.

Titania, a grey and white cat known also as 'Tatty' or 'White Face', often wore a strange mystical expression. Silent for long periods, she looked at people with intensity and gave the impression that she was about to speak. In old age she gained local fame because she appeared in the *60 Minutes* television show when George Negus was interviewing the family. The cameraman must have been intrigued by the sight of her, licking herself and taking no notice of him, and he swung the camera towards her. Responding, she looked up intently, and for some time her face remained taut and expectant as if she was about to address the nation. Some viewers declared that Tatty ruled our house.

I had entered my early forties and was still learning to be a historian; but history itself, and the importance of it in national life, was changing faster than I was. Each year vital books on Australian history were seized upon by an eager, expanding audience. Talented painters and poets followed by filmmakers were illuminating our past; archaeologists dug it up, and politicians appealed to it in national debates. Few other nations in the early 1970s were so absorbed in understanding their history, and debating it on so many fronts. A rising wave of clashing ideas, 'history' here was to grow like thunder.

NOTES

Here and there in this book sentences have been borrowed from some of my other writings, though not always word for word. In some years I contributed regularly – even writing a weekly or fortnightly column – to *The Australian*, Melbourne's *Herald* and *Herald Sun*, *Australian Book Review*, *The Age*, Sydney *Bulletin* and *Australian Business Monthly*. I express my thanks to the editors of all these publications.

Chapter 2

Parts of this chapter were published earlier in G. Blainey, 'A Methodist Childhood', *Proceedings of the Uniting Church Historical Society: Synod of Victoria*, vol. 6, no. 2, December 1999.

The trial of Sodeman: Philip Ayres, *Owen Dixon* (The Miegunyah Press, 2003), pp. 74-7; Gideon Haigh, *A Scandal in Bohemia* (Hamish Hamilton, 2018), pp. 211–13.

Chapter 3

Memories of childhood were aided by those of my older brother John and sister Joan and in several places by recollections written by my mother and father.

Jimmy Knight, footballer and airman: G. Blainey, 'Football the way it was', Melbourne *Herald*, 16 August 1984.

Visit to 1940 football grand final: G. Blainey, 'War, but the game went on', Melbourne *Herald*, 26 September 1986.

Henry Lanyon's wartime manifesto: see *The Advocate*, Melbourne, 25 August 1917.

Chapter 5

The kinsman who was an Orientalist: Professor Frederick Thomas, *Dictionary of National Biography 1951–1960* (Oxford University Press, 1971), pp. 964–5. He was my grandfather Blainey's first cousin but the two never met.

Chapter 6

Of the Wesley students who were in the same year as me, or a year or so before or after, some later made a name. Those who became judges, QCs, professors of law or high members of the legal profession included Robert Brooking, Alan Dixon, S. E. K. Hulme, Jim Morrissey, Robin Sharwood, Ted Sikk, Clive Tadgell and G. R. D. Waldron. Geoff Harcourt became a distinguished economist as well as president of his Cambridge college; he married Joan Bartrop, the daughter of one of our family's close Ballarat friends. Those who rose high in medicine or medical research included Carl (short for Carlyle) Wood and John Leeton, world famous for their successful experiments in gynaecology; Carl produced the world's first in-vitro fertilised human egg and implanted it back into the mother. Several others, especially K. Vernon Bailey, were distinguished medical specialists in Indonesia, the Congo and other parts of the developing world. Peter Bailey, who was a boarder in my time, became deputy head of the prime minister's department.

Of those entering politics, Peter Nixon was a federal minister who served under every non-Labor prime minister from Holt to Fraser; we have lunch together regularly. Lionel Fredman, later a professor of history at Newcastle University, was the first biographer of Sir John Quick, a federation father, and also author of a perceptive survey of the strong Jewish strand in Wesley College's history. Many other Wesley colleagues went successfully into business and farming. Several became shire presidents or rural mayors. One, 'Cocky' Merlo, became a popular part-time bookmaker at country race meetings as well as Castlemaine's mayor. Able sportsmen there were many. To these fellow students I owe much.

Chapter 7

Shann and the Chinese diggers: Edward Shann, *An Economic History of Australia* (Cambridge, 1948), p. 181.

Chapter 8

A book in praise of Dr Raynor Johnson was written by Alan Moore, *Raynor Johnson: A Biographical Memoir* (Lakeland, Melbourne, 2007). He maintained that I had once called Johnson an intellectual 'possibly without peer in this country'. When in 2018 I enquired where and when I had written these words, Moore consulted his notes and found, apologetically, that I had made no such statement.

While I respected Johnson and admired his intellectual curiosity, I was unable, being no physicist, to assess his main work.

Chapter 9

Clark and my student-essay: C. M. H. Clark, *The Quest for Grace* (Penguin, 1991), p. 170.

On Manning Clark, I wrote at two hours' notice an obituary which *The Age* published on 24 May 1991, the day after he died.

Chapter 10

Warner Max Corden: *Lucky Boy in the Lucky Country* (Palgrave Macmillan, 2018), chapter 3.

The Parker-Blainey controversy on the causes of federation began with articles in the journal *Historical Studies* (Melbourne) in November 1949 and May 1950. The controversy was summarised by Helen Irving in *To Constitute a Nation* (Cambridge University Press, 1997), p. 214.

Chapter 11

A version of these pages on Mt Lyell first appeared in G. Blainey, 'Tasmania! Tasmania!', in *Papers and Proceedings, Tasmanian Historical Research Association*, Hobart, 2008. *The Peaks of Lyell*, published in 1954, was enlarged in successive editions by Melbourne University Press. In 1993 appeared a fifth edition (St. David's Park Publishing, Hobart, 1993).

Chapter 13

The two books written on university history were: Norman H. Olver (illustrations) and G. Blainey (narrative), *The University of Melbourne: A Centenary Portrait* (MUP, 1956); and G. Blainey, *A Centenary History of the University of Melbourne* (MUP, 1957).

Chapter 14

The history of the National Bank was called *Gold and Paper* (Georgian House, Melbourne, 1958). In 1983 came a new, enlarged edition, *Gold and Paper 1958–1982* (Macmillan, Melbourne), to which Geoffrey Hutton added 10 new chapters, while I condensed my earlier chapters so that the book was not too large.

Chapter 16

Churchill and Roosevelt: Bernard M. Baruch, *Baruch: The Public Years* (Pocket Books, New York, 1962), esp. chapters 14 and 18.

Mawby's funeral: G. Blainey, *A Remarkable Man: Sir Maurice Mawby CBE 1904–1977* (tribute booklet, 5 pp.), 8 August 1977.

Chapter 17

Across the Red World was first published by Macmillan in April 1968 and was reprinted in the following month. A cheap paperback edition, printed in Hong Kong, was published in 1971.

The title of Ann Blainey's first biography, published by Longmans in London in 1968, was *The Farthing Poet: A Biography of Richard Hengist Horne 1802–1884*. His celebrated work was the long poem *Orion* (1843), which he insisted should be sold for the trifling sum of one farthing. Amongst her later books were *I am Melba: A Biography* (Text Publishing, Melbourne, 2008) which won the national biography award, and *King of the Air: The Turbulent Life of Charles Kingsford Smith* (Black Inc., Melbourne, 2018).

Chapter 18

Tyranny of distance and modern warfare: Report by Center for Strategic and International Studies [CSIS] on US 'Pacific Command' area, submitted by Dept. of Defense to Congress, Washington, 26 July 2012. If 'Tyranny of distance, Guam' is googled, numerous references appear. I thank Tim Warner of East Melbourne for these references.

Chapter 19

Sir Grenfell Price: I wrote the foreword to his life by Colin Kerr, *Archie: The Biography of Sir Archibald Grenfell Price* (Macmillan, 1983).

My article on 'Climate and Australia's History' appeared in the *Melbourne Historical Journal*, vol. 10, 1971. Alas, it was silent on Aboriginal history. My book, *Triumph of the Nomads* (Macmillan, 1975) gave much space to the rising of the seas and its effects on Aboriginal life.

INDEX